D1283638

DISCARDED
from the Nashville Public Library

BATMAN

KING TUT'S TOMB

A NEW DAWN

Nunzio DeFilippis & Christina Weir Writers
José Luis García-López Penciller
Kevin Nowlan Inker
David Baron Colorist
Ken Lopez Letterer

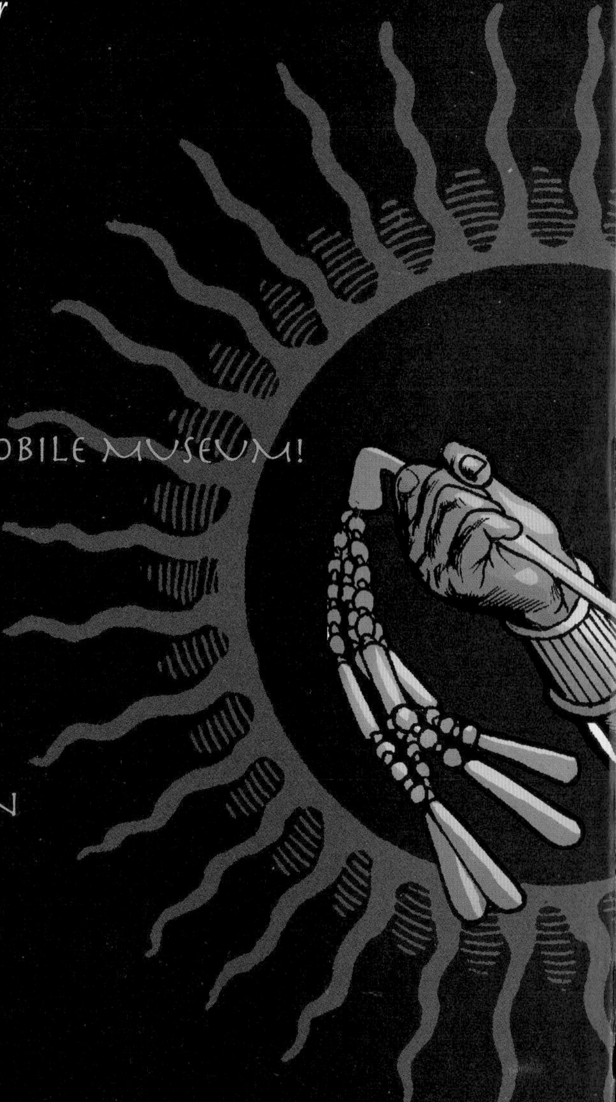

Plus three rare treasures featuring the art of
José Luis García-López

THE MYSTERY OF THE MOBILE MUSEUM!

J.M. De Matteis Writer
José Luis García-López Penciller
Steven Mitchell Inker
Adrienne Roy Colorist
Ben Oda Letterer

A CANNON FOR BATMAN

Gerry Conway Writer
José Luis García-López Artist
Tatjana Wood Colorist

LAST LAUGH

Gerry Conway Writer
José Luis García-López Penciller
Dan Adkins Inker
Adrienne Roy Colorist
Ben Oda Letterer

Batman created by Bob Kane

BATMAN

KING TUT'S TOMB

Dan DiDio SVP-Executive Editor
Mike Carlin Paul Levitz Len Wein Editors-original series
Rachel Gluckstern Associate Editor-original series
Georg Brewer VP-Design & DC Direct Creative
Bob Harras Group Editor-Collected Editions
Bob Joy Editor
Robbin Brosterman Design Director-Books

DC COMICS
Paul Levitz President & Publisher
Richard Bruning SVP-Creative Director
Patrick Caldon EVP-Finance & Operations
Amy Genkins SVP-Business & Legal Affairs
Jim Lee Editorial Director-WildStorm
Gregory Noveck SVP-Creative Affairs
Steve Rotterdam SVP-Sales & Marketing
Cheryl Rubin SVP-Brand Management

Cover by José Luis García-López and Kevin Nowlan
with David Baron

BATMAN: KING TUT'S TOMB

Published by DC Comics. Cover, text and compilation
Copyright © 2010 DC Comics. All Rights Reserved.

Originally published in single magazine form in BATMAN
CONFIDENTIAL 26-28, THE BRAVE & THE BOLD 164, 171,
BATMAN 353 Copyright © 1980, 1981, 1982, 2009 DC Comics.
All Rights Reserved.
All characters, their distinctive likenesses and related
elements featured in this publication are trademarks
of DC Comics. The stories, characters and incidents
featured in this publication are entirely fictional.
DC Comics does not read or accept unsolicited
submissions of ideas, stories or artwork.

DC Comics, 1700 Broadway, New York, NY 10019
A Warner Bros. Entertainment Company
Printed by World Color Press, Inc., St-Romuald, QC, Canada 1/27/10.
First Printing.
ISBN: 978-1-4012-2577-3

SUSTAINABLE FORESTRY INITIATIVE

Certified Fiber Sourcing
www.sfiprogram.org

Fiber used in this product line meets the sourcing requirements
of the SFI program. www.sfiprogram.org PWC-SFICOC-260

A NEW DAWN PART ONE ■ Cover by José Luis García-López, Kevin Nowlan and David Baron

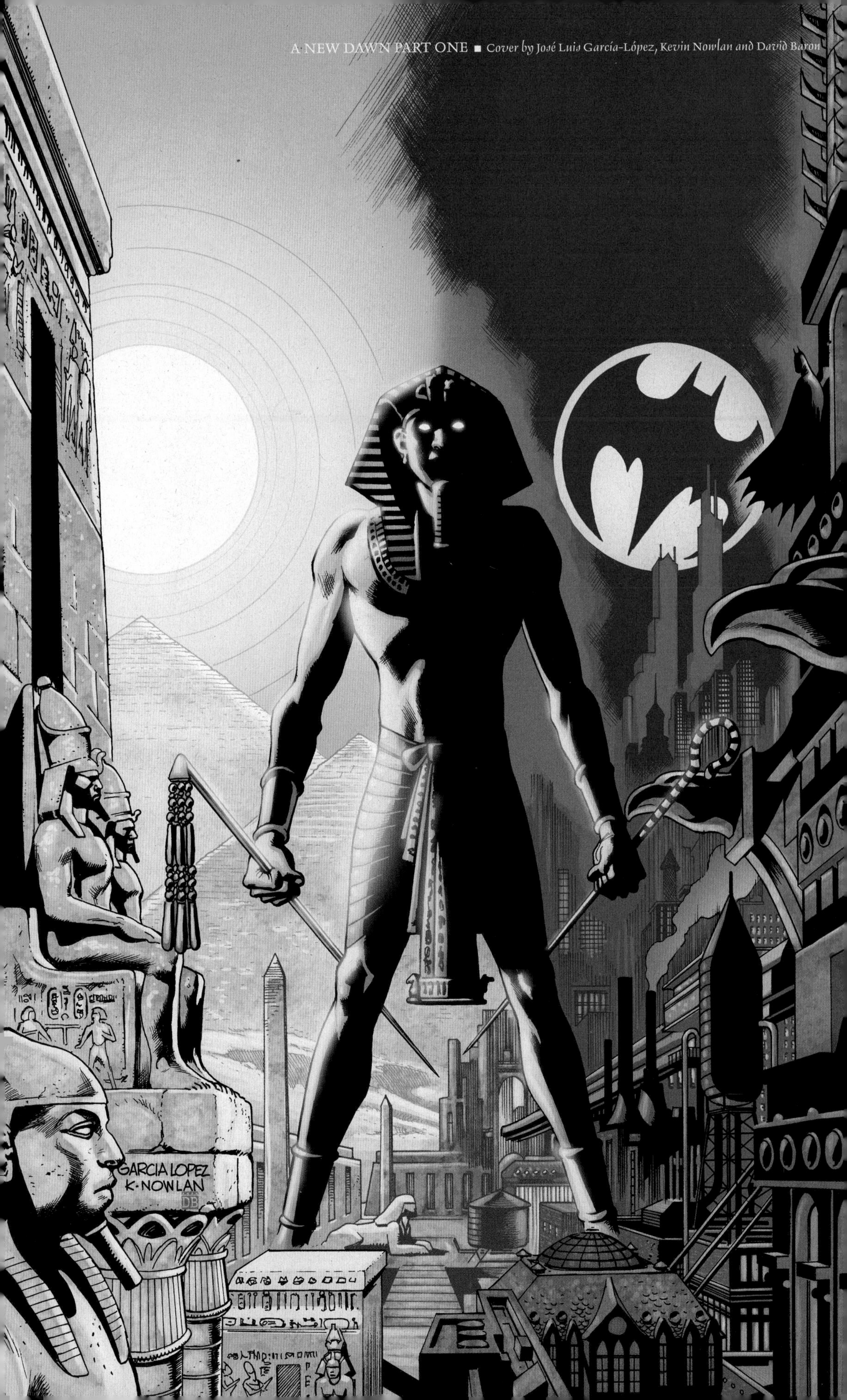
GARCIA LOPEZ
K·NOWLAN
DB

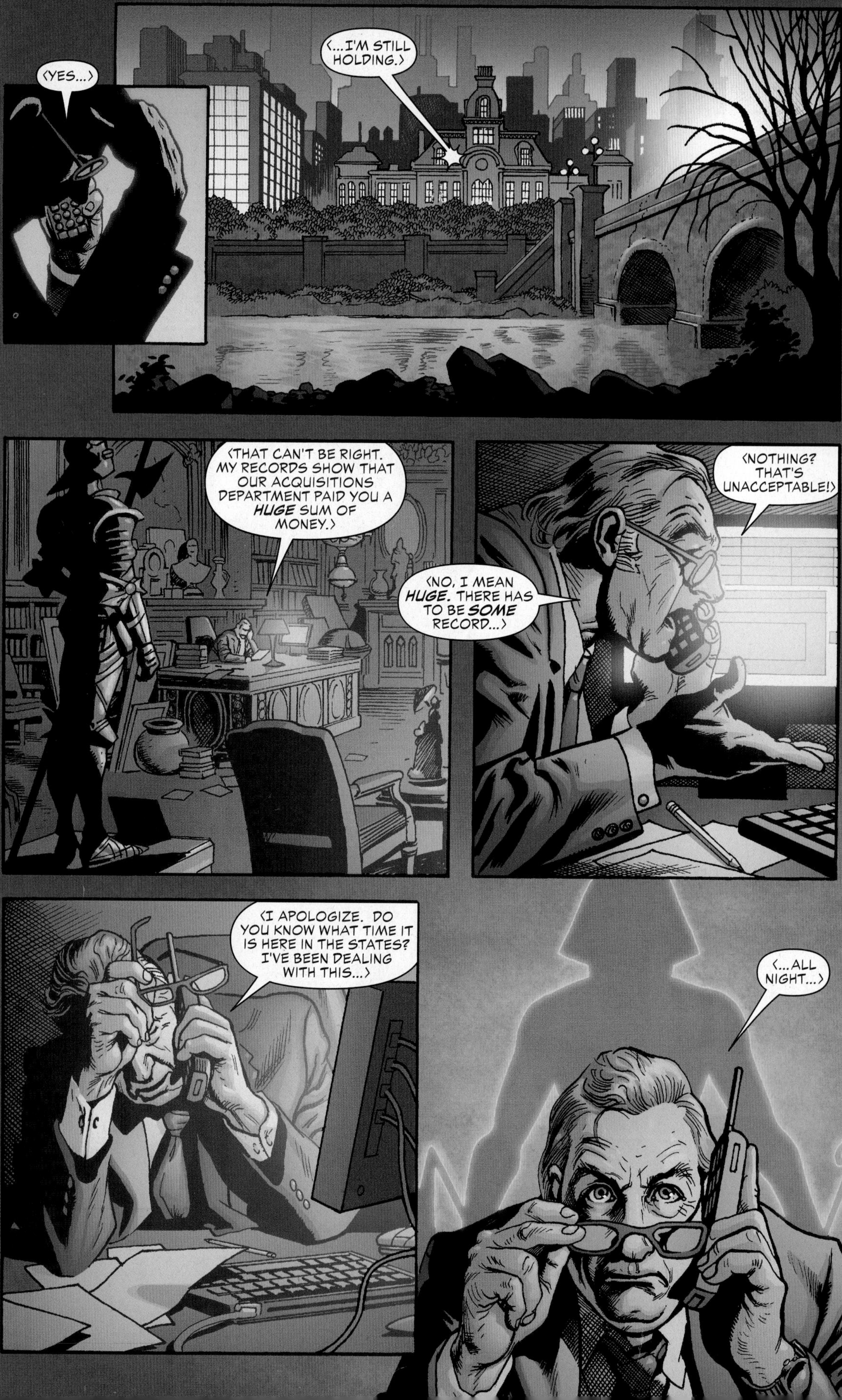
<YES...>
<...I'M STILL HOLDING.>
<THAT CAN'T BE RIGHT. MY RECORDS SHOW THAT OUR ACQUISITIONS DEPARTMENT PAID YOU A HUGE SUM OF MONEY.>
<NOTHING? THAT'S UNACCEPTABLE!>
<NO, I MEAN HUGE. THERE HAS TO BE SOME RECORD...>
<I APOLOGIZE. DO YOU KNOW WHAT TIME IT IS HERE IN THE STATES? I'VE BEEN DEALING WITH THIS...>
<...ALL NIGHT...>

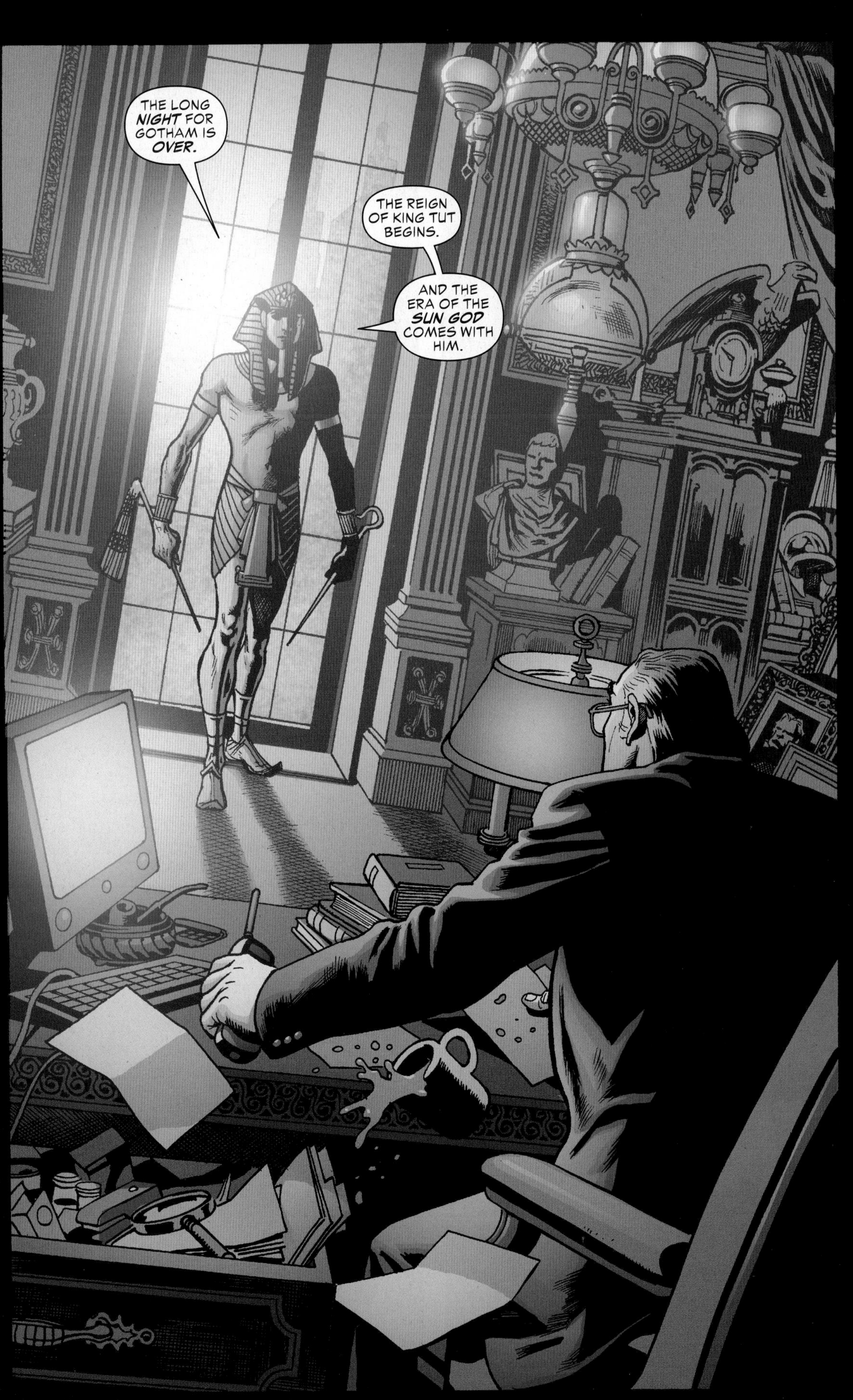
THE LONG NIGHT FOR GOTHAM IS OVER.
THE REIGN OF KING TUT BEGINS.
AND THE ERA OF THE SUN GOD COMES WITH HIM.

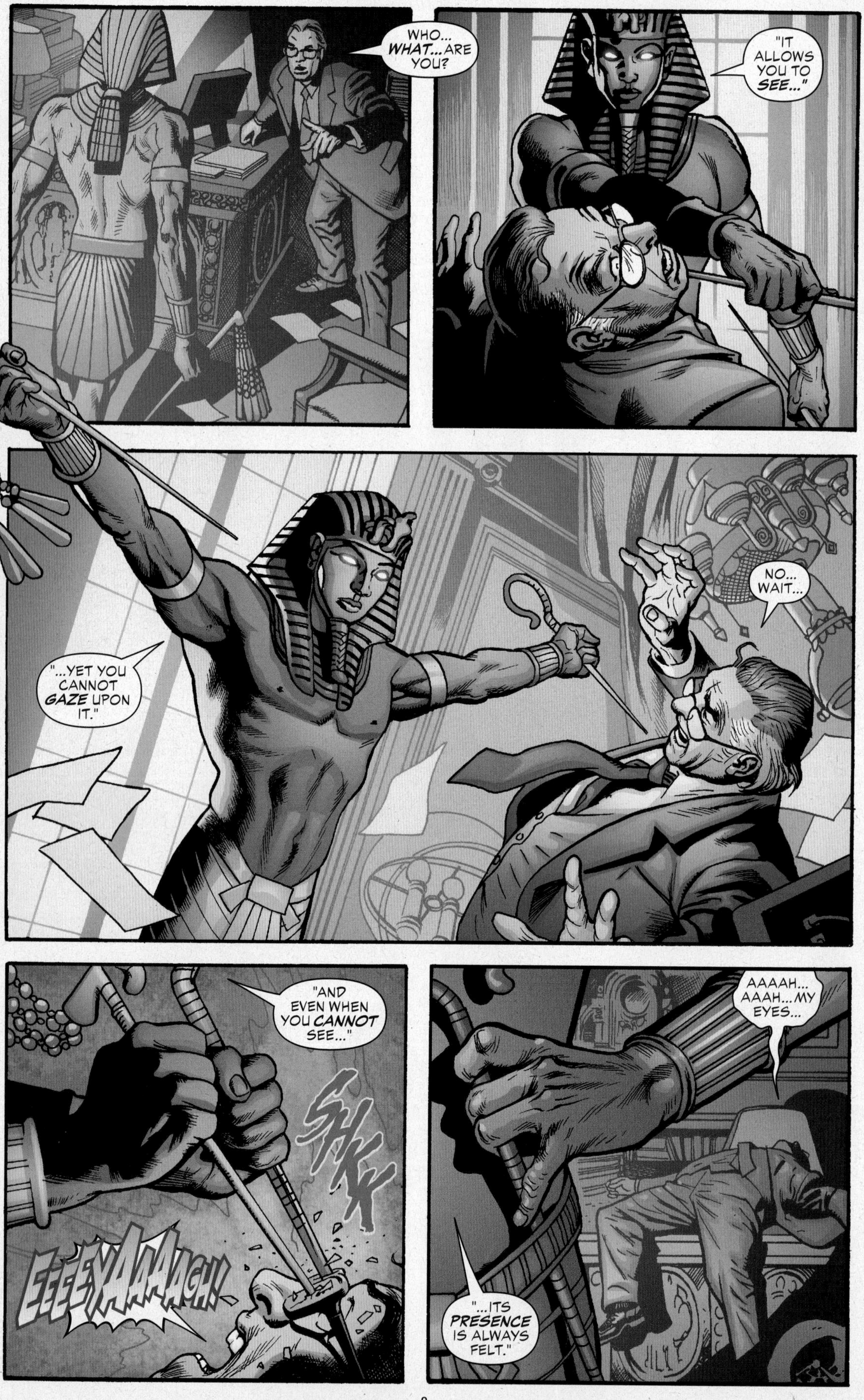
WHO... WHAT... ARE YOU?
"IT ALLOWS YOU TO SEE..."
"...YET YOU CANNOT GAZE UPON IT."
NO... WAIT...
"AND EVEN WHEN YOU CANNOT SEE..."
SHKK
EEEEYAAAAAGH!
AAAAH... AAAH... MY EYES...
"...ITS PRESENCE IS ALWAYS FELT."

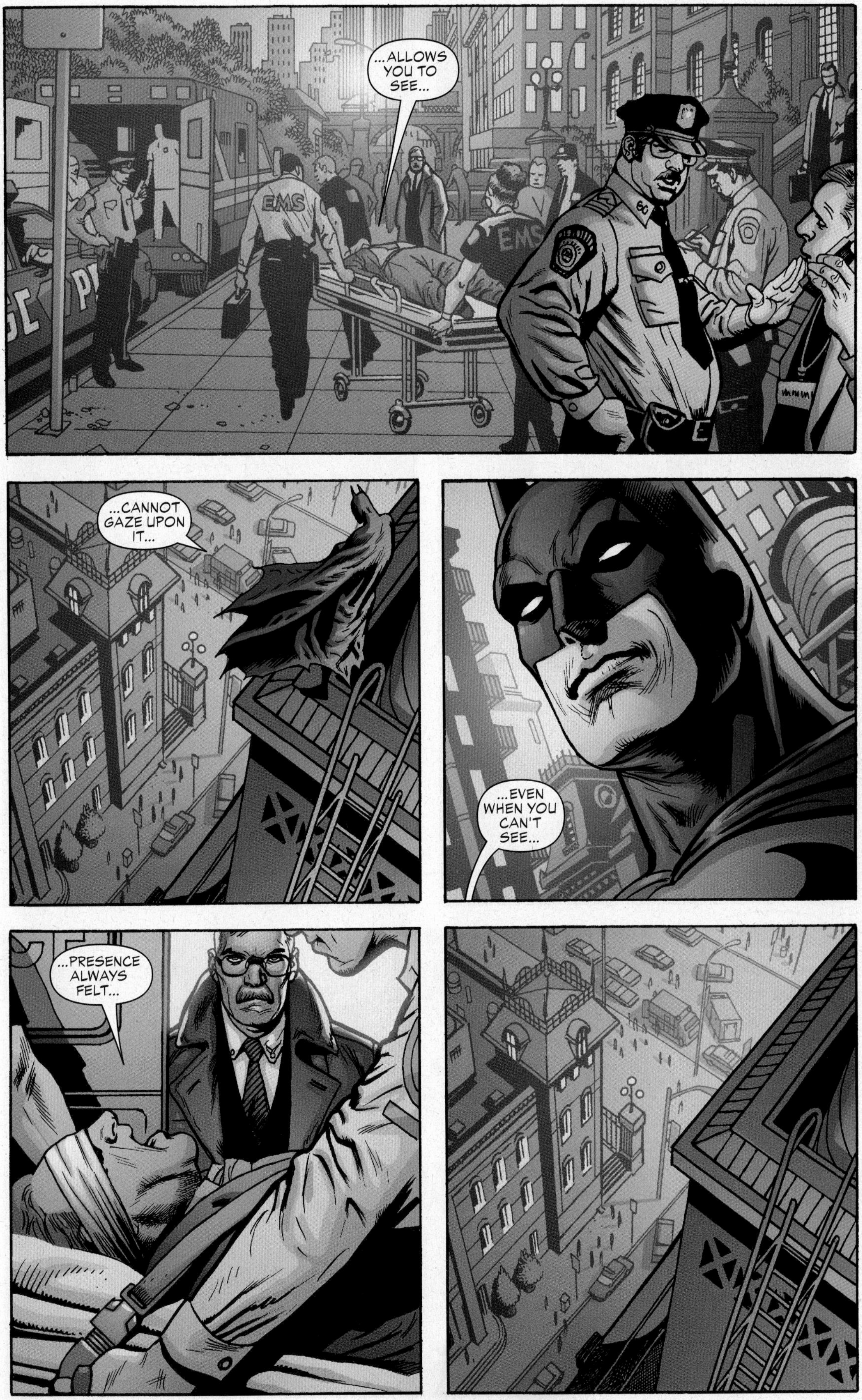
...ALLOWS YOU TO SEE...
...CANNOT GAZE UPON IT...
...EVEN WHEN YOU CAN'T SEE...
...PRESENCE ALWAYS FELT...

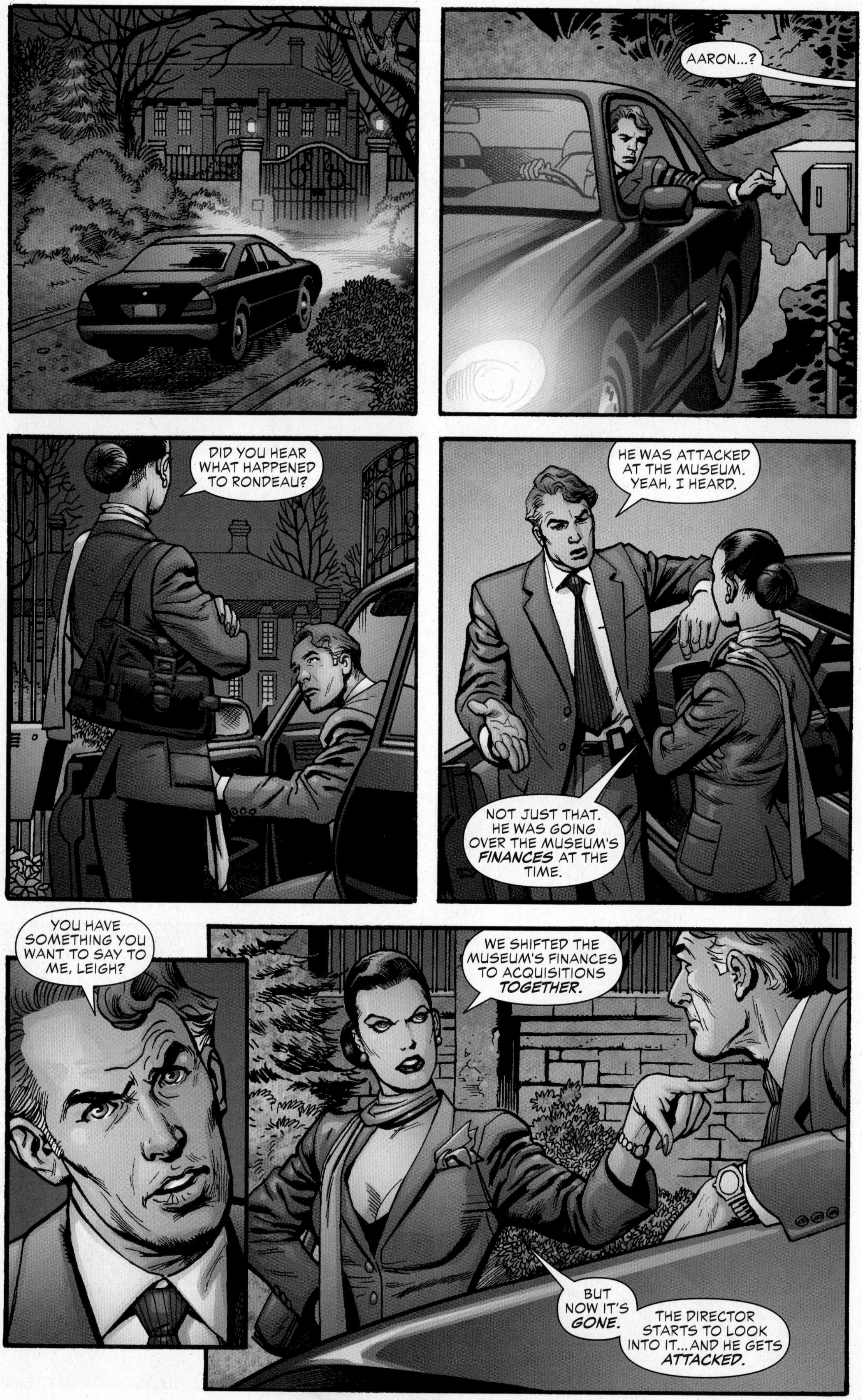
AARON...?
DID YOU HEAR WHAT HAPPENED TO RONDEAU?
HE WAS ATTACKED AT THE MUSEUM. YEAH, I HEARD.
NOT JUST THAT. HE WAS GOING OVER THE MUSEUM'S *FINANCES* AT THE TIME.
YOU HAVE SOMETHING YOU WANT TO SAY TO ME, LEIGH?
WE SHIFTED THE MUSEUM'S FINANCES TO ACQUISITIONS *TOGETHER.*
BUT NOW IT'S *GONE.*
THE DIRECTOR STARTS TO LOOK INTO IT...AND HE GETS *ATTACKED.*

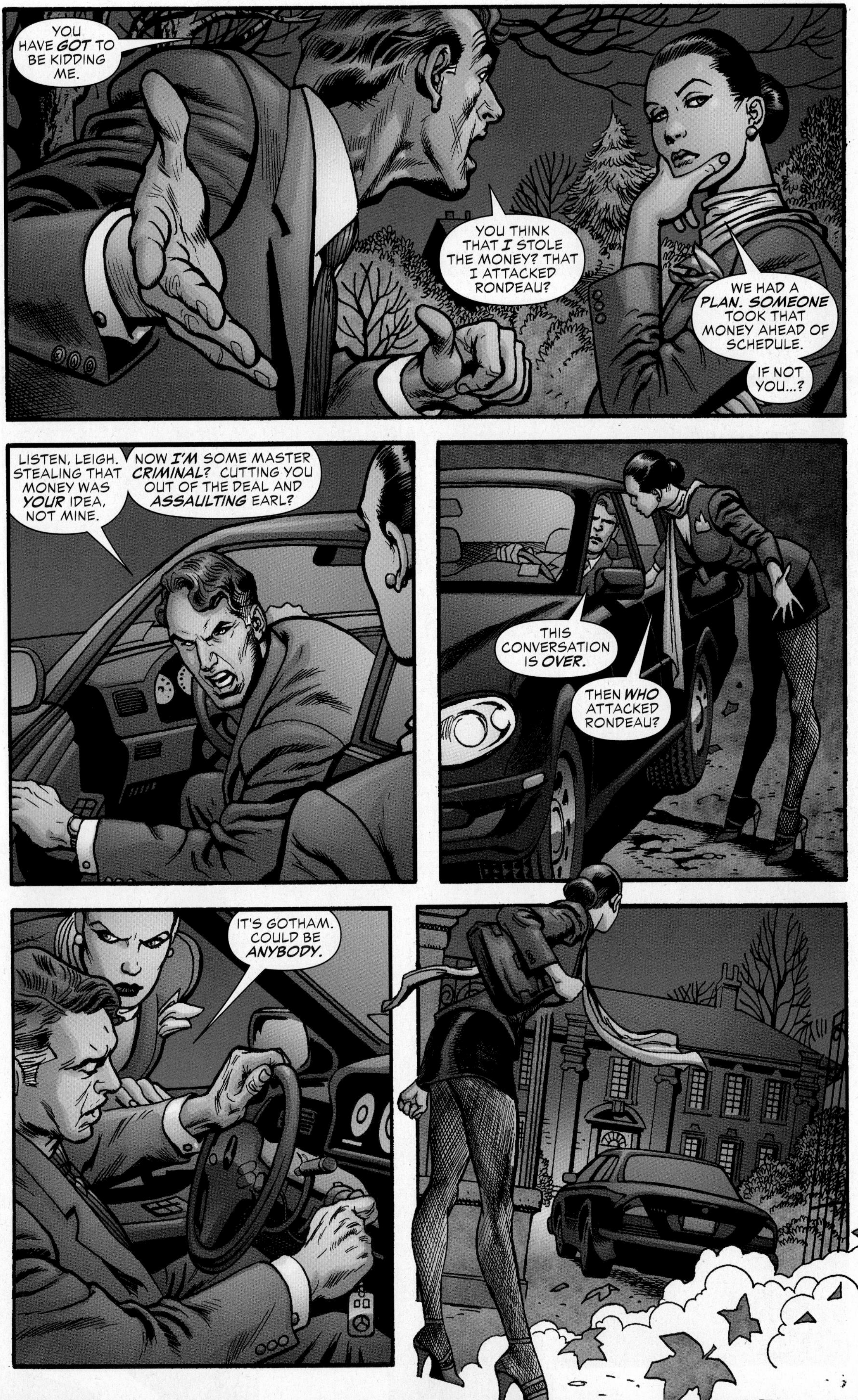
YOU HAVE GOT TO BE KIDDING ME.
YOU THINK THAT I STOLE THE MONEY? THAT I ATTACKED RONDEAU?
WE HAD A PLAN. SOMEONE TOOK THAT MONEY AHEAD OF SCHEDULE.
IF NOT YOU...?
LISTEN, LEIGH. STEALING THAT MONEY WAS YOUR IDEA, NOT MINE.
NOW I'M SOME MASTER CRIMINAL? CUTTING YOU OUT OF THE DEAL AND ASSAULTING EARL?
THIS CONVERSATION IS OVER.
THEN WHO ATTACKED RONDEAU?
IT'S GOTHAM. COULD BE ANYBODY.

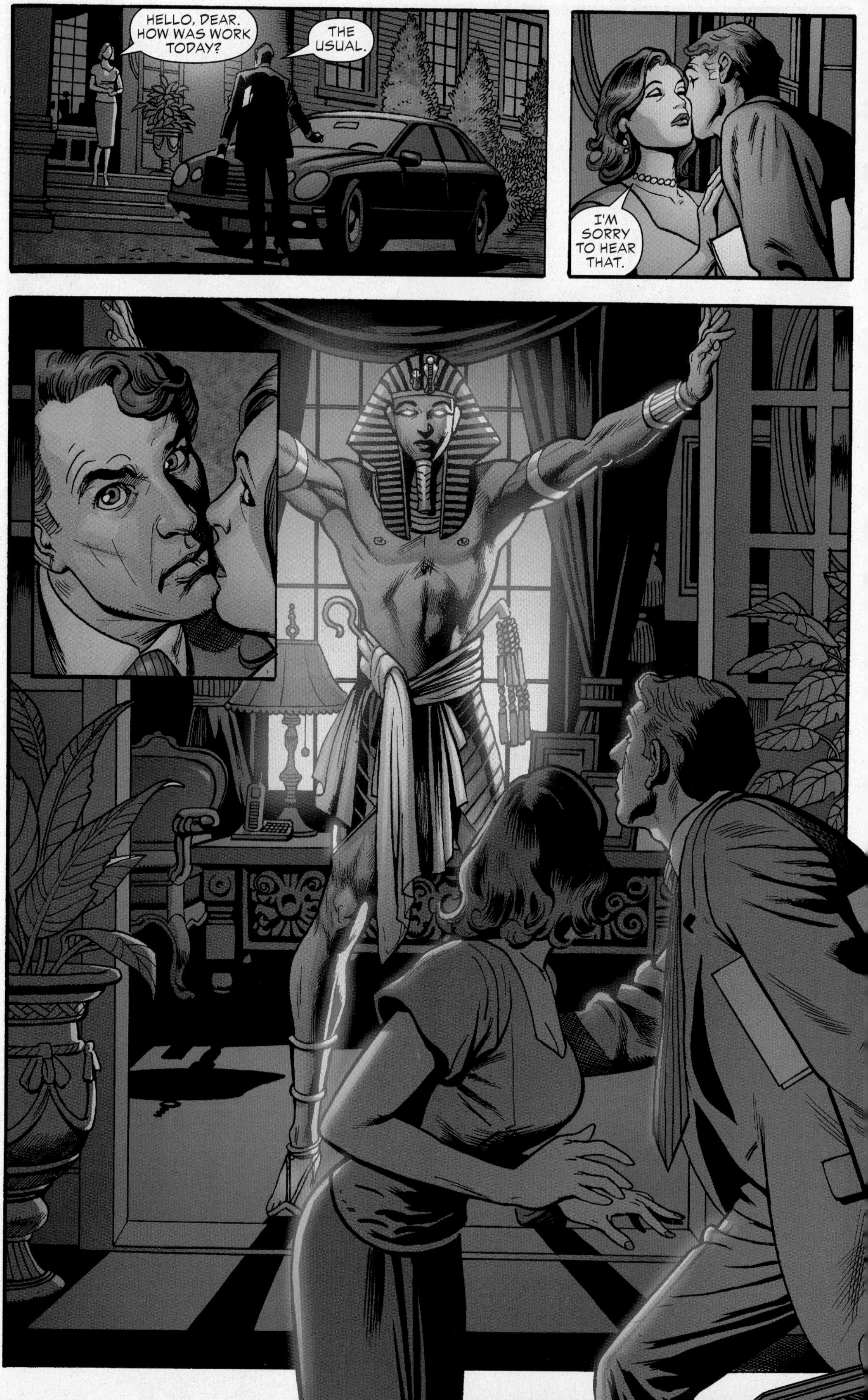
HELLO, DEAR. HOW WAS WORK TODAY?
THE USUAL.
I'M SORRY TO HEAR THAT.

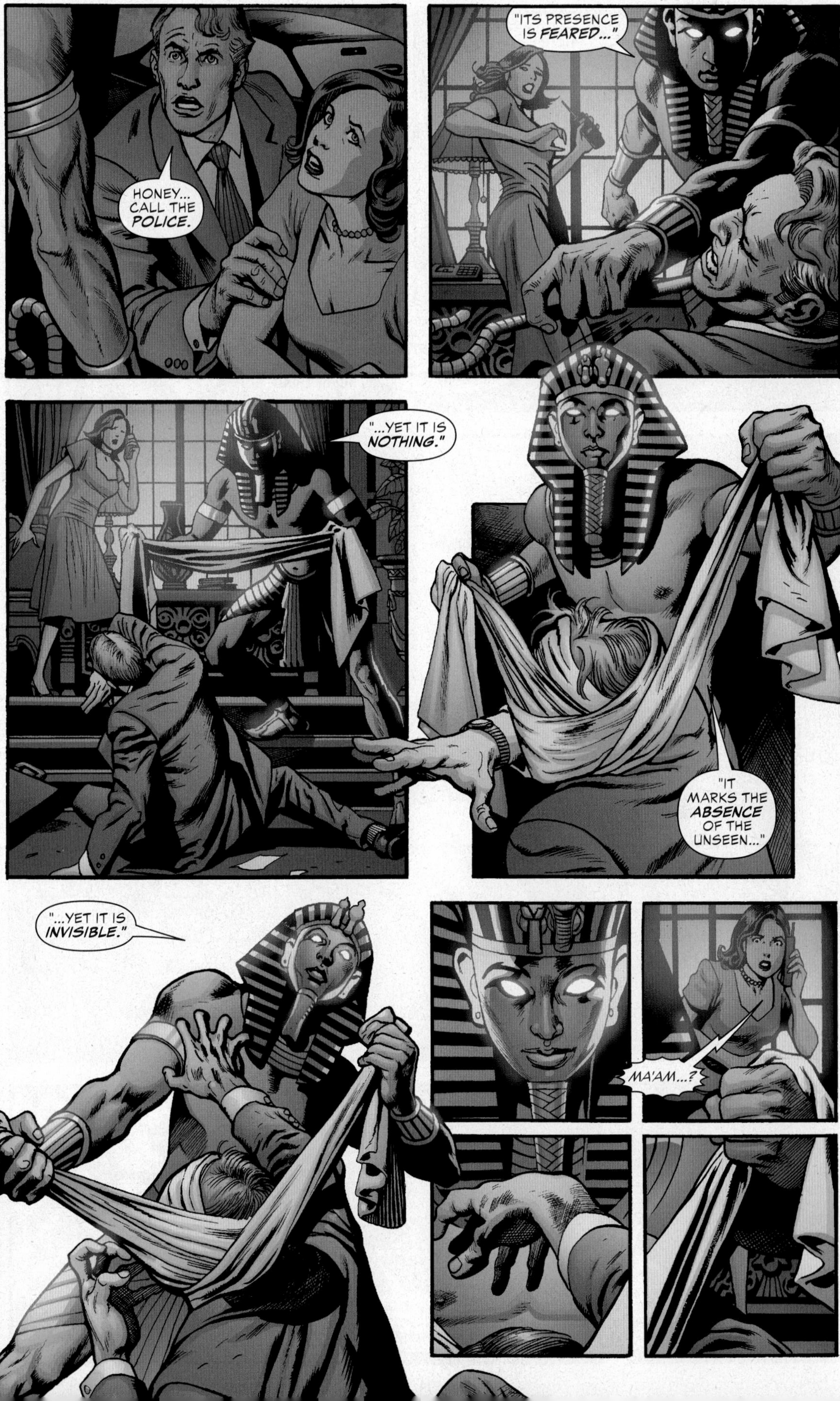
HONEY... CALL THE POLICE.
"ITS PRESENCE IS FEARED..."
"...YET IT IS NOTHING."
"IT MARKS THE ABSENCE OF THE UNSEEN..."
"...YET IT IS INVISIBLE."
MA'AM...?

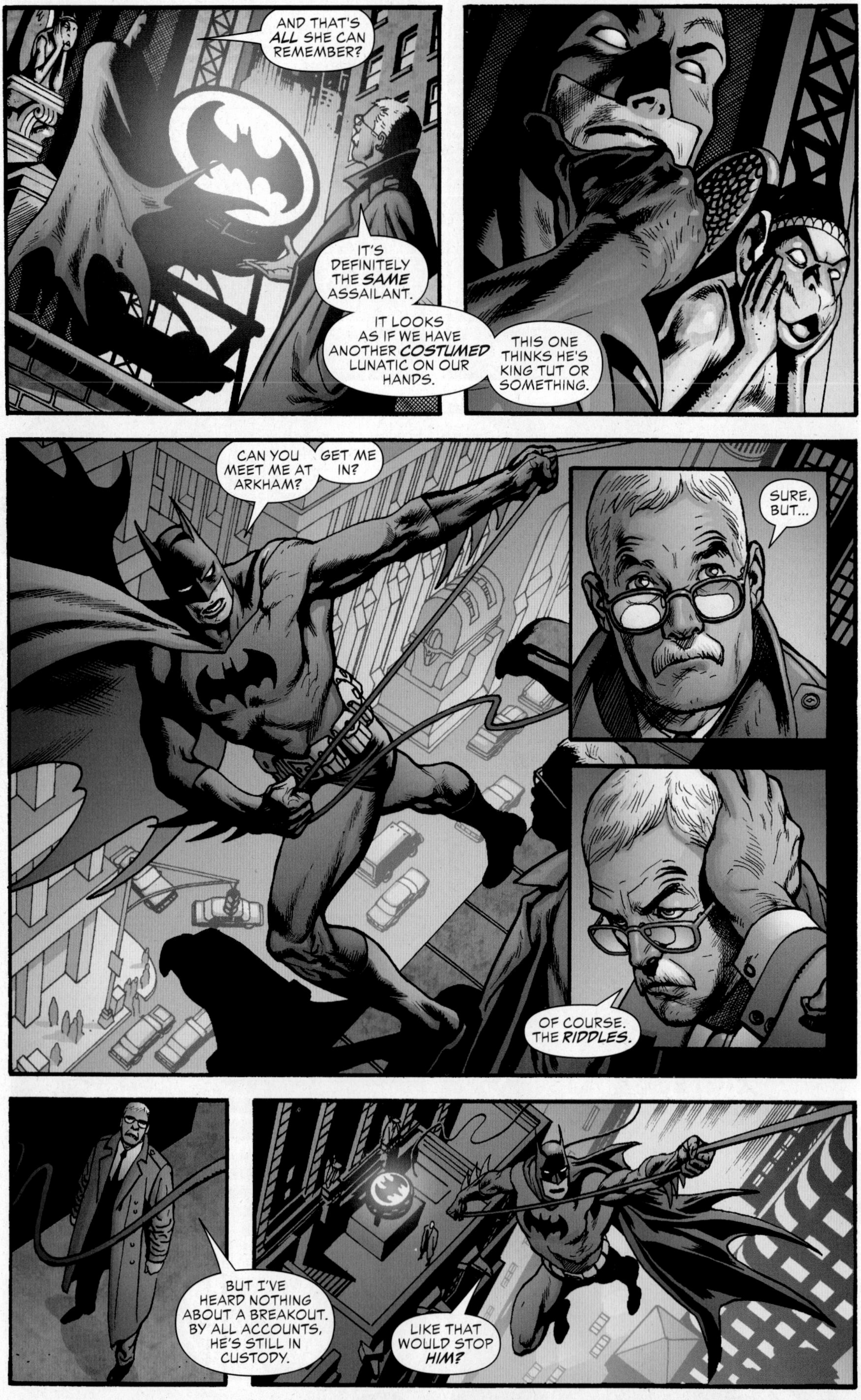
AND THAT'S ALL SHE CAN REMEMBER?
IT'S DEFINITELY THE SAME ASSAILANT.
IT LOOKS AS IF WE HAVE ANOTHER COSTUMED LUNATIC ON OUR HANDS.
THIS ONE THINKS HE'S KING TUT OR SOMETHING.
CAN YOU MEET ME AT ARKHAM?
GET ME IN?
SURE, BUT...
OF COURSE. THE RIDDLES.
BUT I'VE HEARD NOTHING ABOUT A BREAKOUT. BY ALL ACCOUNTS, HE'S STILL IN CUSTODY.
LIKE THAT WOULD STOP HIM?

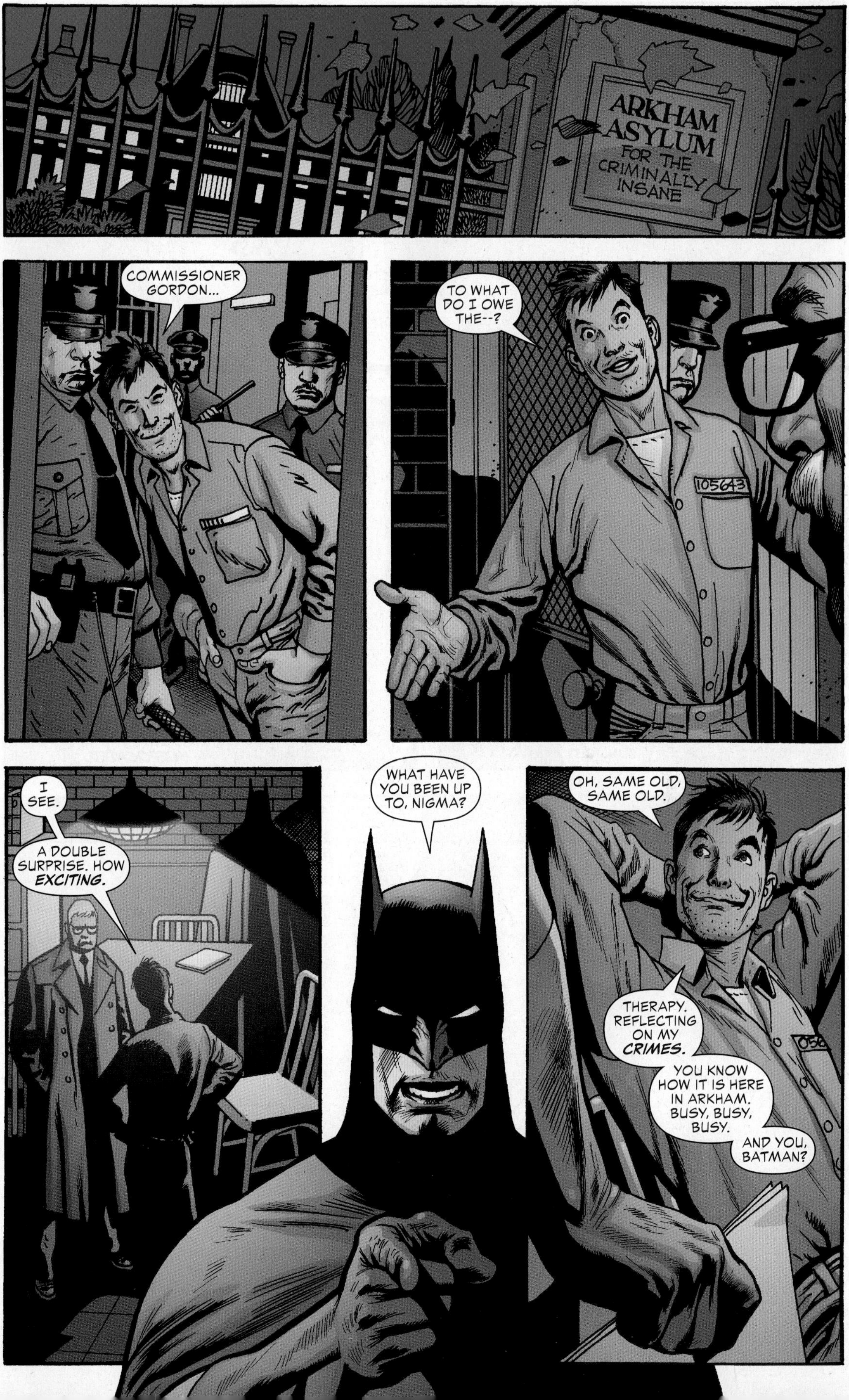
ARKHAM ASYLUM FOR THE CRIMINALLY INSANE
COMMISSIONER GORDON...
TO WHAT DO I OWE THE--?
105643
I SEE.
A DOUBLE SURPRISE. HOW *EXCITING.*
WHAT HAVE YOU BEEN UP TO, NIGMA?
OH, SAME OLD, SAME OLD.
THERAPY. REFLECTING ON MY *CRIMES.*
YOU KNOW HOW IT IS HERE IN ARKHAM. BUSY, BUSY, BUSY.
AND YOU, BATMAN?

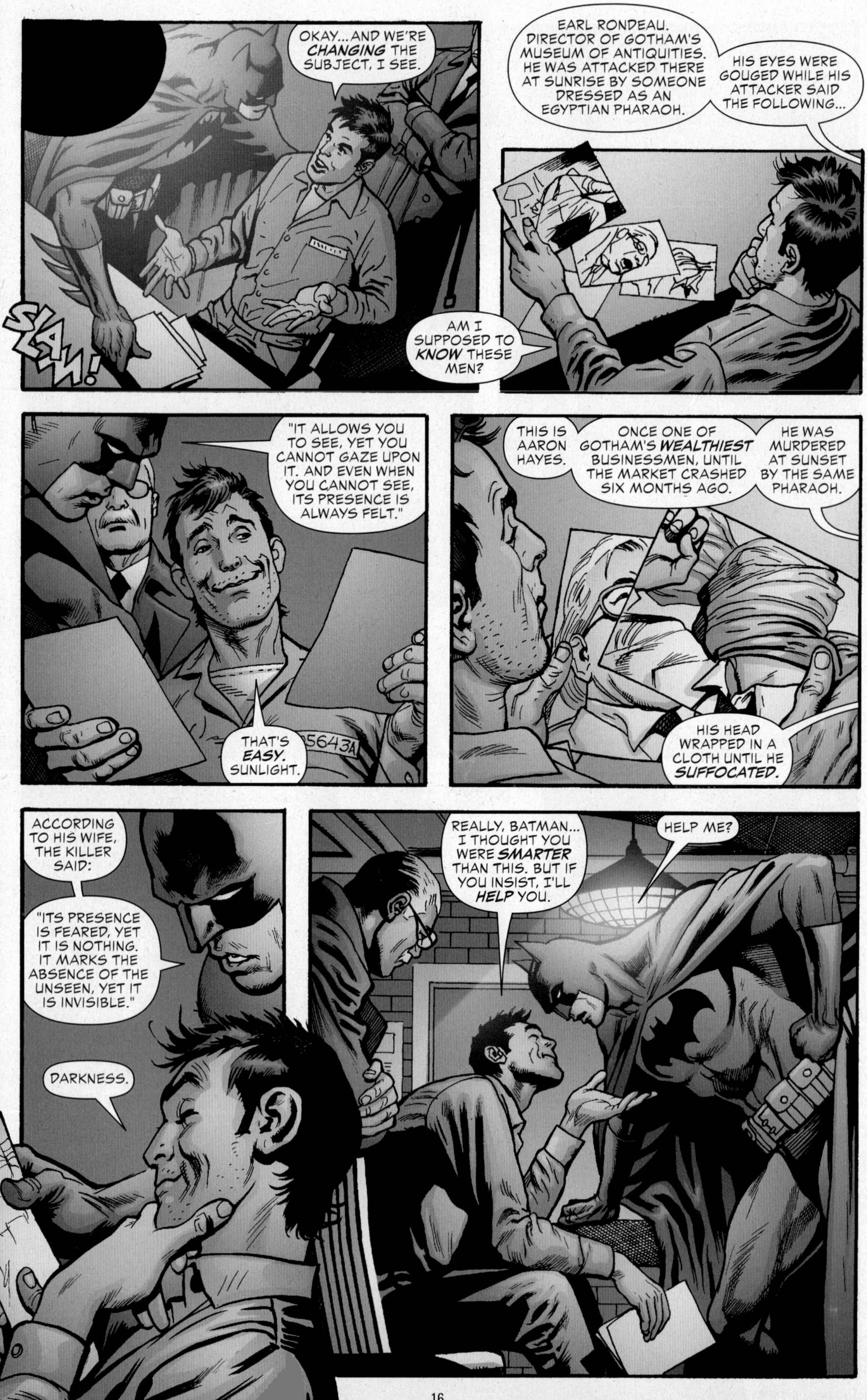
OKAY... AND WE'RE CHANGING THE SUBJECT, I SEE.
SLAM!
EARL RONDEAU. DIRECTOR OF GOTHAM'S MUSEUM OF ANTIQUITIES. HE WAS ATTACKED THERE AT SUNRISE BY SOMEONE DRESSED AS AN EGYPTIAN PHARAOH.
HIS EYES WERE GOUGED WHILE HIS ATTACKER SAID THE FOLLOWING...
AM I SUPPOSED TO KNOW THESE MEN?
"IT ALLOWS YOU TO SEE, YET YOU CANNOT GAZE UPON IT. AND EVEN WHEN YOU CANNOT SEE, ITS PRESENCE IS ALWAYS FELT."
THAT'S EASY. SUNLIGHT.
5643A
THIS IS AARON HAYES.
ONCE ONE OF GOTHAM'S WEALTHIEST BUSINESSMEN, UNTIL THE MARKET CRASHED SIX MONTHS AGO.
HE WAS MURDERED AT SUNSET BY THE SAME PHARAOH.
HIS HEAD WRAPPED IN A CLOTH UNTIL HE SUFFOCATED.
ACCORDING TO HIS WIFE, THE KILLER SAID:
"ITS PRESENCE IS FEARED, YET IT IS NOTHING. IT MARKS THE ABSENCE OF THE UNSEEN, YET IT IS INVISIBLE."
DARKNESS.
REALLY, BATMAN... I THOUGHT YOU WERE SMARTER THAN THIS. BUT IF YOU INSIST, I'LL HELP YOU.
HELP ME?

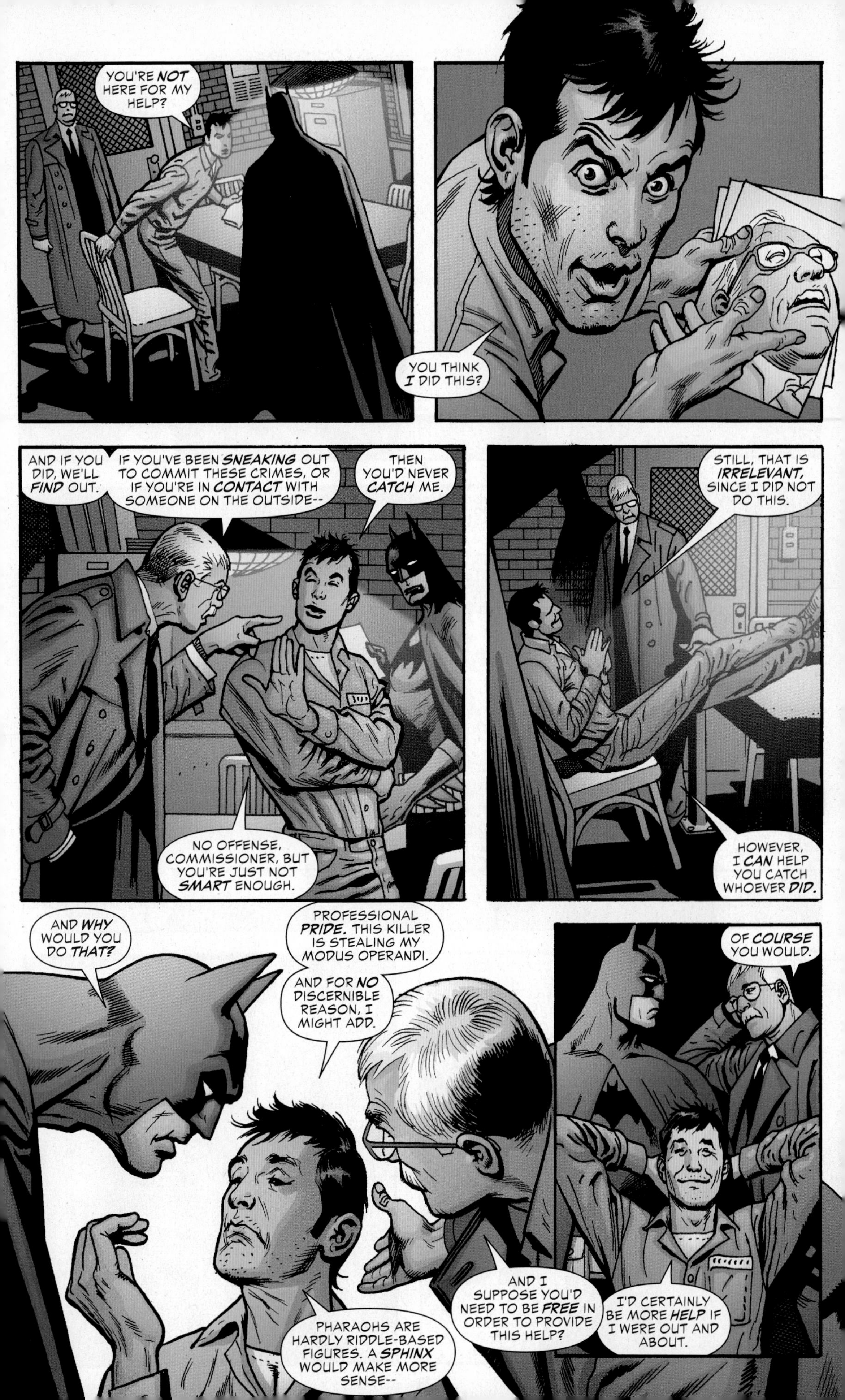
YOU'RE NOT HERE FOR MY HELP?
YOU THINK I DID THIS?
AND IF YOU DID, WE'LL FIND OUT.
IF YOU'VE BEEN SNEAKING OUT TO COMMIT THESE CRIMES, OR IF YOU'RE IN CONTACT WITH SOMEONE ON THE OUTSIDE--
THEN YOU'D NEVER CATCH ME.
NO OFFENSE, COMMISSIONER, BUT YOU'RE JUST NOT SMART ENOUGH.
STILL, THAT IS IRRELEVANT, SINCE I DID NOT DO THIS.
HOWEVER, I CAN HELP YOU CATCH WHOEVER DID.
AND WHY WOULD YOU DO THAT?
PROFESSIONAL PRIDE. THIS KILLER IS STEALING MY MODUS OPERANDI.
AND FOR NO DISCERNIBLE REASON, I MIGHT ADD.
PHARAOHS ARE HARDLY RIDDLE-BASED FIGURES. A SPHINX WOULD MAKE MORE SENSE--
OF COURSE YOU WOULD.
AND I SUPPOSE YOU'D NEED TO BE FREE IN ORDER TO PROVIDE THIS HELP?
I'D CERTAINLY BE MORE HELP IF I WERE OUT AND ABOUT.

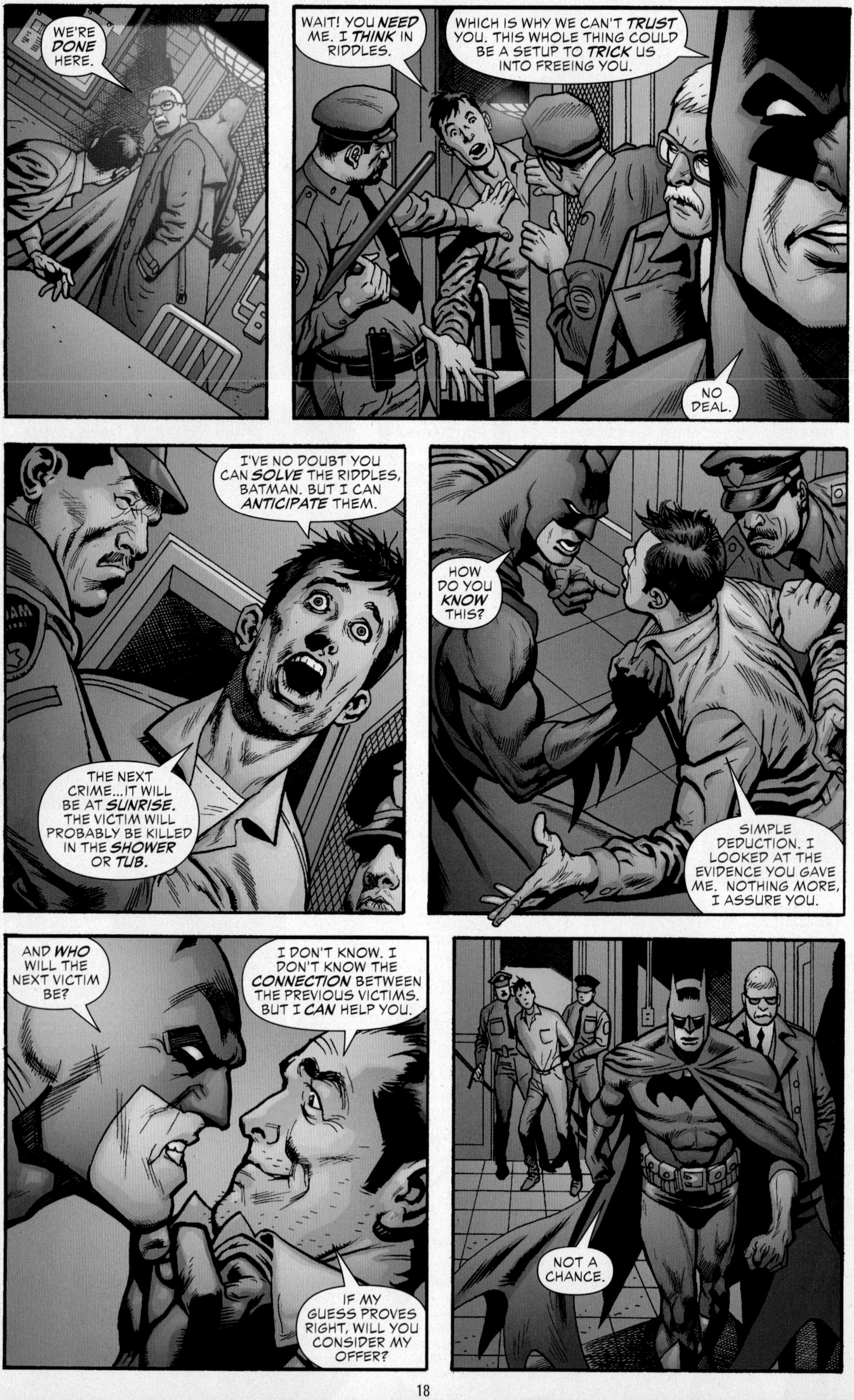
WE'RE DONE HERE.
WAIT! YOU NEED ME. I THINK IN RIDDLES.
WHICH IS WHY WE CAN'T TRUST YOU. THIS WHOLE THING COULD BE A SETUP TO TRICK US INTO FREEING YOU.
NO DEAL.
I'VE NO DOUBT YOU CAN SOLVE THE RIDDLES, BATMAN. BUT I CAN ANTICIPATE THEM.
THE NEXT CRIME...IT WILL BE AT SUNRISE. THE VICTIM WILL PROBABLY BE KILLED IN THE SHOWER OR TUB.
HOW DO YOU KNOW THIS?
SIMPLE DEDUCTION. I LOOKED AT THE EVIDENCE YOU GAVE ME. NOTHING MORE, I ASSURE YOU.
AND WHO WILL THE NEXT VICTIM BE?
I DON'T KNOW. I DON'T KNOW THE CONNECTION BETWEEN THE PREVIOUS VICTIMS. BUT I CAN HELP YOU.
IF MY GUESS PROVES RIGHT, WILL YOU CONSIDER MY OFFER?
NOT A CHANCE.

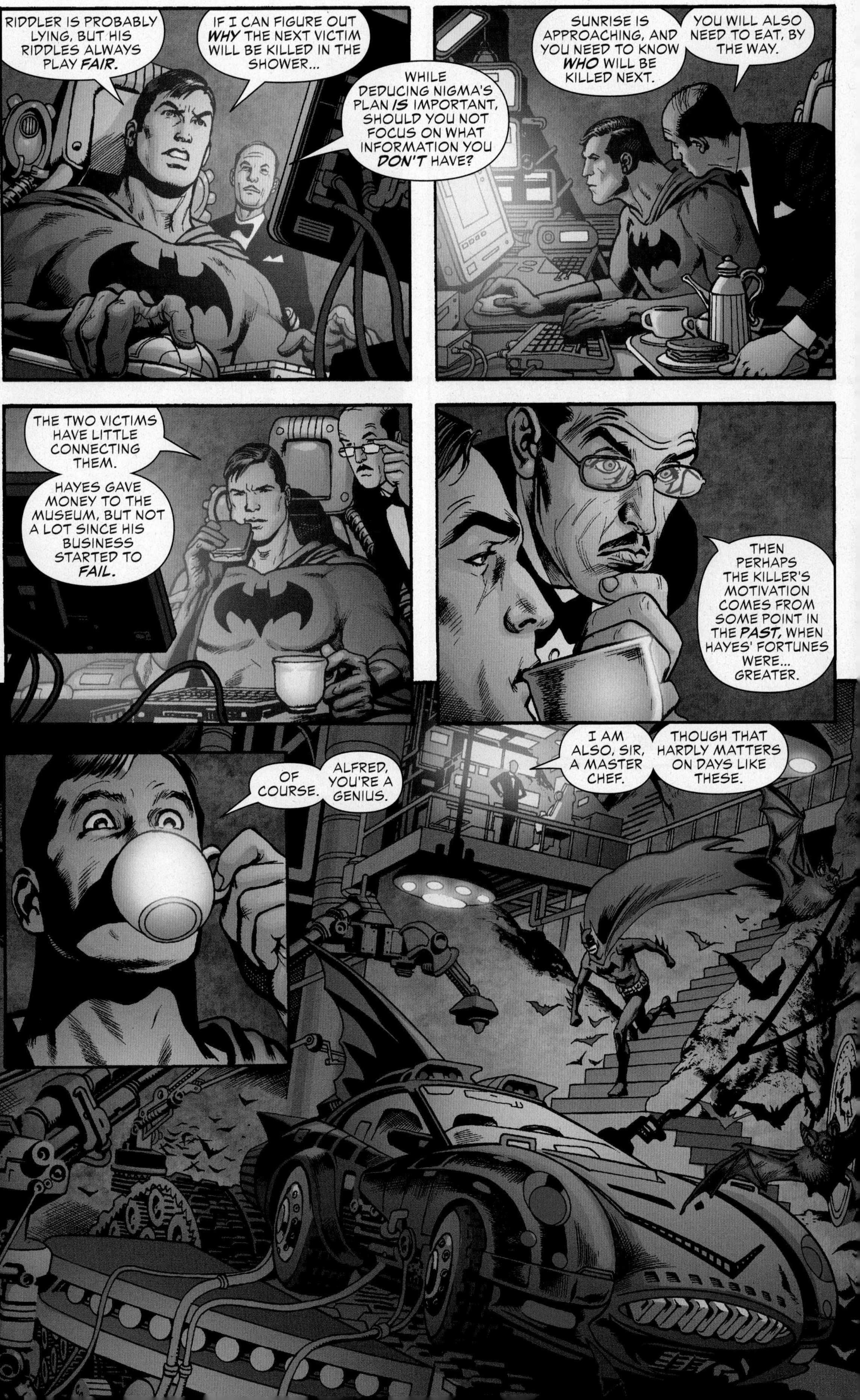
RIDDLER IS PROBABLY LYING, BUT HIS RIDDLES ALWAYS PLAY FAIR.
IF I CAN FIGURE OUT WHY THE NEXT VICTIM WILL BE KILLED IN THE SHOWER...
WHILE DEDUCING NIGMA'S PLAN IS IMPORTANT, SHOULD YOU NOT FOCUS ON WHAT INFORMATION YOU DON'T HAVE?
SUNRISE IS APPROACHING, AND YOU NEED TO KNOW WHO WILL BE KILLED NEXT.
YOU WILL ALSO NEED TO EAT, BY THE WAY.
THE TWO VICTIMS HAVE LITTLE CONNECTING THEM.
HAYES GAVE MONEY TO THE MUSEUM, BUT NOT A LOT SINCE HIS BUSINESS STARTED TO FAIL.
THEN PERHAPS THE KILLER'S MOTIVATION COMES FROM SOME POINT IN THE PAST, WHEN HAYES' FORTUNES WERE... GREATER.
OF COURSE.
ALFRED, YOU'RE A GENIUS.
I AM ALSO, SIR, A MASTER CHEF.
THOUGH THAT HARDLY MATTERS ON DAYS LIKE THESE.

THE MUSEUM'S BOARD OF *TRUSTEES.*

AARON HAYES WAS ON THE BOARD UNTIL SIX MONTHS AGO. HERE'S A LIST OF TRUSTEES AT THAT TIME.

IF YOU'RE RIGHT, THE NEXT VICTIM IS SOMEONE ON THIS LIST.

GET UNITS TO EVERY HOUSE ON THAT LIST.

THERE ARE *THIRTEEN* NAMES HERE, INCLUDING HAYES.

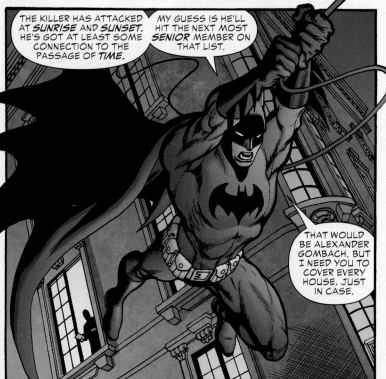

THE KILLER HAS ATTACKED AT *SUNRISE* AND *SUNSET.* HE'S GOT AT LEAST SOME CONNECTION TO THE PASSAGE OF *TIME.*

MY GUESS IS HE'LL HIT THE NEXT MOST *SENIOR* MEMBER ON THAT LIST.

THAT WOULD BE ALEXANDER GOMBACH. BUT I NEED YOU TO COVER EVERY HOUSE, JUST IN CASE.

BULLOCK! I'M GONNA NEED SQUAD CARS SENT TO TWELVE ADDRESSES.

NOW!

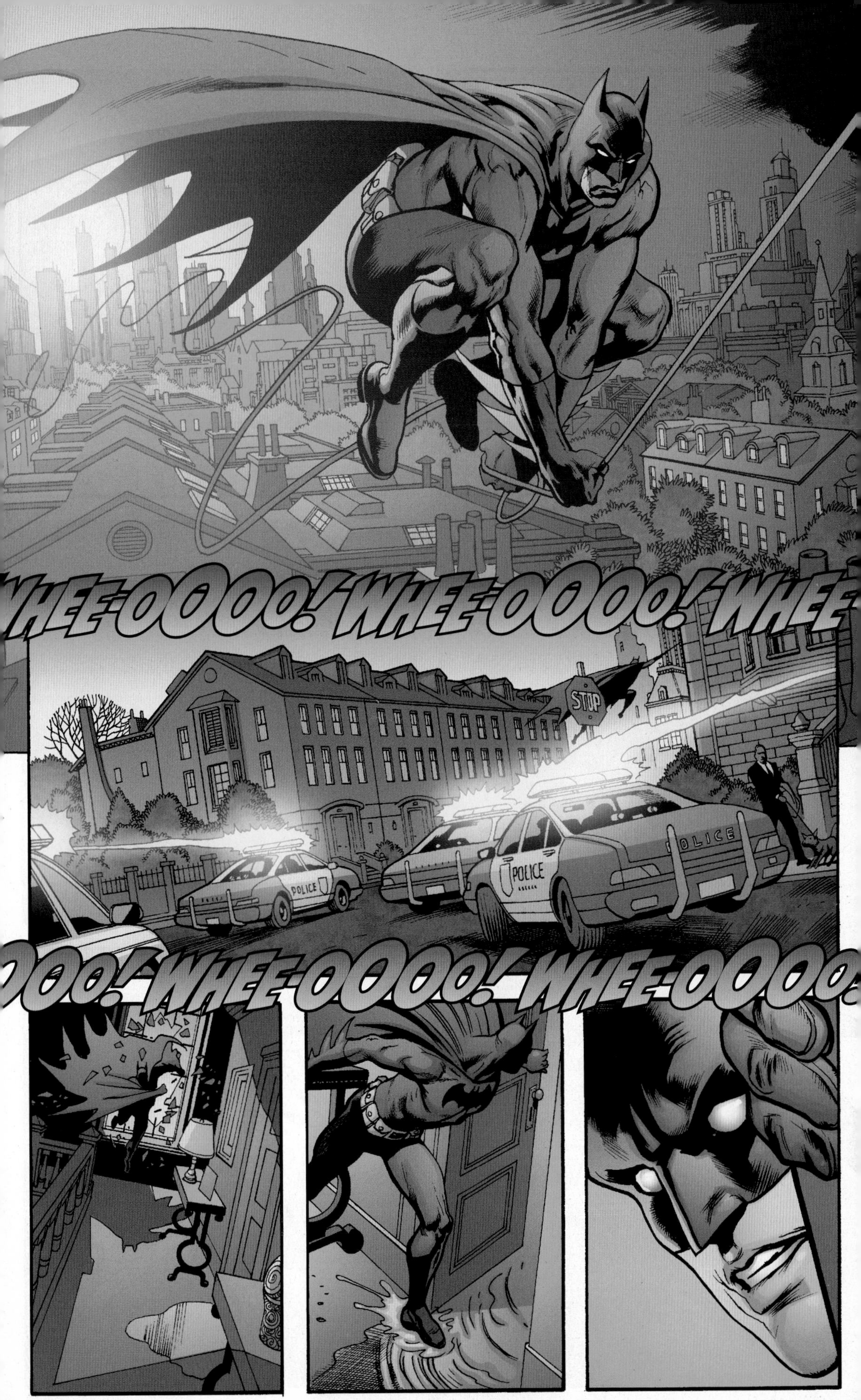
WHEE-OOOO! WHEE-OOOO! WHEE
STOP
POLICE
POLICE
POLICE
OOO! WHEE-OOOO! WHEE-OOOO

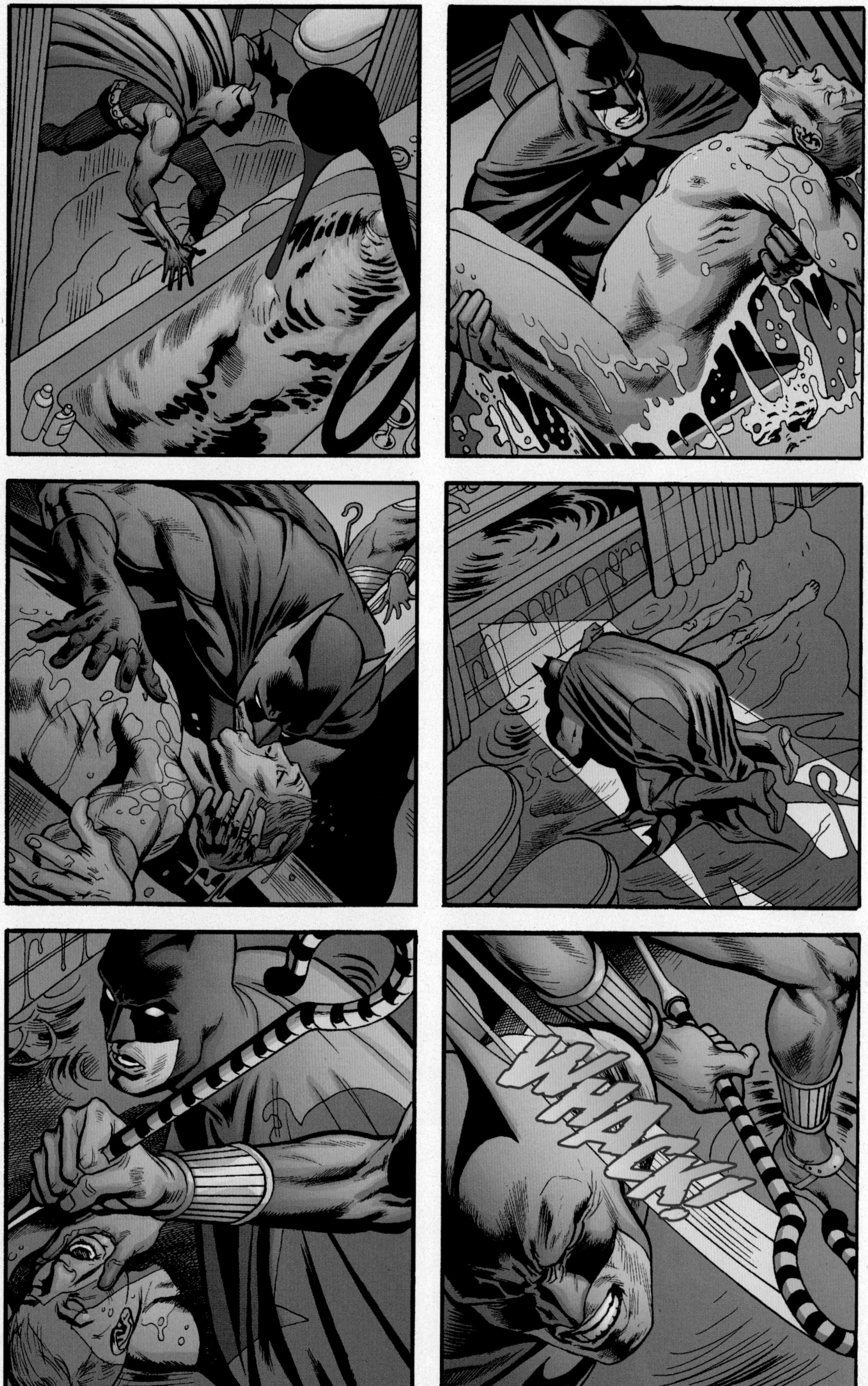
WHACK!

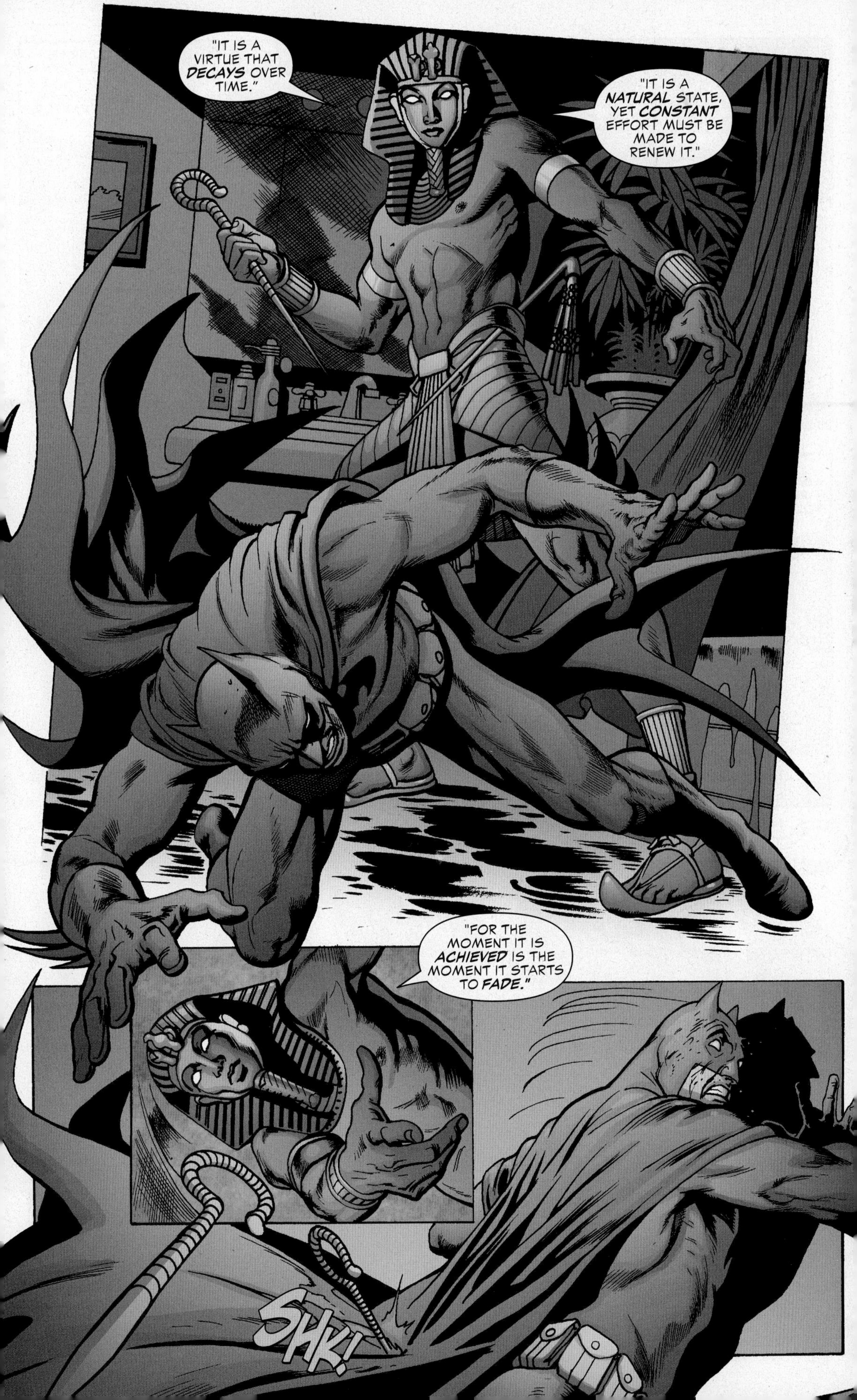
"IT IS A VIRTUE THAT DECAYS OVER TIME."
"IT IS A NATURAL STATE, YET CONSTANT EFFORT MUST BE MADE TO RENEW IT."
"FOR THE MOMENT IT IS ACHIEVED IS THE MOMENT IT STARTS TO FADE."
SHK!

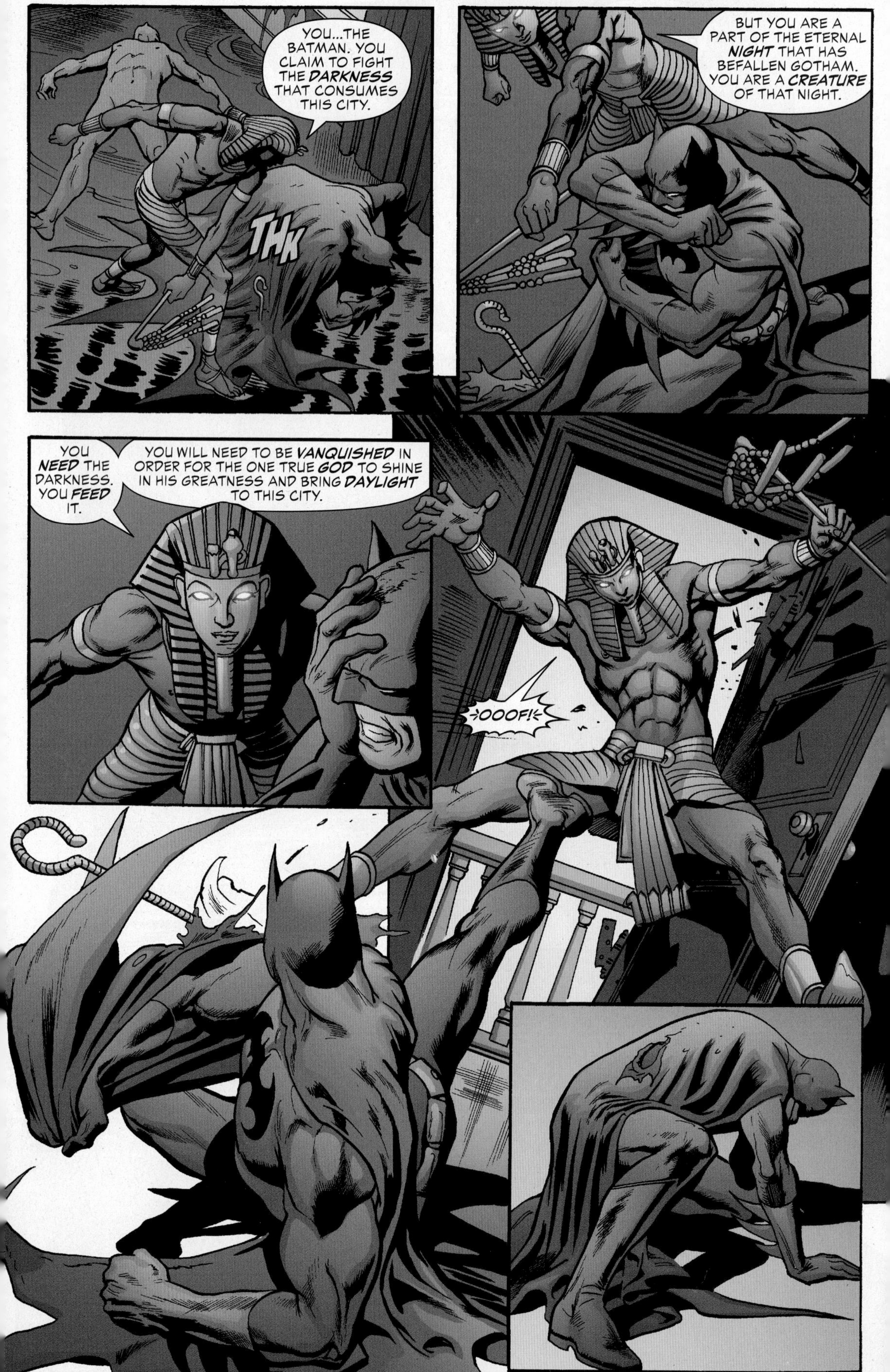
YOU...THE BATMAN. YOU CLAIM TO FIGHT THE DARKNESS THAT CONSUMES THIS CITY.
THK
BUT YOU ARE A PART OF THE ETERNAL NIGHT THAT HAS BEFALLEN GOTHAM. YOU ARE A CREATURE OF THAT NIGHT.
YOU NEED THE DARKNESS. YOU FEED IT.
YOU WILL NEED TO BE VANQUISHED IN ORDER FOR THE ONE TRUE GOD TO SHINE IN HIS GREATNESS AND BRING DAYLIGHT TO THIS CITY.
OOOF!

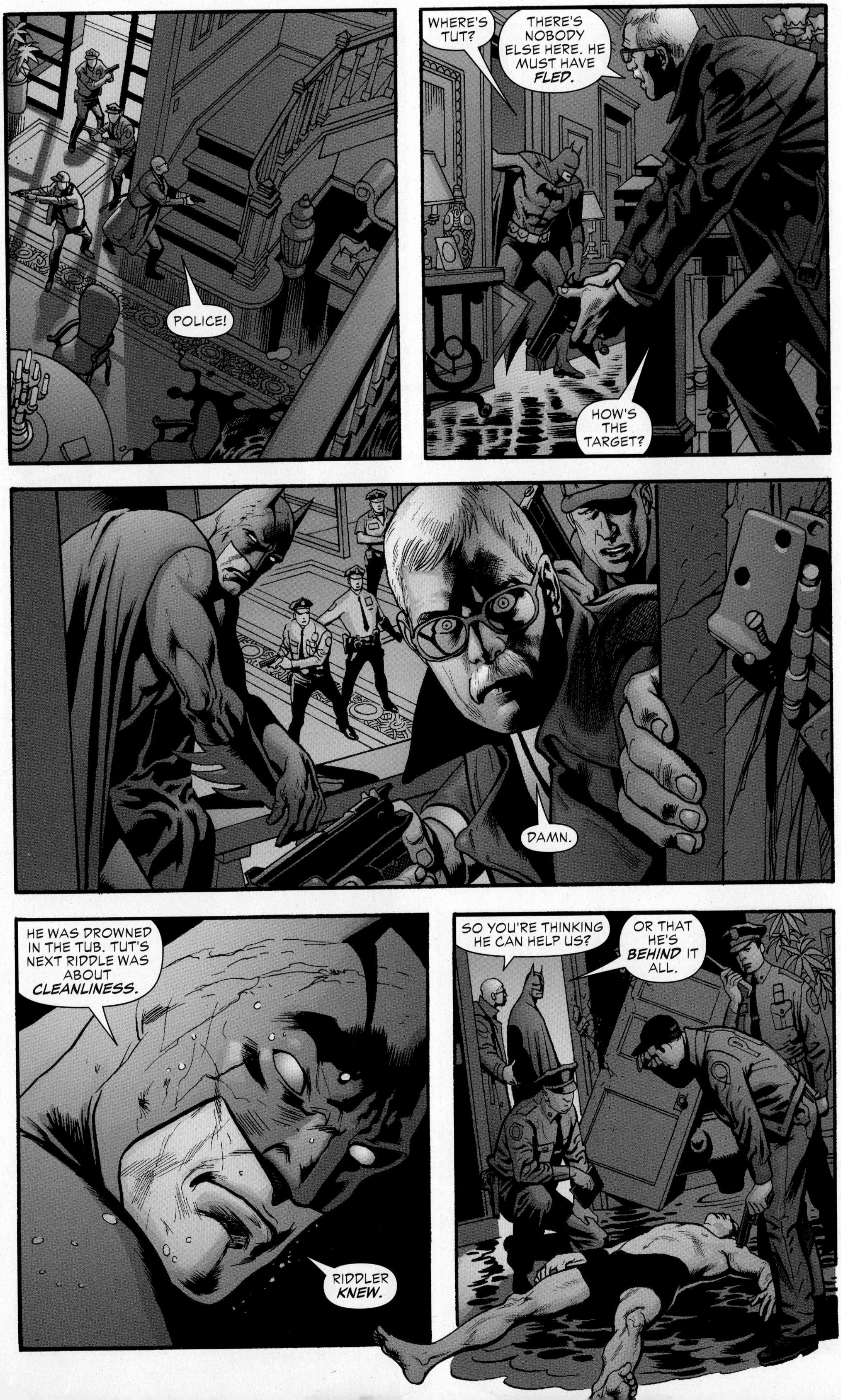
POLICE!
WHERE'S TUT?
THERE'S NOBODY ELSE HERE. HE MUST HAVE FLED.
HOW'S THE TARGET?
DAMN.
HE WAS DROWNED IN THE TUB. TUT'S NEXT RIDDLE WAS ABOUT CLEANLINESS.
RIDDLER KNEW.
SO YOU'RE THINKING HE CAN HELP US?
OR THAT HE'S BEHIND IT ALL.

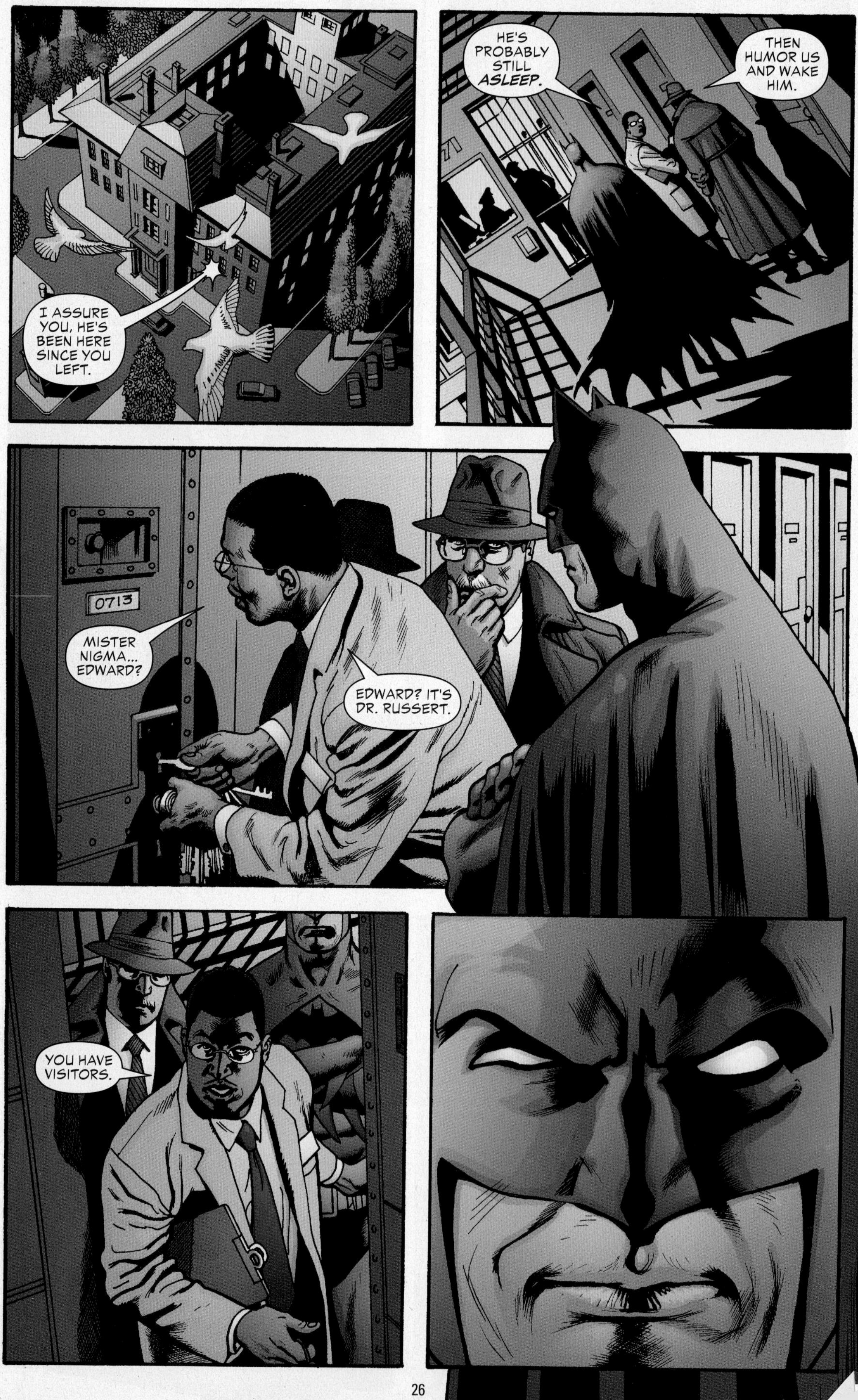
I ASSURE YOU, HE'S BEEN HERE SINCE YOU LEFT.
HE'S PROBABLY STILL ASLEEP.
THEN HUMOR US AND WAKE HIM.
0713
MISTER NIGMA... EDWARD?
EDWARD? IT'S DR. RUSSERT.
YOU HAVE VISITORS.

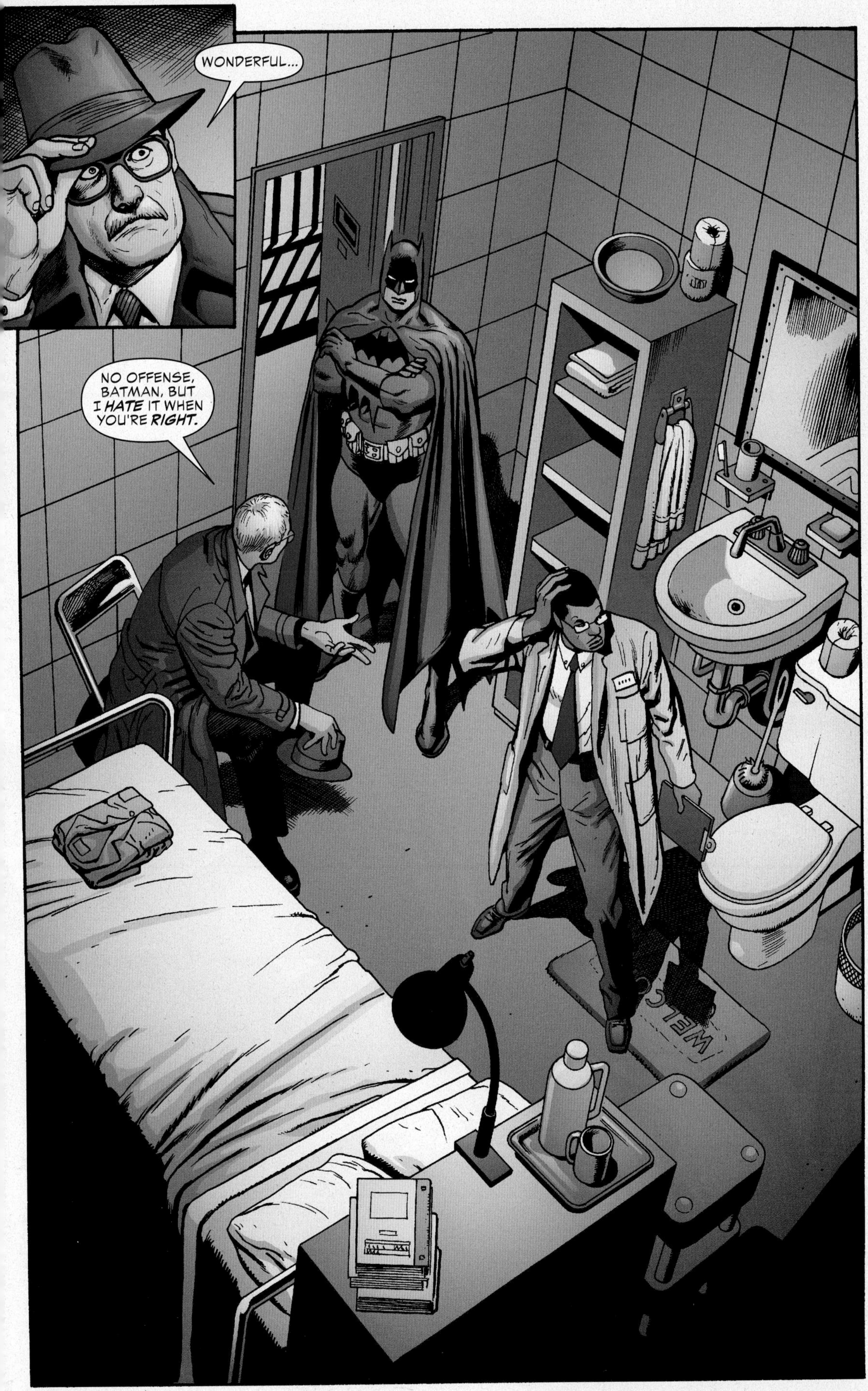
WONDERFUL...
NO OFFENSE, BATMAN, BUT I *HATE* IT WHEN YOU'RE *RIGHT.*
WELC

A NEW DAWN PART TWO ■ *Cover by José Luis García-López, Kevin Nowlan and David Baron*

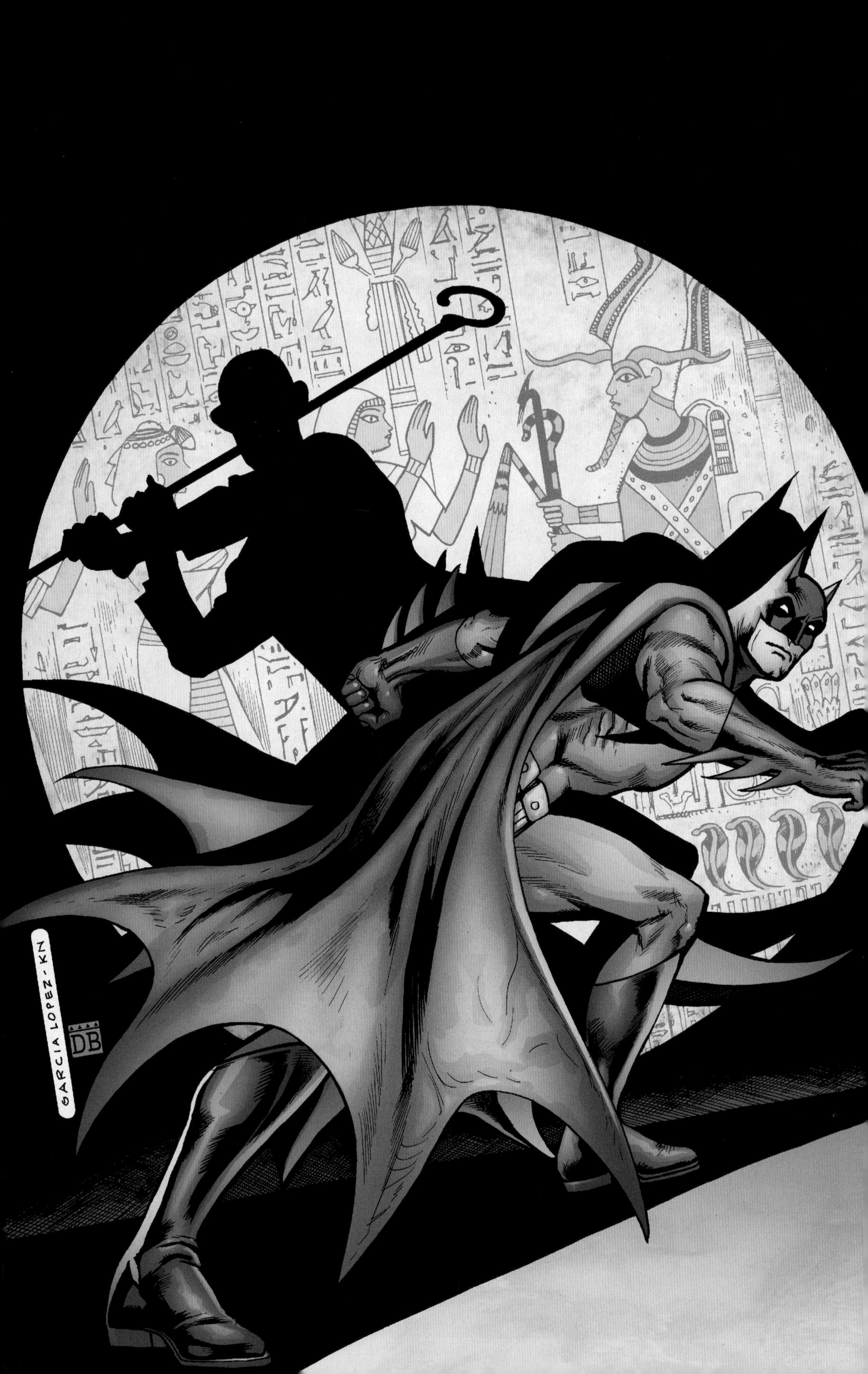
GARCIA LOPEZ - KN
DB

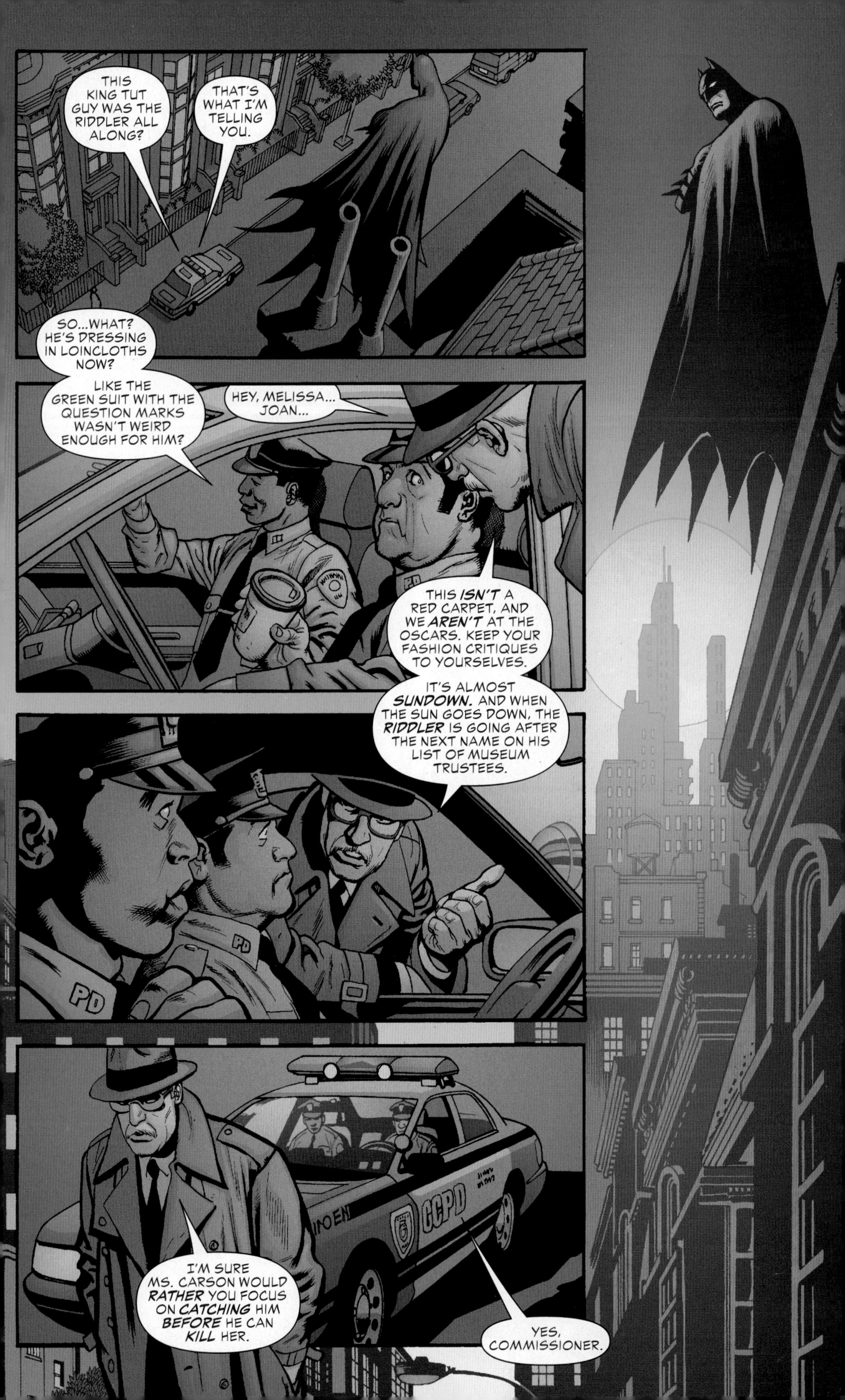
THIS KING TUT GUY WAS THE RIDDLER ALL ALONG?
THAT'S WHAT I'M TELLING YOU.
SO...WHAT? HE'S DRESSING IN LOINCLOTHS NOW?
LIKE THE GREEN SUIT WITH THE QUESTION MARKS WASN'T WEIRD ENOUGH FOR HIM?
HEY, MELISSA... JOAN...
THIS ISN'T A RED CARPET, AND WE AREN'T AT THE OSCARS. KEEP YOUR FASHION CRITIQUES TO YOURSELVES.
IT'S ALMOST SUNDOWN. AND WHEN THE SUN GOES DOWN, THE RIDDLER IS GOING AFTER THE NEXT NAME ON HIS LIST OF MUSEUM TRUSTEES.
I'M SURE MS. CARSON WOULD RATHER YOU FOCUS ON CATCHING HIM BEFORE HE CAN KILL HER.
YES, COMMISSIONER.

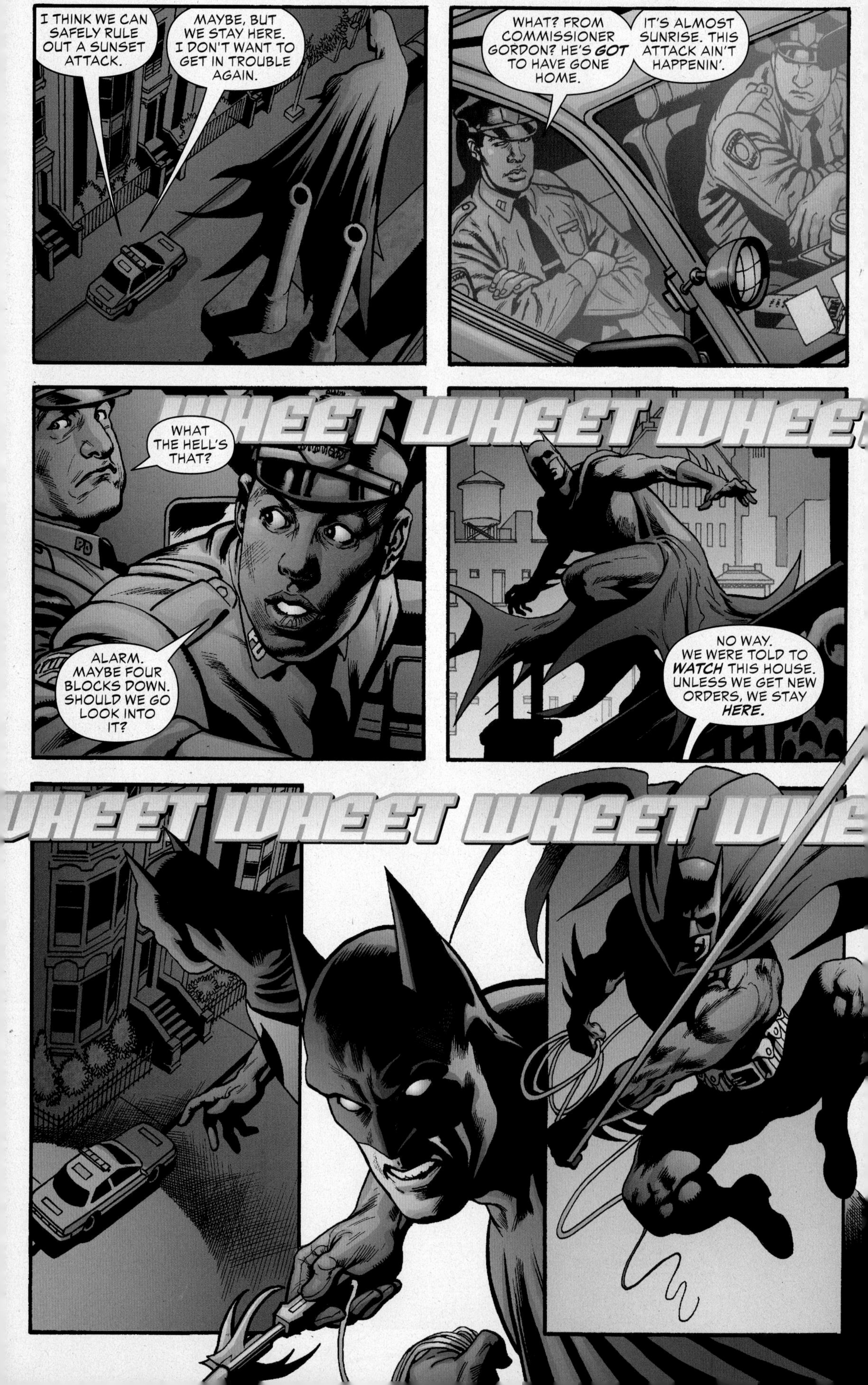
I THINK WE CAN SAFELY RULE OUT A SUNSET ATTACK.
MAYBE, BUT WE STAY HERE. I DON'T WANT TO GET IN TROUBLE AGAIN.
WHAT? FROM COMMISSIONER GORDON? HE'S GOT TO HAVE GONE HOME.
IT'S ALMOST SUNRISE. THIS ATTACK AIN'T HAPPENIN'.
WHEET WHEET WHEE
WHAT THE HELL'S THAT?
ALARM. MAYBE FOUR BLOCKS DOWN. SHOULD WE GO LOOK INTO IT?
NO WAY. WE WERE TOLD TO WATCH THIS HOUSE. UNLESS WE GET NEW ORDERS, WE STAY HERE.
WHEET WHEET WHEET WHE

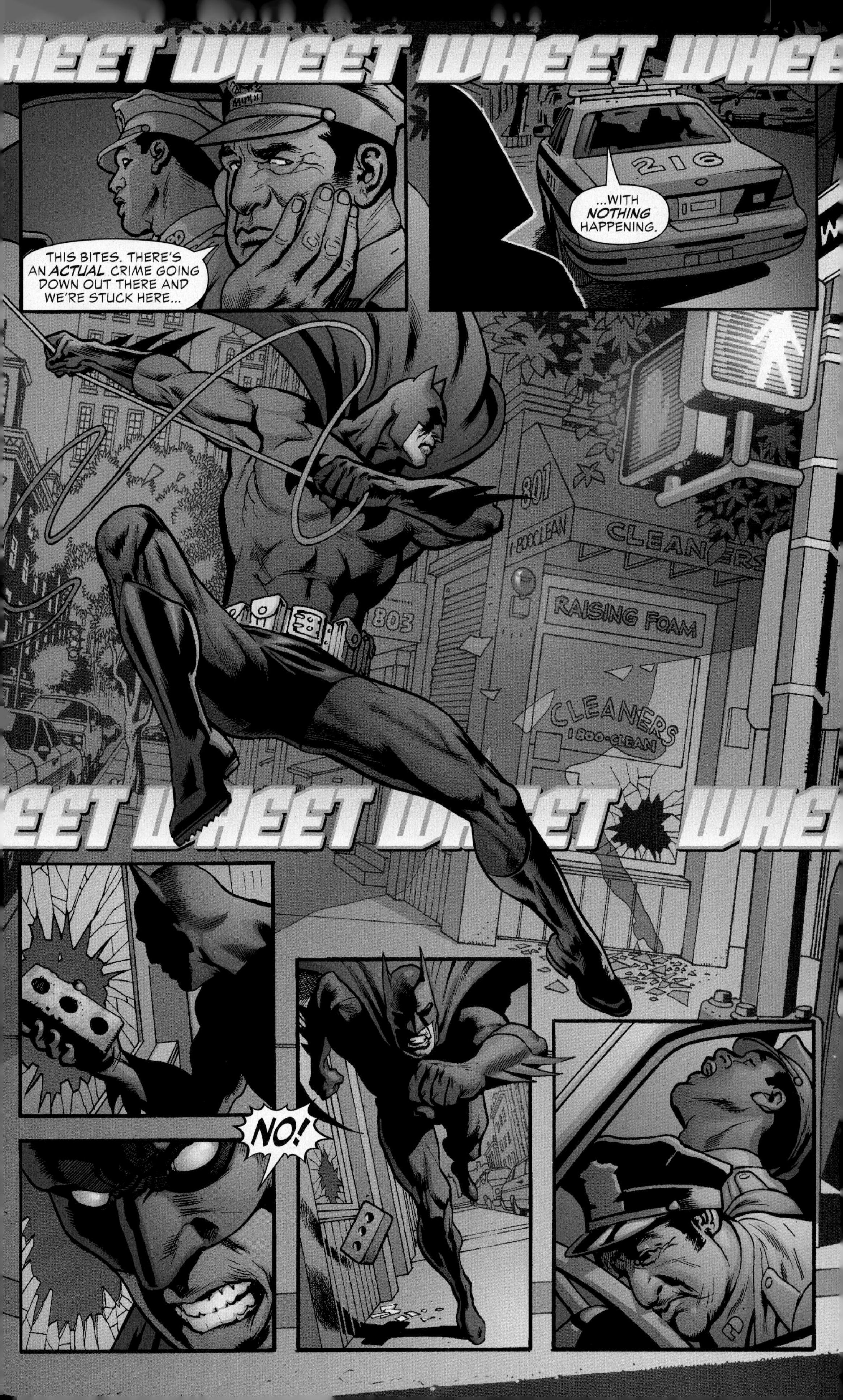
HEET WHEET WHEET WHEE
THIS BITES. THERE'S AN ACTUAL CRIME GOING DOWN OUT THERE AND WE'RE STUCK HERE...
216
...WITH NOTHING HAPPENING.
801
1-800CLEAN
CLEANERS
RAISING FOAM
803
CLEANERS 1 800-CLEAN
EET WHEET WHEET WHE
NO!

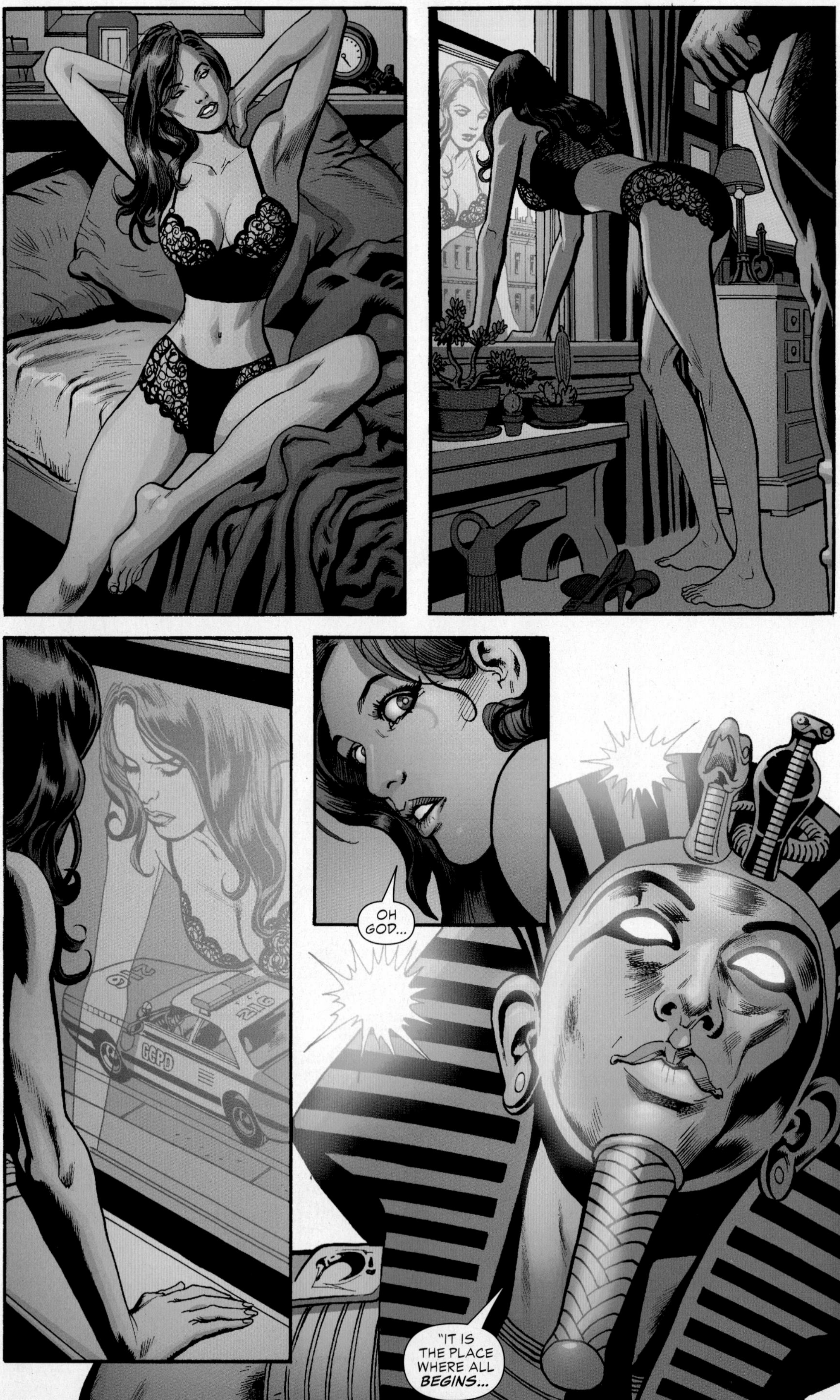
OH GOD...
"IT IS THE PLACE WHERE ALL BEGINS...

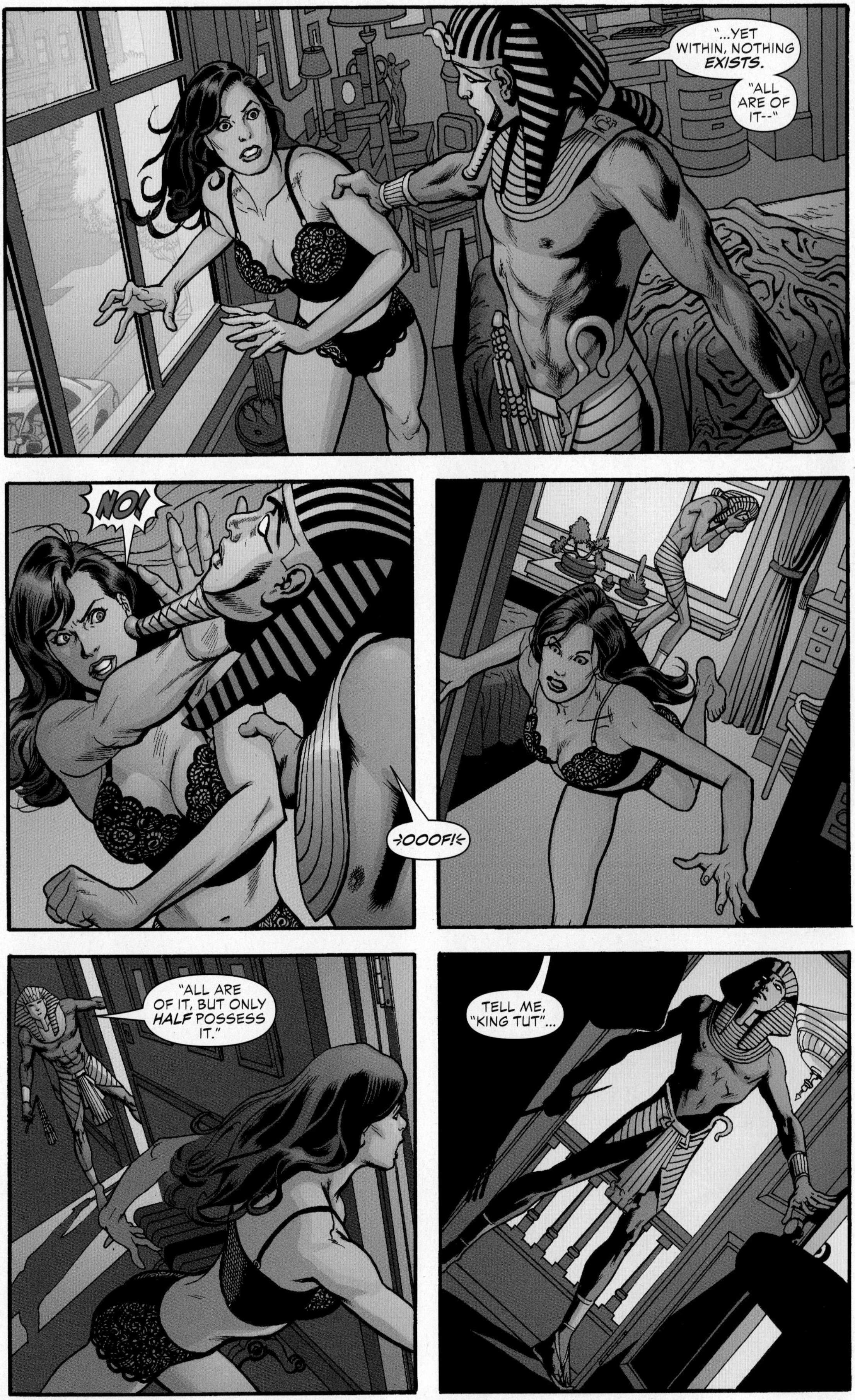
"...YET WITHIN, NOTHING EXISTS.
"ALL ARE OF IT--"
NO!
OOOF!
"ALL ARE OF IT, BUT ONLY HALF POSSESS IT."
TELL ME, "KING TUT"...

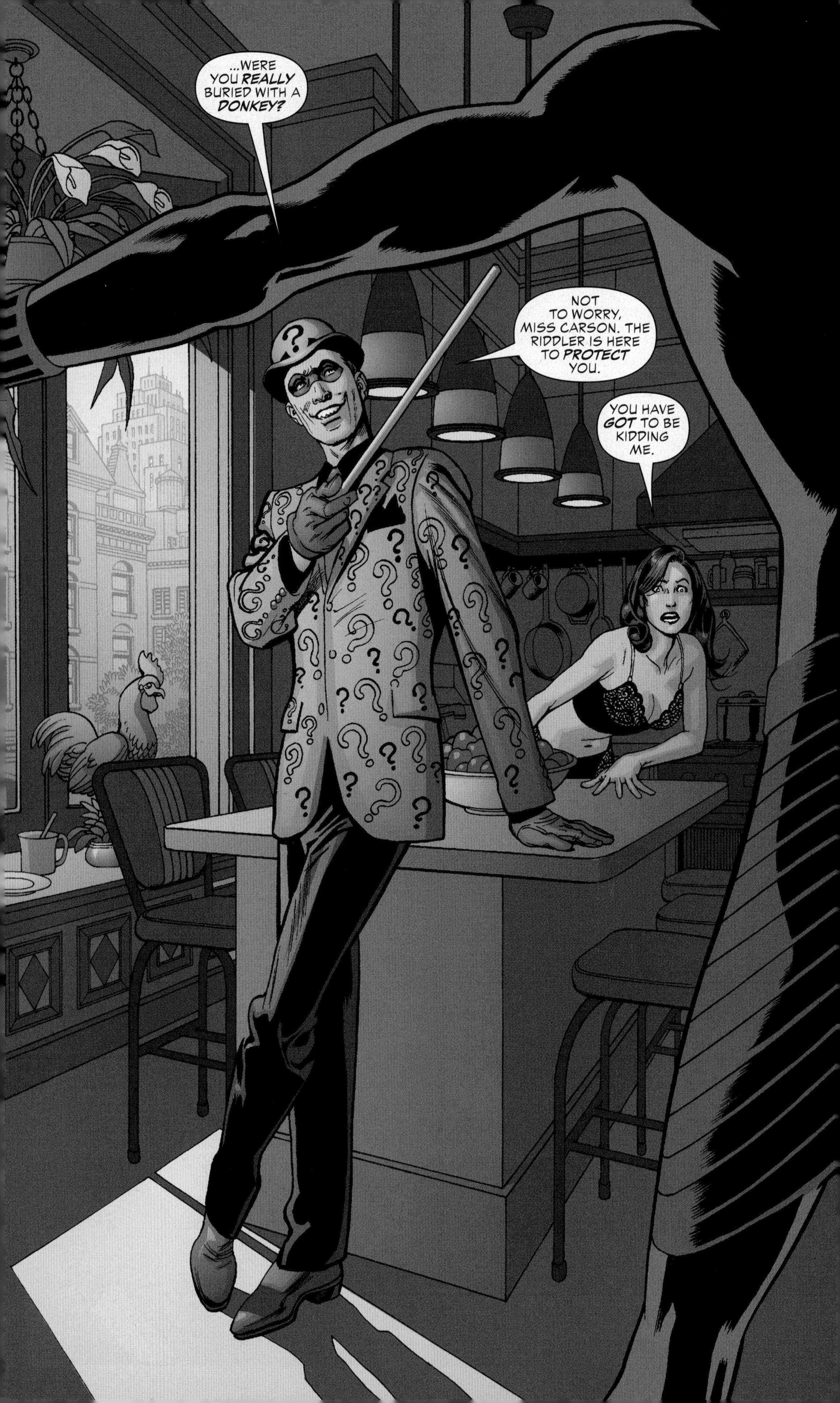
...WERE YOU REALLY BURIED WITH A DONKEY?
NOT TO WORRY, MISS CARSON. THE RIDDLER IS HERE TO PROTECT YOU.
YOU HAVE GOT TO BE KIDDING ME.

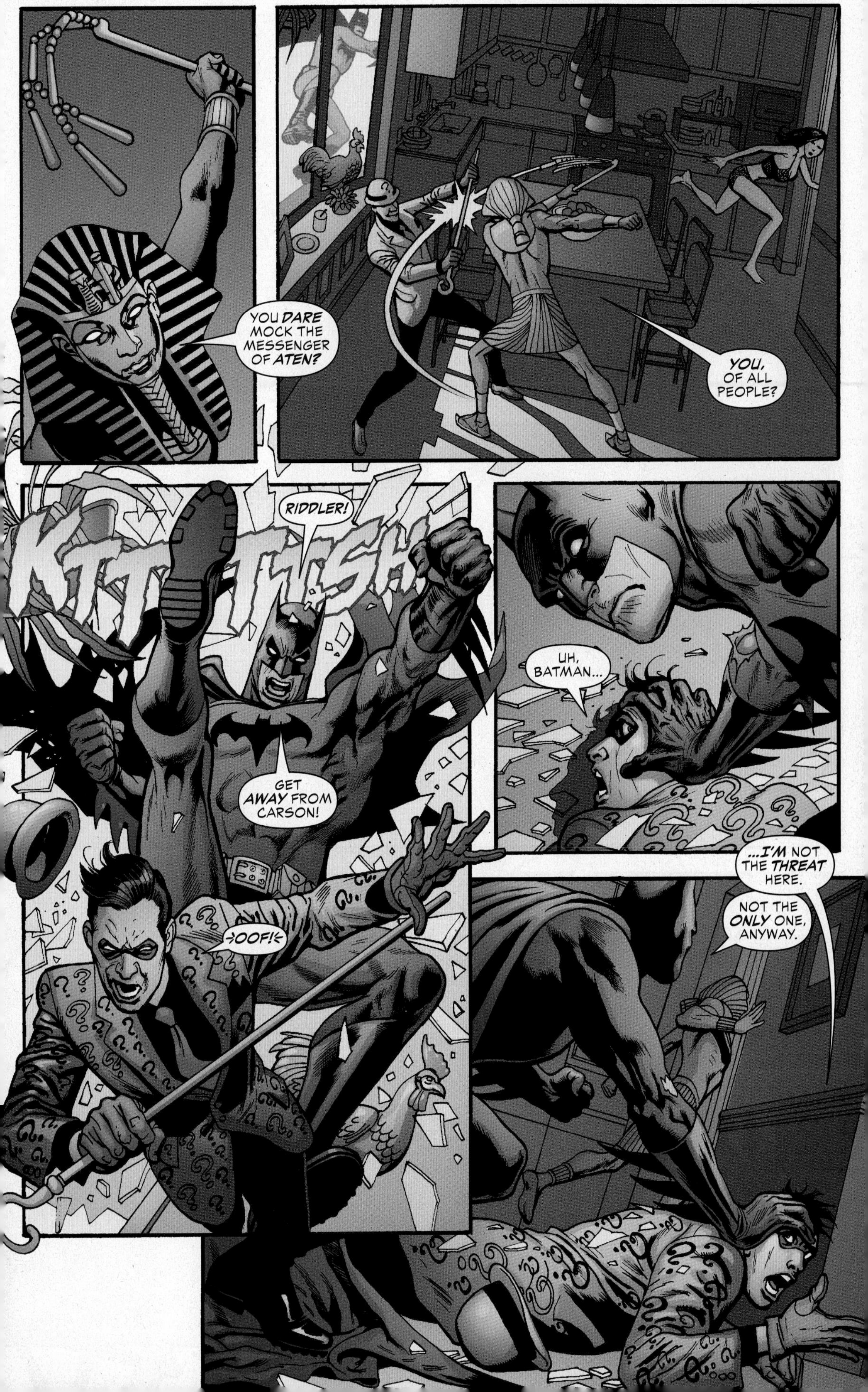
YOU DARE MOCK THE MESSENGER OF ATEN?
YOU, OF ALL PEOPLE?
RIDDLER!
GET AWAY FROM CARSON!
OOF!
UH, BATMAN...
...I'M NOT THE THREAT HERE.
NOT THE ONLY ONE, ANYWAY.

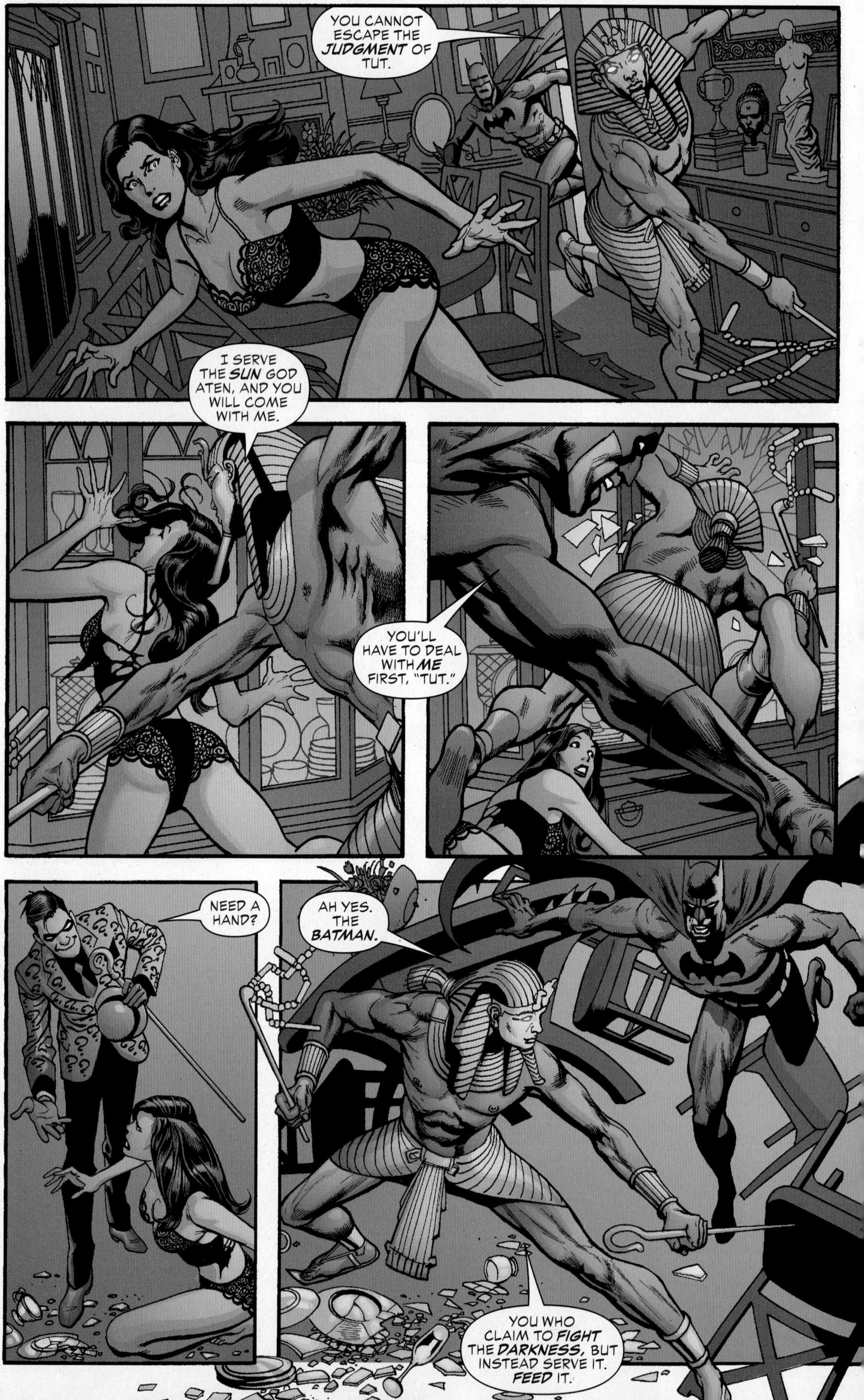
YOU CANNOT ESCAPE THE JUDGMENT OF TUT.
I SERVE THE SUN GOD ATEN, AND YOU WILL COME WITH ME.
YOU'LL HAVE TO DEAL WITH ME FIRST, "TUT."
NEED A HAND?
AH YES. THE BATMAN.
YOU WHO CLAIM TO FIGHT THE DARKNESS, BUT INSTEAD SERVE IT. FEED IT.

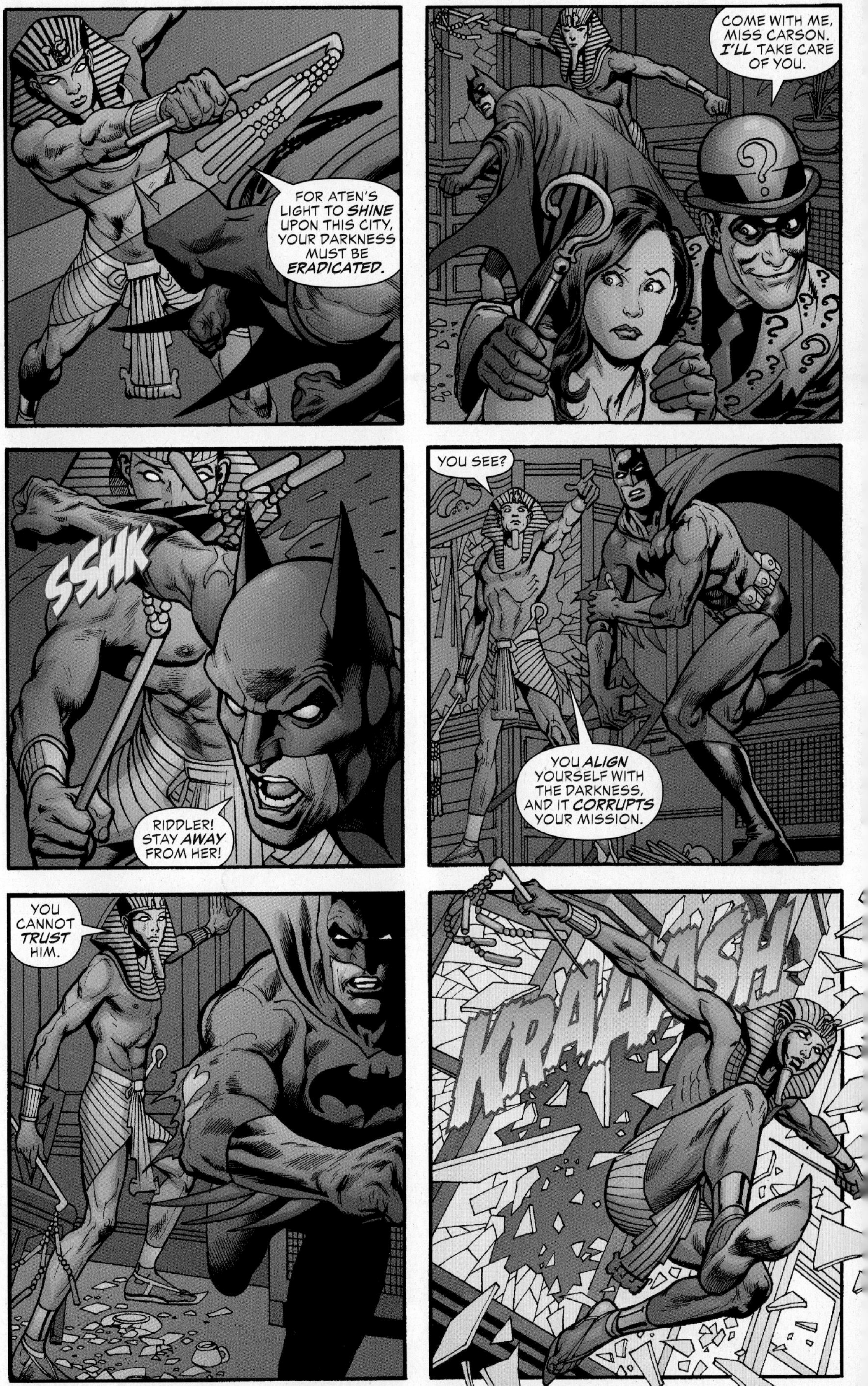

FOR ATEN'S LIGHT TO SHINE UPON THIS CITY, YOUR DARKNESS MUST BE ERADICATED.
COME WITH ME, MISS CARSON. I'LL TAKE CARE OF YOU.
SSHK
RIDDLER! STAY AWAY FROM HER!
YOU SEE?
YOU ALIGN YOURSELF WITH THE DARKNESS, AND IT CORRUPTS YOUR MISSION.
YOU CANNOT TRUST HIM.
KRAAASH

RIDDLER...

...I SAID...

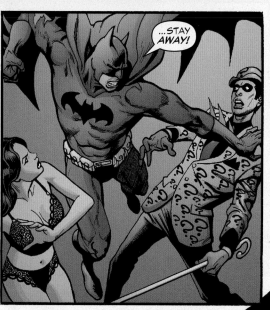

...STAY AWAY!

BATMAN, PLEASE. IS THERE THIS LITTLE TRUST BETWEEN YOU AND ROBIN?

WAIT. HE'S YOUR PARTNER NOW?

NO. HE'S NOT. ARE YOU ALL RIGHT, MS. CARSON?

I'M FINE.

DID TUT SAY ANYTHING...?

YES, ACTUALLY. IT WAS CONFUSING. LIKE A RIDDLE. SOMETHING ABOUT--

THE WOMB.

WHAT?

I TOLD YOU. I DON'T JUST SOLVE RIDDLES. I ANTICIPATE

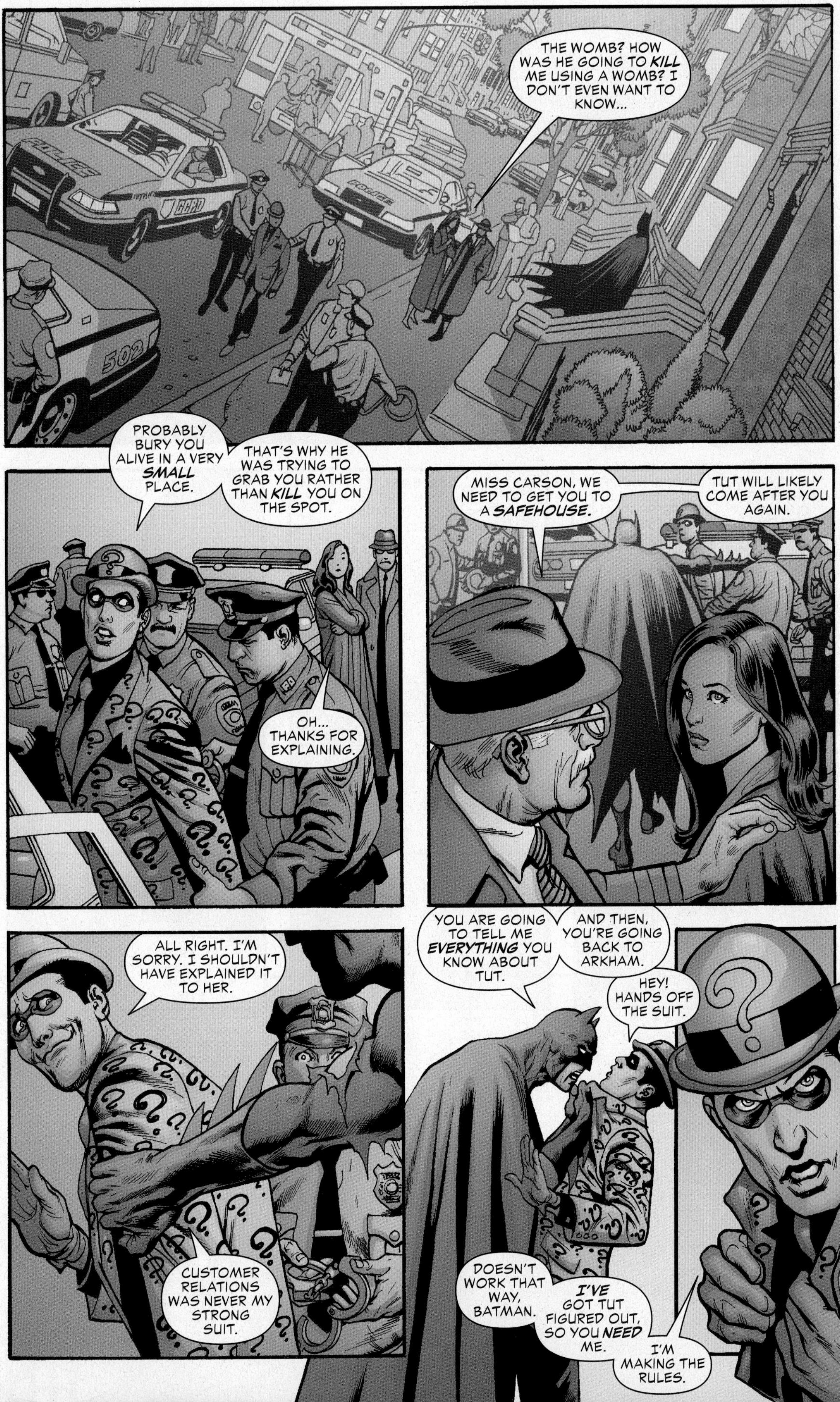
THE WOMB? HOW WAS HE GOING TO KILL ME USING A WOMB? I DON'T EVEN WANT TO KNOW...
PROBABLY BURY YOU ALIVE IN A VERY SMALL PLACE.
THAT'S WHY HE WAS TRYING TO GRAB YOU RATHER THAN KILL YOU ON THE SPOT.
OH... THANKS FOR EXPLAINING.
MISS CARSON, WE NEED TO GET YOU TO A SAFEHOUSE.
TUT WILL LIKELY COME AFTER YOU AGAIN.
ALL RIGHT. I'M SORRY. I SHOULDN'T HAVE EXPLAINED IT TO HER.
CUSTOMER RELATIONS WAS NEVER MY STRONG SUIT.
YOU ARE GOING TO TELL ME EVERYTHING YOU KNOW ABOUT TUT.
AND THEN, YOU'RE GOING BACK TO ARKHAM.
HEY! HANDS OFF THE SUIT.
DOESN'T WORK THAT WAY, BATMAN.
I'VE GOT TUT FIGURED OUT, SO YOU NEED ME.
I'M MAKING THE RULES.

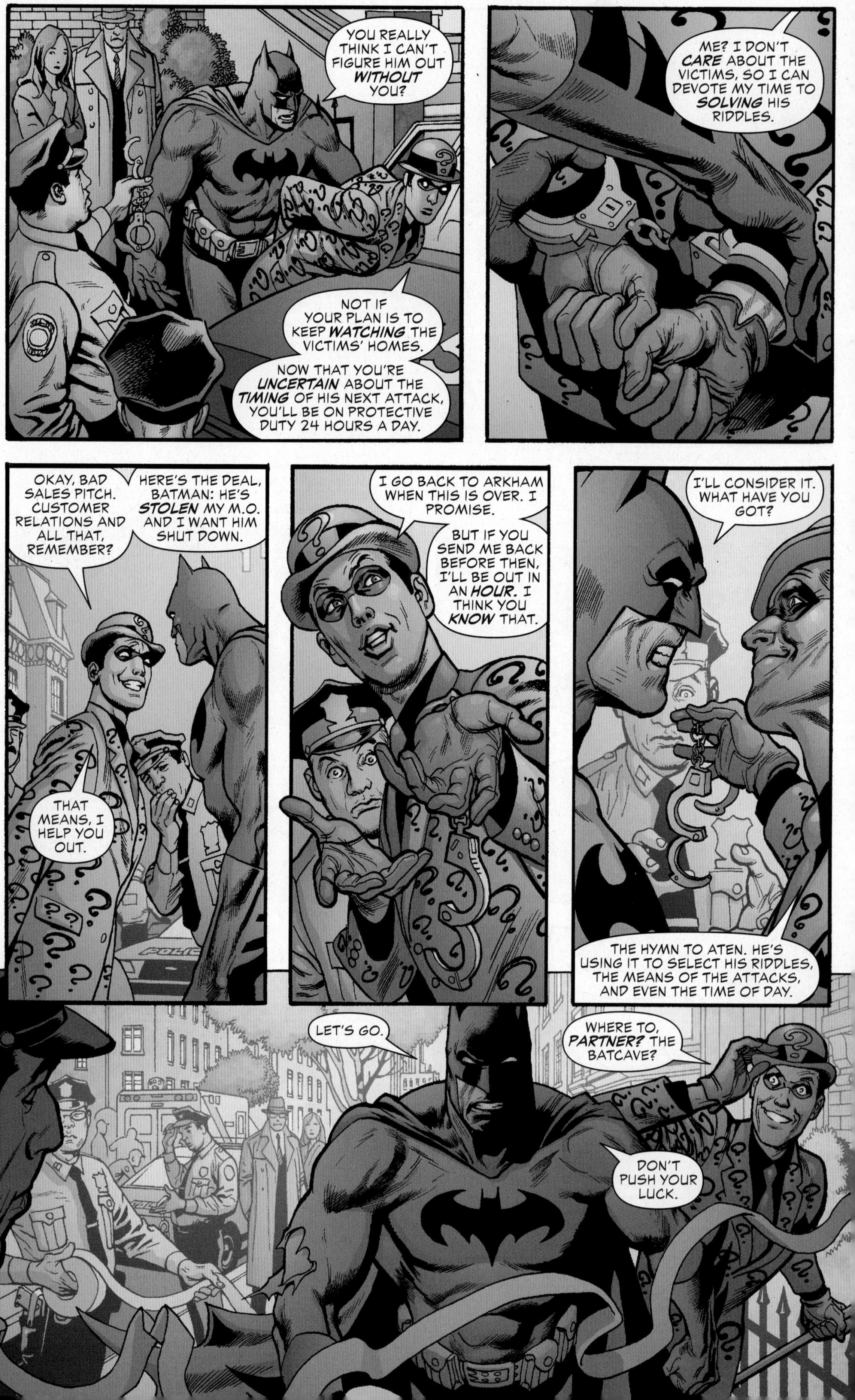

YOU REALLY THINK I CAN'T FIGURE HIM OUT WITHOUT YOU?
NOT IF YOUR PLAN IS TO KEEP WATCHING THE VICTIMS' HOMES.
NOW THAT YOU'RE UNCERTAIN ABOUT THE TIMING OF HIS NEXT ATTACK, YOU'LL BE ON PROTECTIVE DUTY 24 HOURS A DAY.
ME? I DON'T CARE ABOUT THE VICTIMS, SO I CAN DEVOTE MY TIME TO SOLVING HIS RIDDLES.
OKAY, BAD SALES PITCH. CUSTOMER RELATIONS AND ALL THAT, REMEMBER?
THAT MEANS, I HELP YOU OUT.
HERE'S THE DEAL, BATMAN: HE'S STOLEN MY M.O. AND I WANT HIM SHUT DOWN.
I GO BACK TO ARKHAM WHEN THIS IS OVER. I PROMISE.
BUT IF YOU SEND ME BACK BEFORE THEN, I'LL BE OUT IN AN HOUR. I THINK YOU KNOW THAT.
I'LL CONSIDER IT. WHAT HAVE YOU GOT?
THE HYMN TO ATEN. HE'S USING IT TO SELECT HIS RIDDLES, THE MEANS OF THE ATTACKS, AND EVEN THE TIME OF DAY.
LET'S GO.
WHERE TO, PARTNER? THE BATCAVE?
DON'T PUSH YOUR LUCK.

HERE?

YES, *HERE*. WHERE A HUNDRED COPS CAN KEEP AN *EYE* ON YOU.

DOESN'T LOOK LIKE *HE'S* ANY HAPPIER ABOUT THIS THAN I AM.

HEY, AREN'T THEY SUPPOSED TO HAVE DOUGHNUTS AROUND HERE?

...DOES HE EVEN *ASK* ME BEFORE BRINGING A KNOWN *FELON* IN HERE AS A *CONSULTANT*? NO!

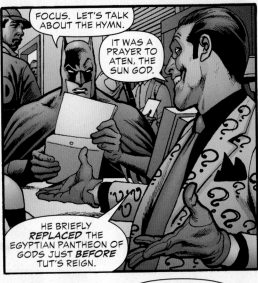

FOCUS. LET'S TALK ABOUT THE HYMN.

IT WAS A PRAYER TO ATEN, THE SUN GOD.

HE BRIEFLY *REPLACED* THE EGYPTIAN PANTHEON OF GODS JUST *BEFORE* TUT'S REIGN.

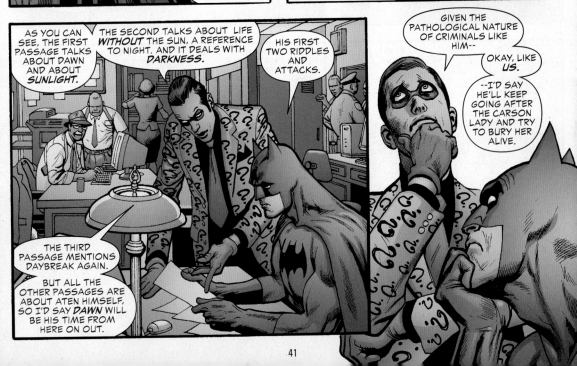

AS YOU CAN SEE, THE FIRST PASSAGE TALKS ABOUT DAWN AND ABOUT *SUNLIGHT*.

THE SECOND TALKS ABOUT LIFE *WITHOUT* THE SUN, A REFERENCE TO NIGHT. AND IT DEALS WITH *DARKNESS*.

HIS FIRST TWO RIDDLES AND ATTACKS.

THE THIRD PASSAGE MENTIONS DAYBREAK AGAIN.

BUT ALL THE OTHER PASSAGES ARE ABOUT ATEN HIMSELF, SO I'D SAY *DAWN* WILL BE HIS TIME FROM HERE ON OUT.

GIVEN THE PATHOLOGICAL NATURE OF CRIMINALS LIKE HIM--

OKAY, LIKE *US*.

--I'D SAY HE'LL KEEP GOING AFTER THE CARSON LADY AND TRY TO BURY HER ALIVE.

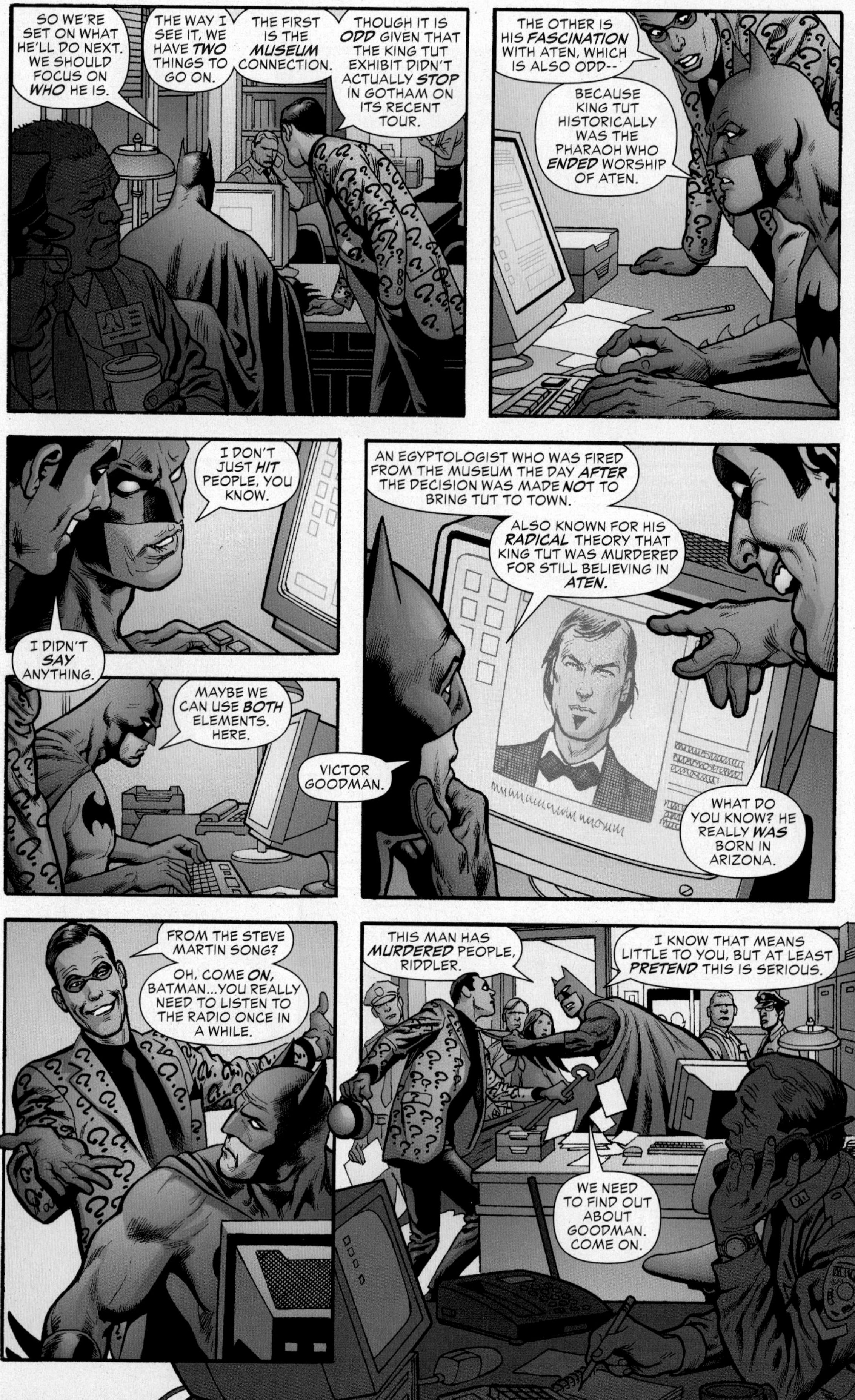
SO WE'RE SET ON WHAT HE'LL DO NEXT. WE SHOULD FOCUS ON WHO HE IS.
THE WAY I SEE IT, WE HAVE TWO THINGS TO GO ON.
THE FIRST IS THE MUSEUM CONNECTION.
THOUGH IT IS ODD GIVEN THAT THE KING TUT EXHIBIT DIDN'T ACTUALLY STOP IN GOTHAM ON ITS RECENT TOUR.
THE OTHER IS HIS FASCINATION WITH ATEN, WHICH IS ALSO ODD--
BECAUSE KING TUT HISTORICALLY WAS THE PHARAOH WHO ENDED WORSHIP OF ATEN.
I DON'T JUST HIT PEOPLE, YOU KNOW.
I DIDN'T SAY ANYTHING.
MAYBE WE CAN USE BOTH ELEMENTS. HERE.
VICTOR GOODMAN.
AN EGYPTOLOGIST WHO WAS FIRED FROM THE MUSEUM THE DAY AFTER THE DECISION WAS MADE NOT TO BRING TUT TO TOWN.
ALSO KNOWN FOR HIS RADICAL THEORY THAT KING TUT WAS MURDERED FOR STILL BELIEVING IN ATEN.
WHAT DO YOU KNOW? HE REALLY WAS BORN IN ARIZONA.
FROM THE STEVE MARTIN SONG?
OH, COME ON, BATMAN...YOU REALLY NEED TO LISTEN TO THE RADIO ONCE IN A WHILE.
THIS MAN HAS MURDERED PEOPLE, RIDDLER.
I KNOW THAT MEANS LITTLE TO YOU, BUT AT LEAST PRETEND THIS IS SERIOUS.
WE NEED TO FIND OUT ABOUT GOODMAN. COME ON.

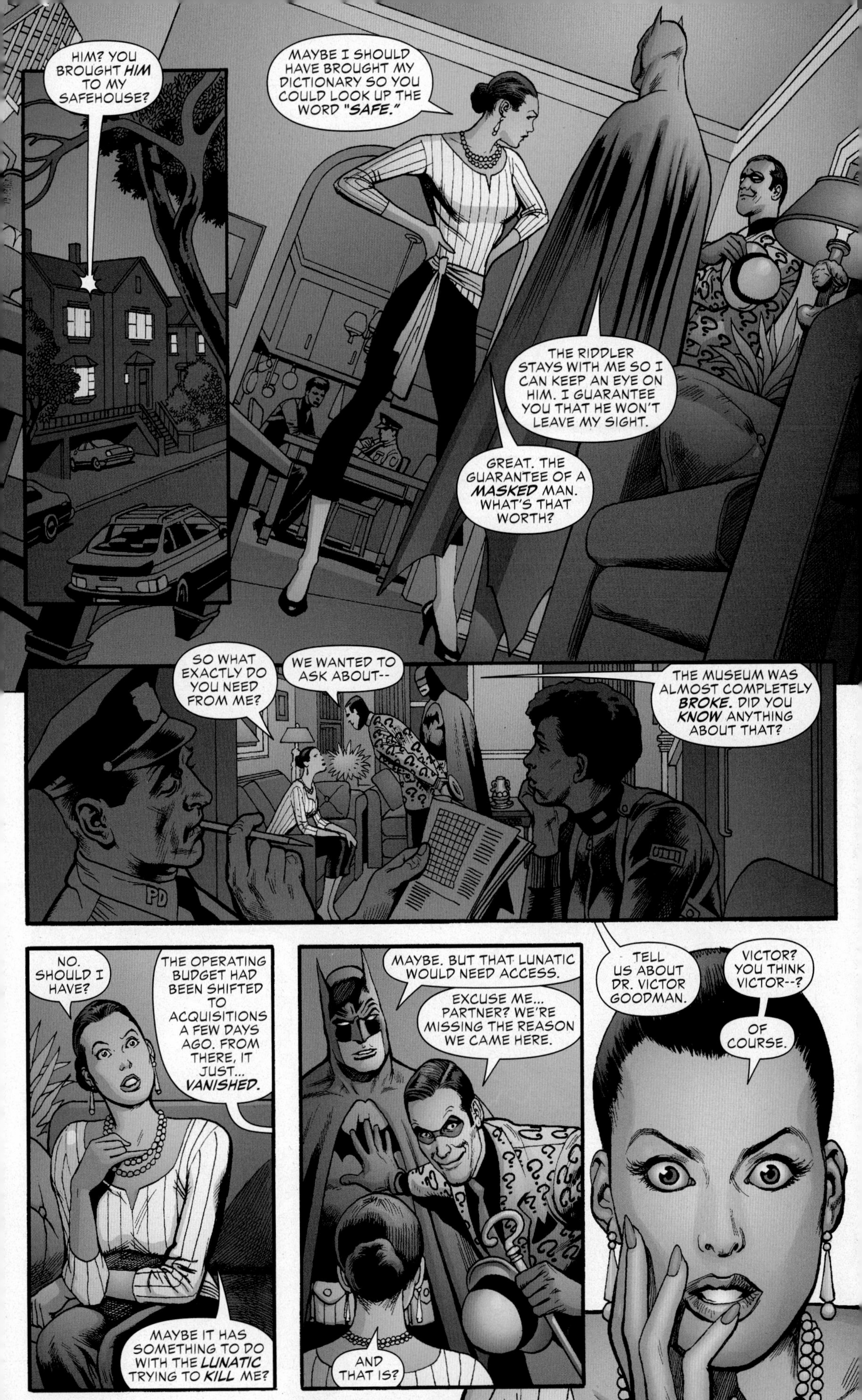
HIM? YOU BROUGHT *HIM* TO MY SAFEHOUSE?
MAYBE I SHOULD HAVE BROUGHT MY DICTIONARY SO YOU COULD LOOK UP THE WORD *"SAFE."*
THE RIDDLER STAYS WITH ME SO I CAN KEEP AN EYE ON HIM. I GUARANTEE YOU THAT HE WON'T LEAVE MY SIGHT.
GREAT. THE GUARANTEE OF A *MASKED* MAN. WHAT'S THAT WORTH?
SO WHAT EXACTLY DO YOU NEED FROM ME?
WE WANTED TO ASK ABOUT--
THE MUSEUM WAS ALMOST COMPLETELY *BROKE.* DID YOU *KNOW* ANYTHING ABOUT THAT?
NO. SHOULD I HAVE?
THE OPERATING BUDGET HAD BEEN SHIFTED TO ACQUISITIONS A FEW DAYS AGO. FROM THERE, IT JUST... *VANISHED.*
MAYBE IT HAS SOMETHING TO DO WITH THE *LUNATIC* TRYING TO *KILL* ME?
MAYBE. BUT THAT LUNATIC WOULD NEED ACCESS.
EXCUSE ME... PARTNER? WE'RE MISSING THE REASON WE CAME HERE.
AND THAT IS?
TELL US ABOUT DR. VICTOR GOODMAN.
VICTOR? YOU THINK VICTOR--?
OF COURSE.

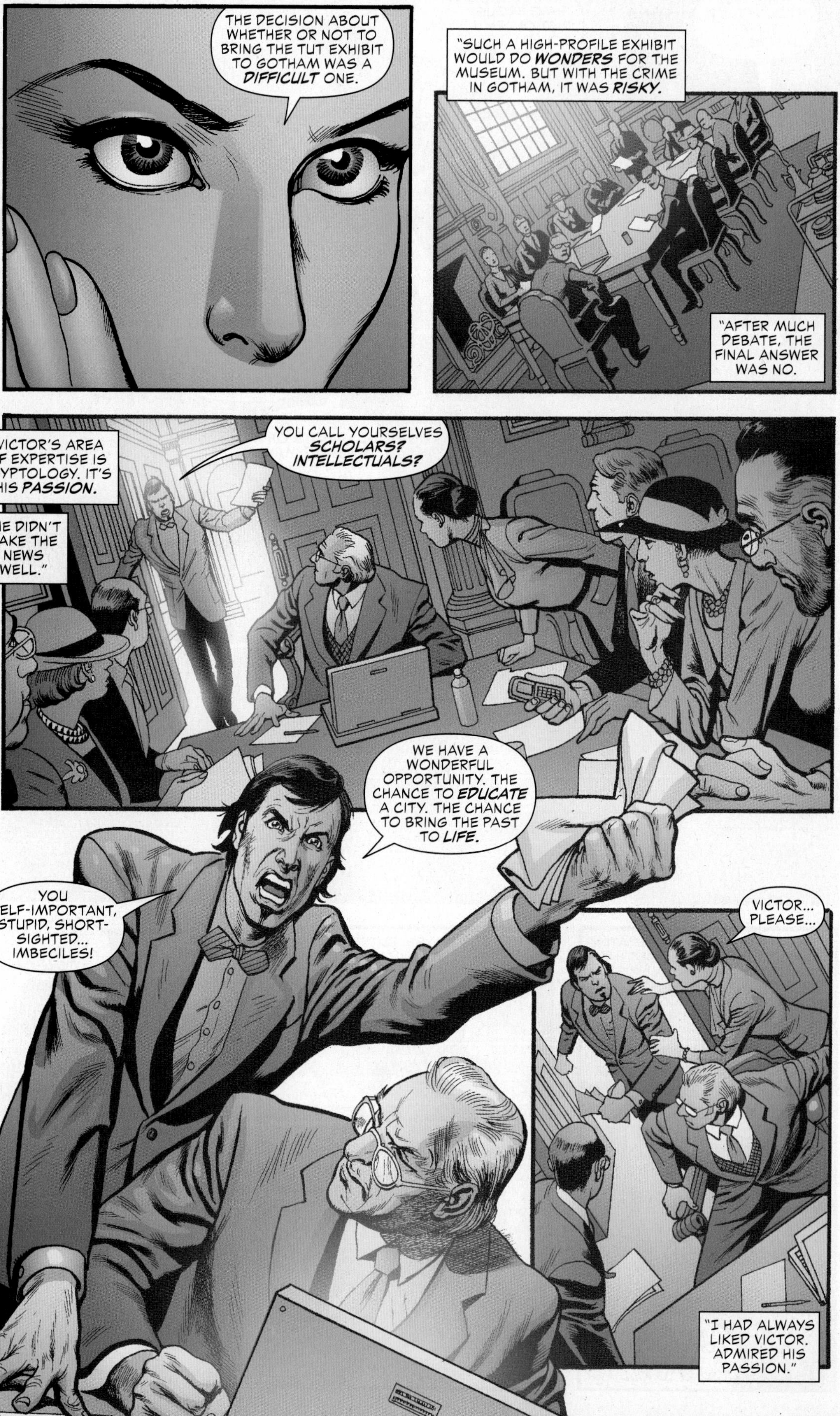
THE DECISION ABOUT WHETHER OR NOT TO BRING THE TUT EXHIBIT TO GOTHAM WAS A DIFFICULT ONE.
"SUCH A HIGH-PROFILE EXHIBIT WOULD DO WONDERS FOR THE MUSEUM. BUT WITH THE CRIME IN GOTHAM, IT WAS RISKY.
"AFTER MUCH DEBATE, THE FINAL ANSWER WAS NO.
"VICTOR'S AREA OF EXPERTISE IS EGYPTOLOGY. IT'S HIS PASSION.
"HE DIDN'T TAKE THE NEWS WELL."
YOU CALL YOURSELVES SCHOLARS? INTELLECTUALS?
WE HAVE A WONDERFUL OPPORTUNITY. THE CHANCE TO EDUCATE A CITY. THE CHANCE TO BRING THE PAST TO LIFE.
YOU SELF-IMPORTANT, STUPID, SHORT-SIGHTED... IMBECILES!
VICTOR... PLEASE...
"I HAD ALWAYS LIKED VICTOR. ADMIRED HIS PASSION."

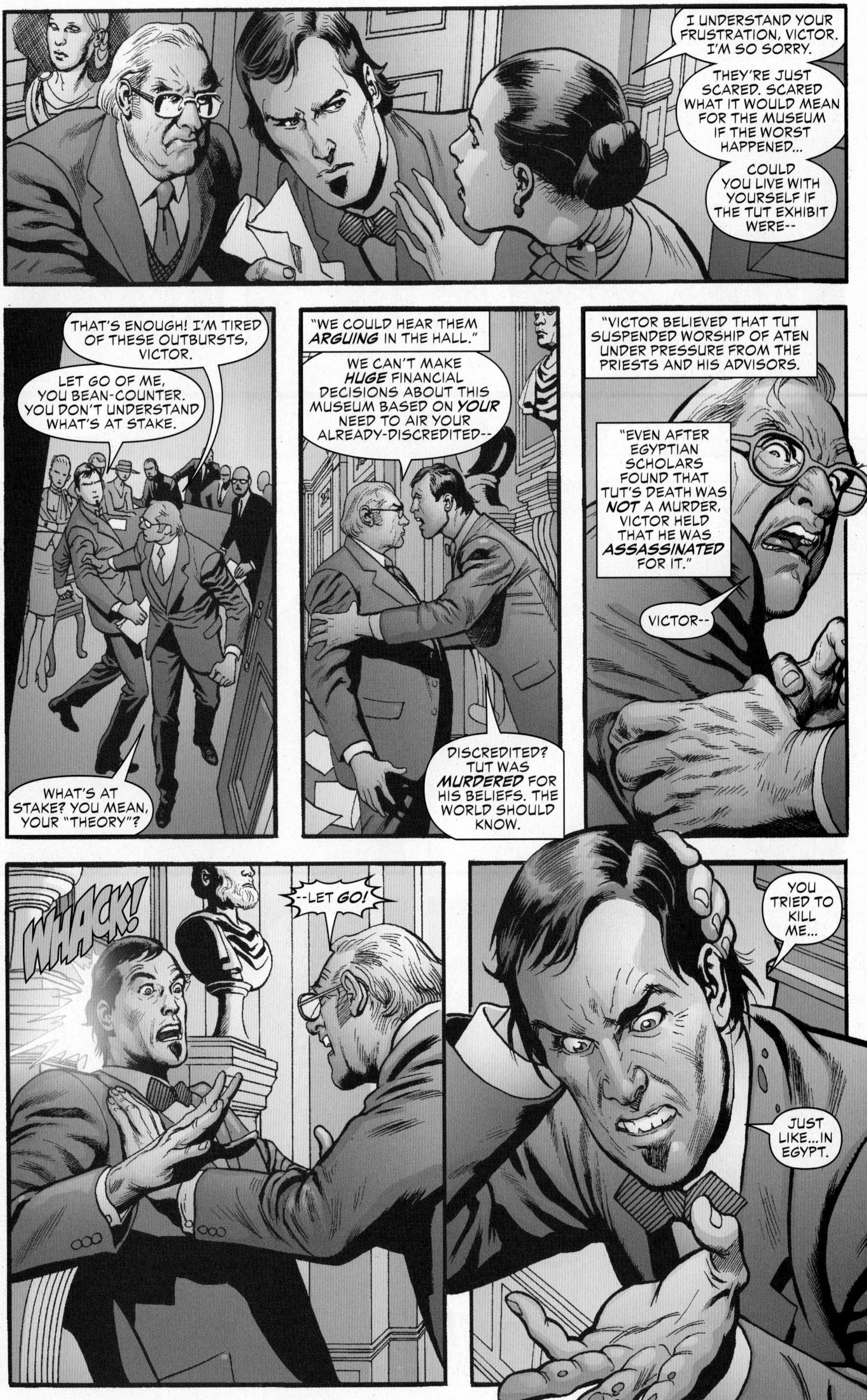
I UNDERSTAND YOUR FRUSTRATION, VICTOR. I'M SO SORRY.
THEY'RE JUST SCARED. SCARED WHAT IT WOULD MEAN FOR THE MUSEUM IF THE WORST HAPPENED...
COULD YOU LIVE WITH YOURSELF IF THE TUT EXHIBIT WERE--
THAT'S ENOUGH! I'M TIRED OF THESE OUTBURSTS, VICTOR.
LET GO OF ME, YOU BEAN-COUNTER. YOU DON'T UNDERSTAND WHAT'S AT STAKE.
WHAT'S AT STAKE? YOU MEAN, YOUR "THEORY"?
"WE COULD HEAR THEM ARGUING IN THE HALL."
WE CAN'T MAKE HUGE FINANCIAL DECISIONS ABOUT THIS MUSEUM BASED ON YOUR NEED TO AIR YOUR ALREADY-DISCREDITED--
DISCREDITED? TUT WAS MURDERED FOR HIS BELIEFS. THE WORLD SHOULD KNOW.
"VICTOR BELIEVED THAT TUT SUSPENDED WORSHIP OF ATEN UNDER PRESSURE FROM THE PRIESTS AND HIS ADVISORS.
"EVEN AFTER EGYPTIAN SCHOLARS FOUND THAT TUT'S DEATH WAS NOT A MURDER, VICTOR HELD THAT HE WAS ASSASSINATED FOR IT."
VICTOR--
WHACK!
--LET GO!
YOU TRIED TO KILL ME...
JUST LIKE...IN EGYPT.

VICTOR WAS A LITTLE *CRAZY* THAT DAY. AND RONDEAU TOLD ME LATER THAT HE FIRED VICTOR BECAUSE OF *THREATS.*

BUT I ALWAYS THOUGHT HE FIRED VICTOR BECAUSE VICTOR WAS GOING TO MAKE *TROUBLE.* NOT *KILL* PEOPLE.

VICTOR WAS PASSIONATE, BUT HE WAS NEVER *DANGEROUS.*

YOU'D BE SURPRISED TO WHAT *LENGTHS* PEOPLE WILL GO TO *PROVE* THEIR INTELLECT.

RIDDLER, LET'S *GO.* WE NEED TO FIND GOODMAN.

THANK YOU FOR YOUR HELP, MISS CARSON.

WE'LL LET YOU KNOW HOW OUR INVESTIGATION PROGRESSES. BOTH OF GOODMAN *AND* THE MUSEUM'S FINANCES...

YOU *DO* THAT.

YOU *SYMPATHIZE* WITH GOODMAN, DON'T YOU? YOU SOUNDED AS IF YOU ALMOST *ADMIRED* HIM BACK THERE.

SYMPATHIZE? NO. THE MAN TOOK A BLOW TO THE HEAD AND THINKS HE'S A DEAD PHARAOH REBORN. WE HAVE *NOTHING* IN COMMON.

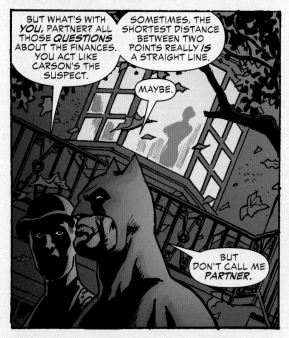

BUT WHAT'S WITH *YOU,* PARTNER? ALL THOSE *QUESTIONS* ABOUT THE FINANCES. YOU ACT LIKE CARSON'S THE SUSPECT.

SOMETIMES, THE SHORTEST DISTANCE BETWEEN TWO POINTS REALLY *IS* A STRAIGHT LINE.

MAYBE.

BUT DON'T CALL ME *PARTNER.*

VICTOR? IT'S LEIGH CARSON.

THEY SAY IT WAS *YOU* WHO ATTACKED ME THIS MORNING. I HOPE NOT. BUT IF SO, WE NEED TO *TALK*...

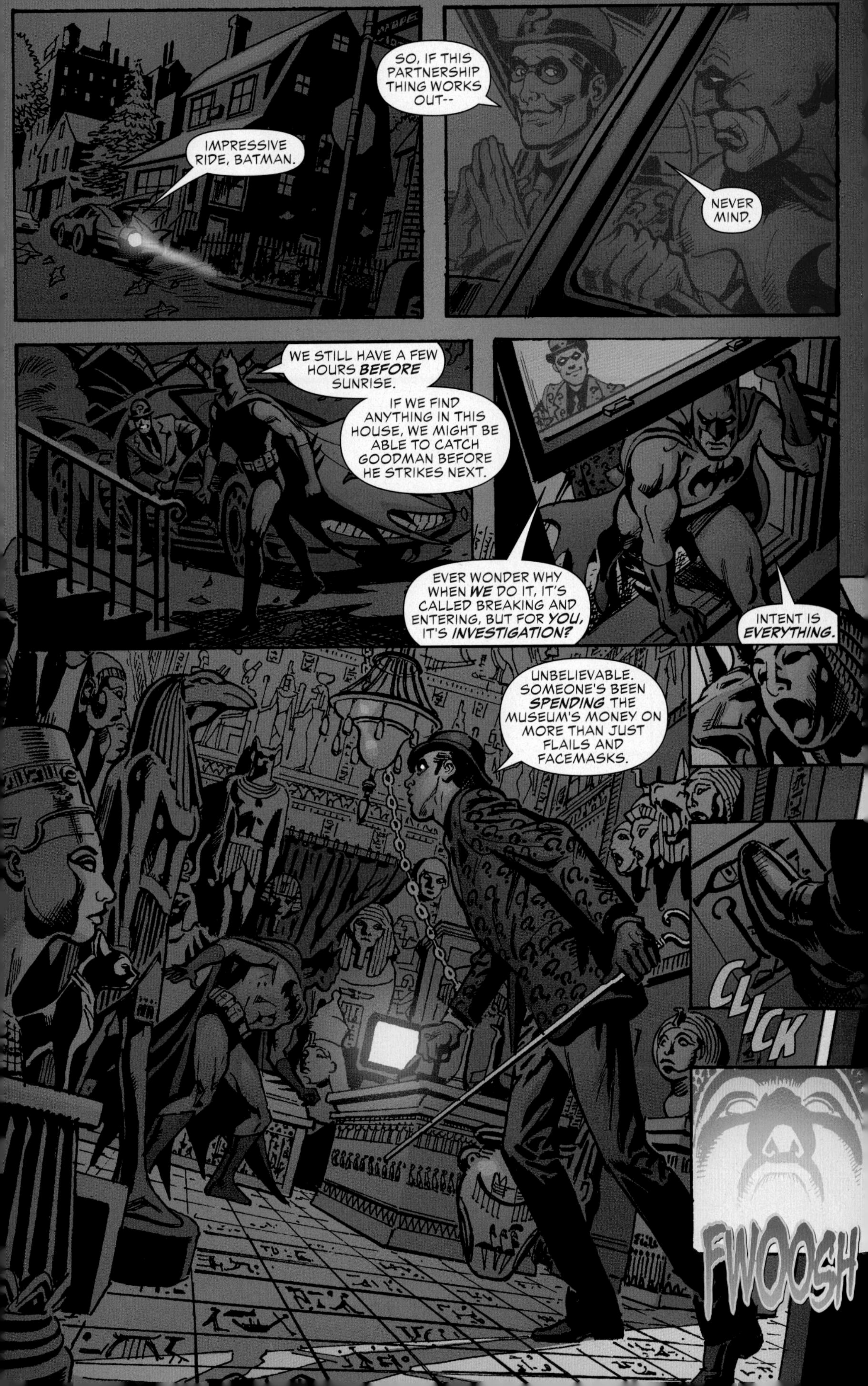
IMPRESSIVE RIDE, BATMAN.
SO, IF THIS PARTNERSHIP THING WORKS OUT--
NEVER MIND.
WE STILL HAVE A FEW HOURS *BEFORE* SUNRISE.
IF WE FIND ANYTHING IN THIS HOUSE, WE MIGHT BE ABLE TO CATCH GOODMAN BEFORE HE STRIKES NEXT.
EVER WONDER WHY WHEN *WE* DO IT, IT'S CALLED BREAKING AND ENTERING, BUT FOR *YOU*, IT'S *INVESTIGATION?*
INTENT IS *EVERYTHING.*
UNBELIEVABLE. SOMEONE'S BEEN *SPENDING* THE MUSEUM'S MONEY ON MORE THAN JUST FLAILS AND FACEMASKS.
CLICK
FWOOSH

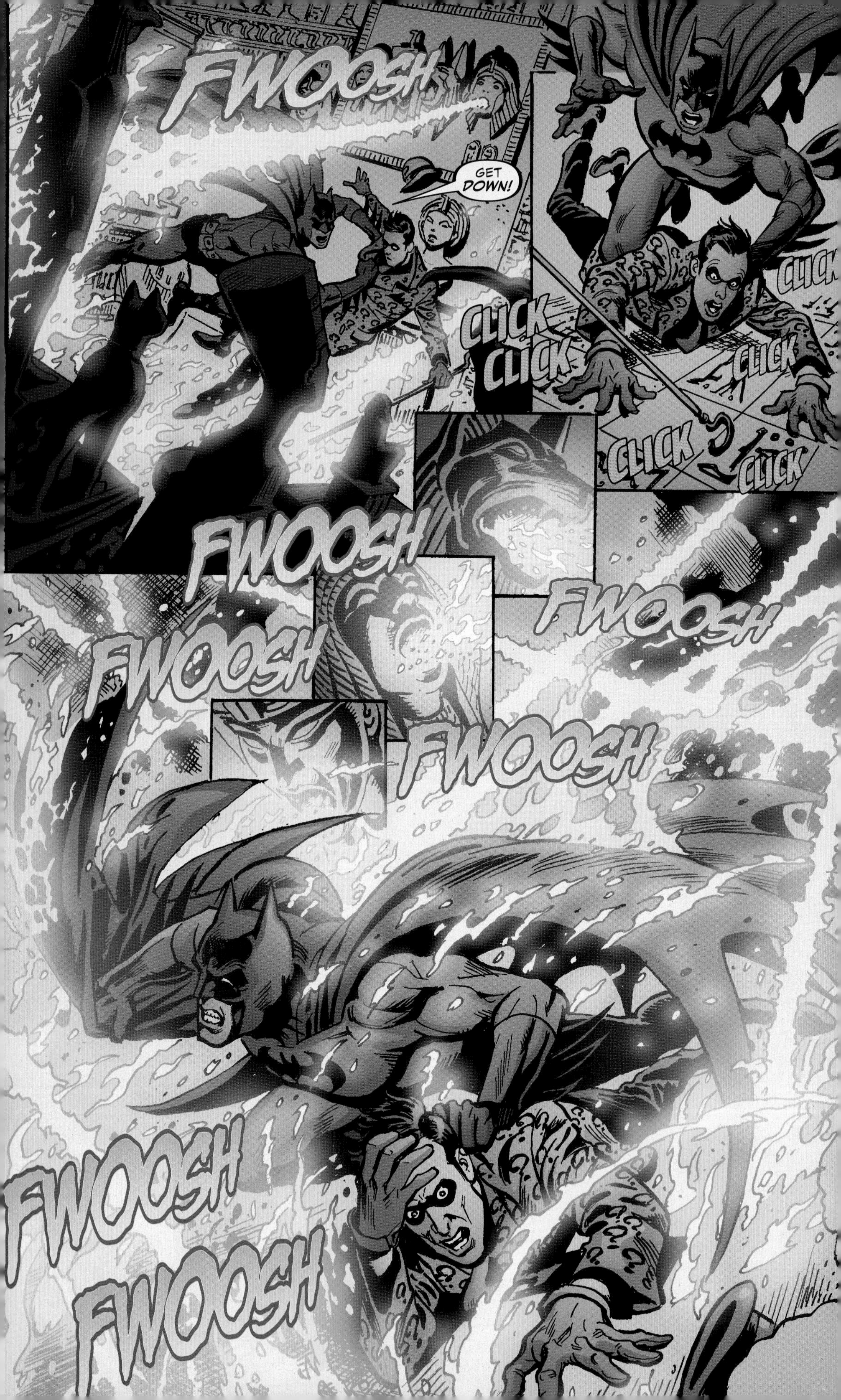
FWOOSH
GET DOWN!
CLICK
CLICK
CLICK
CLICK
CLICK
CLICK
CLICK
FWOOSH
FWOOSH
FWOOSH
FWOOSH
FWOOSH
FWOOSH

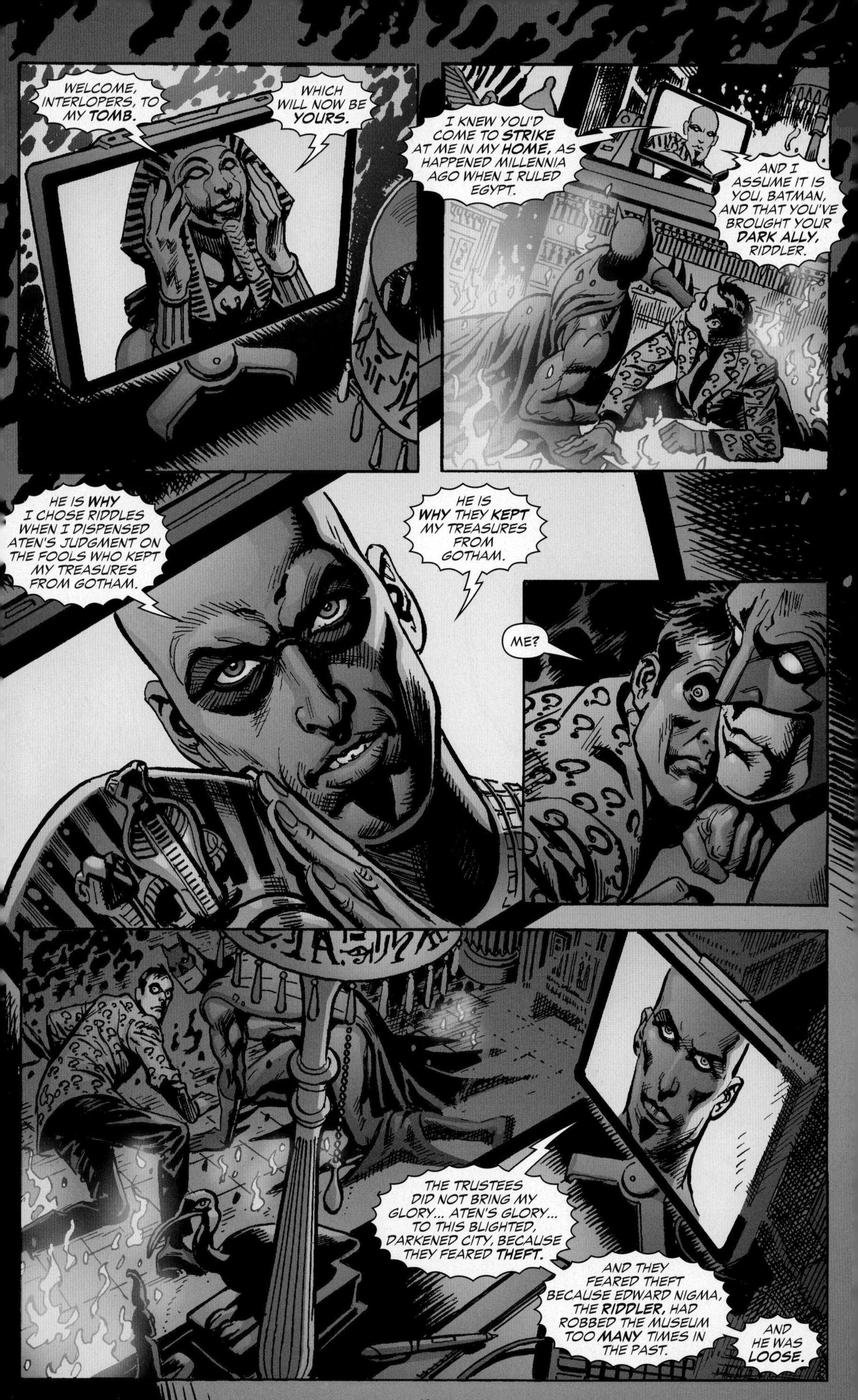
WELCOME, INTERLOPERS, TO MY TOMB.
WHICH WILL NOW BE YOURS.
I KNEW YOU'D COME TO STRIKE AT ME IN MY HOME, AS HAPPENED MILLENNIA AGO WHEN I RULED EGYPT.
AND I ASSUME IT IS YOU, BATMAN, AND THAT YOU'VE BROUGHT YOUR DARK ALLY, RIDDLER.
HE IS WHY I CHOSE RIDDLES WHEN I DISPENSED ATEN'S JUDGMENT ON THE FOOLS WHO KEPT MY TREASURES FROM GOTHAM.
HE IS WHY THEY KEPT MY TREASURES FROM GOTHAM.
ME?
THE TRUSTEES DID NOT BRING MY GLORY... ATEN'S GLORY... TO THIS BLIGHTED, DARKENED CITY, BECAUSE THEY FEARED THEFT.
AND THEY FEARED THEFT BECAUSE EDWARD NIGMA, THE RIDDLER, HAD ROBBED THE MUSEUM TOO MANY TIMES IN THE PAST.
AND HE WAS LOOSE.

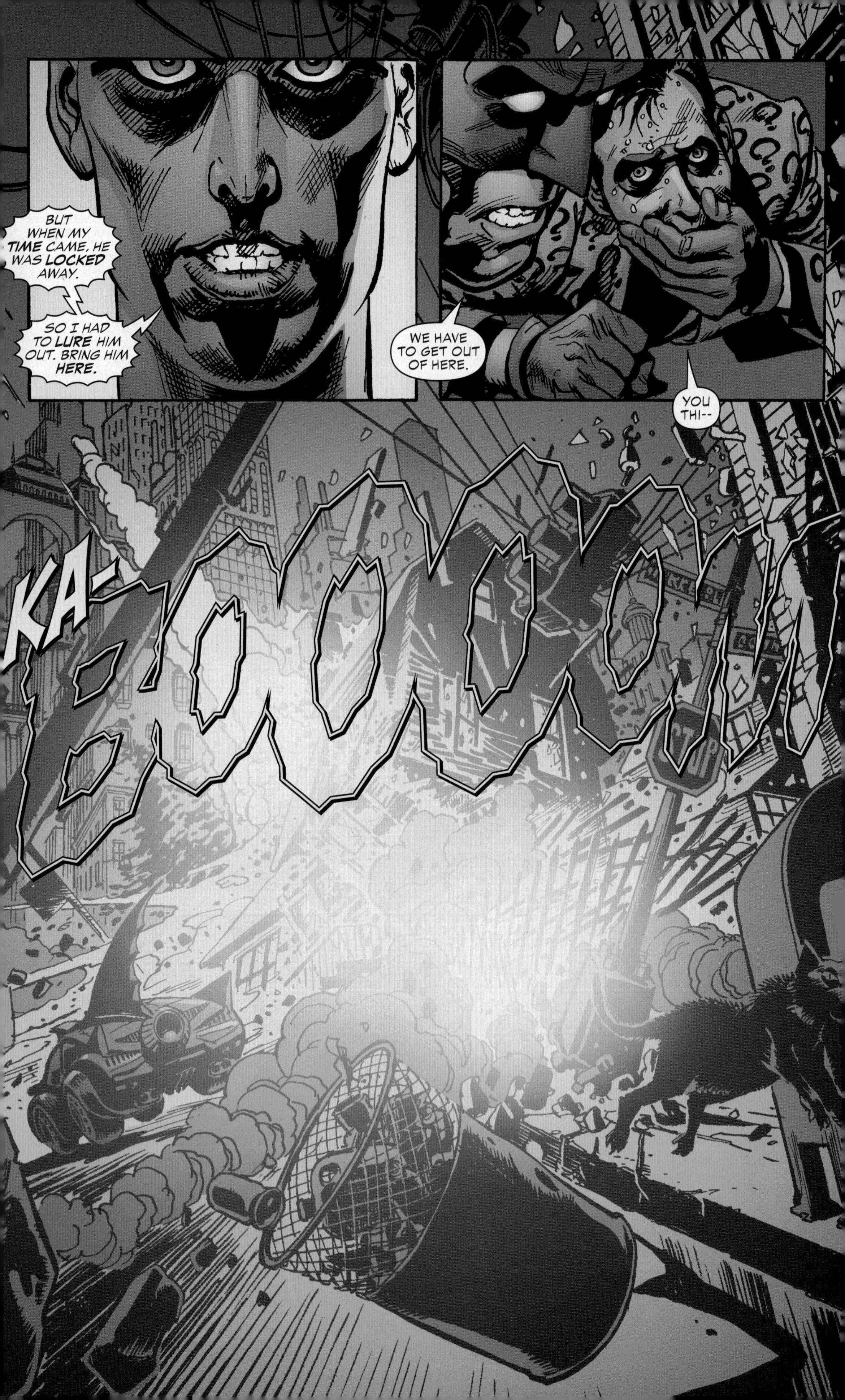
BUT WHEN MY TIME CAME, HE WAS LOCKED AWAY.
SO I HAD TO LURE HIM OUT. BRING HIM HERE.
WE HAVE TO GET OUT OF HERE.
YOU THI--
KA-
BOOOOOOM

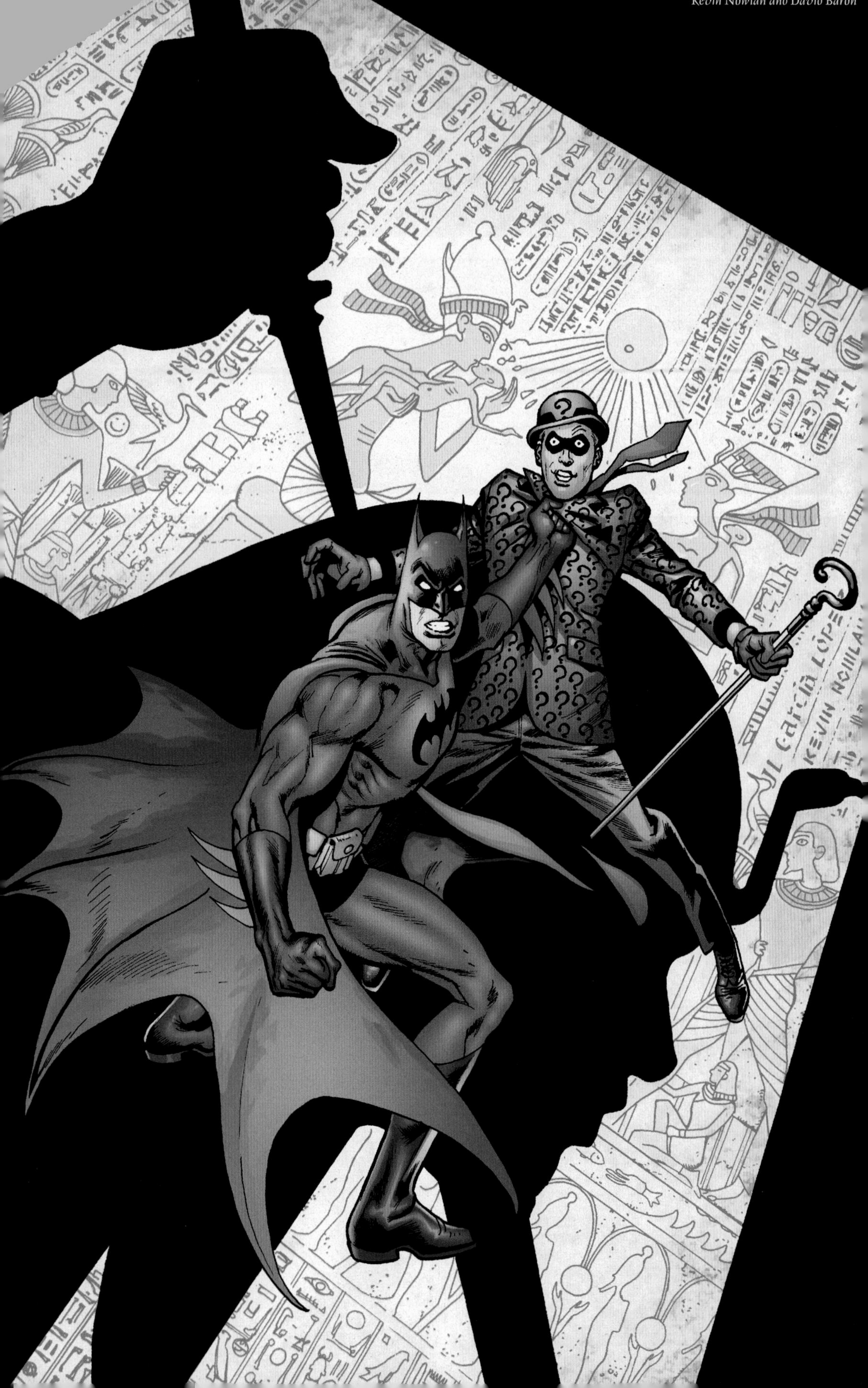

A NEW DAWN PART THREE ■ *Cover by Jose Luis Garcia-Lopez, Kevin Nowlan and David Baron*

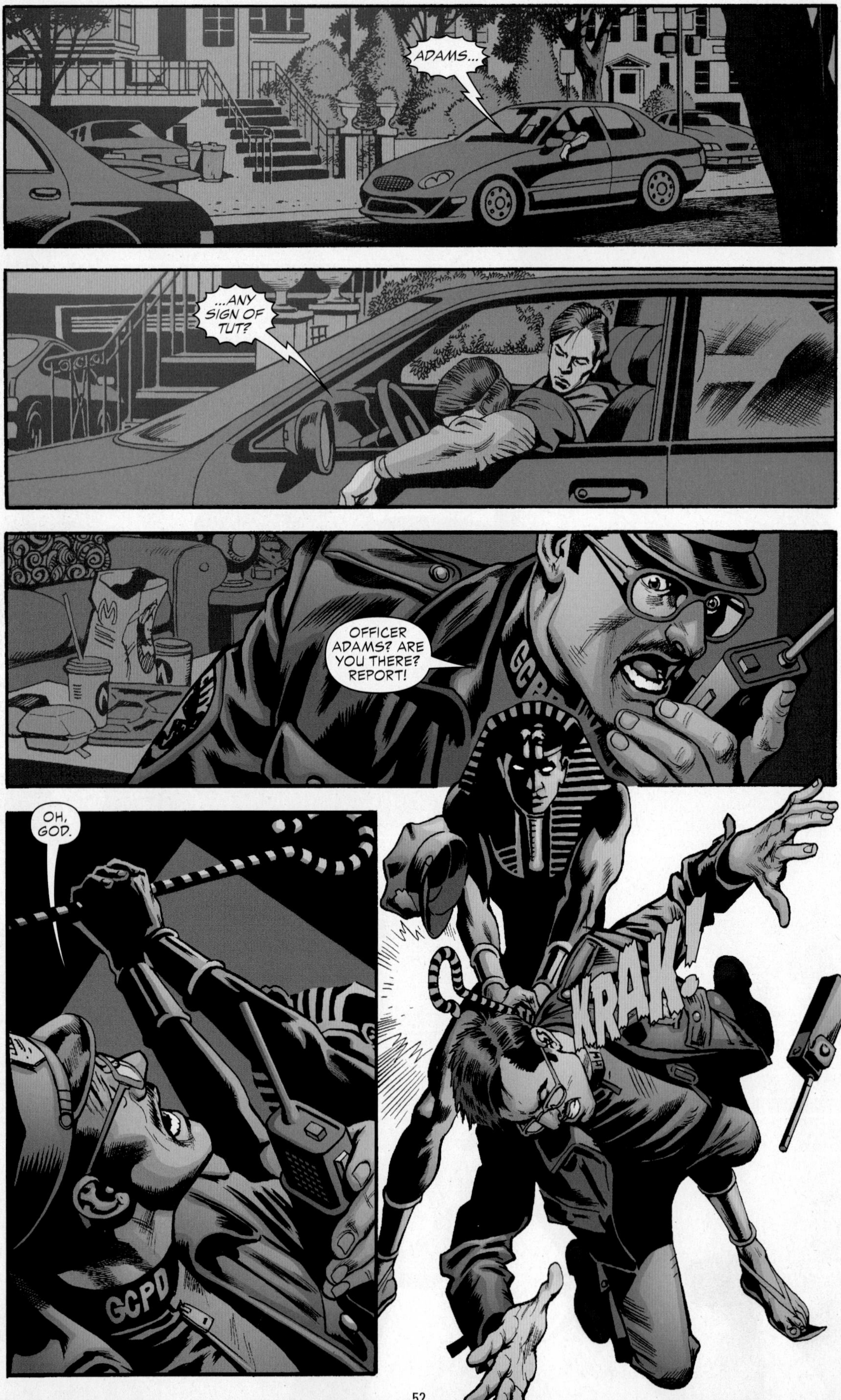
ADAMS...
...ANY SIGN OF TUT?
OFFICER ADAMS? ARE YOU THERE? REPORT!
OH, GOD.
KRAK!

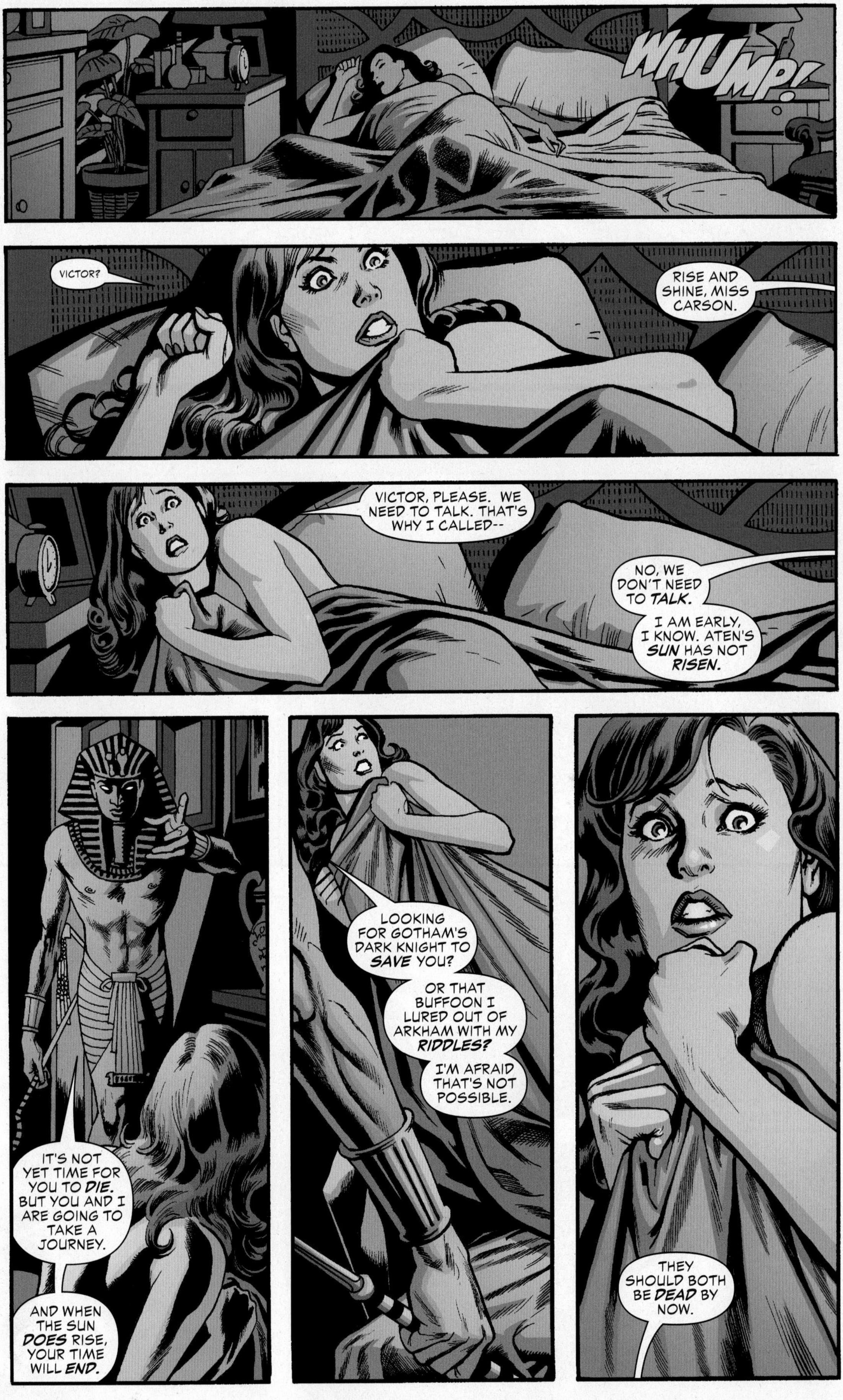
WHUMP!
VICTOR?
RISE AND SHINE, MISS CARSON.
VICTOR, PLEASE. WE NEED TO TALK. THAT'S WHY I CALLED--
NO, WE DON'T NEED TO TALK.
I AM EARLY, I KNOW. ATEN'S SUN HAS NOT RISEN.
IT'S NOT YET TIME FOR YOU TO DIE. BUT YOU AND I ARE GOING TO TAKE A JOURNEY.
AND WHEN THE SUN DOES RISE, YOUR TIME WILL END.
LOOKING FOR GOTHAM'S DARK KNIGHT TO SAVE YOU?
OR THAT BUFFOON I LURED OUT OF ARKHAM WITH MY RIDDLES?
I'M AFRAID THAT'S NOT POSSIBLE.
THEY SHOULD BOTH BE DEAD BY NOW.

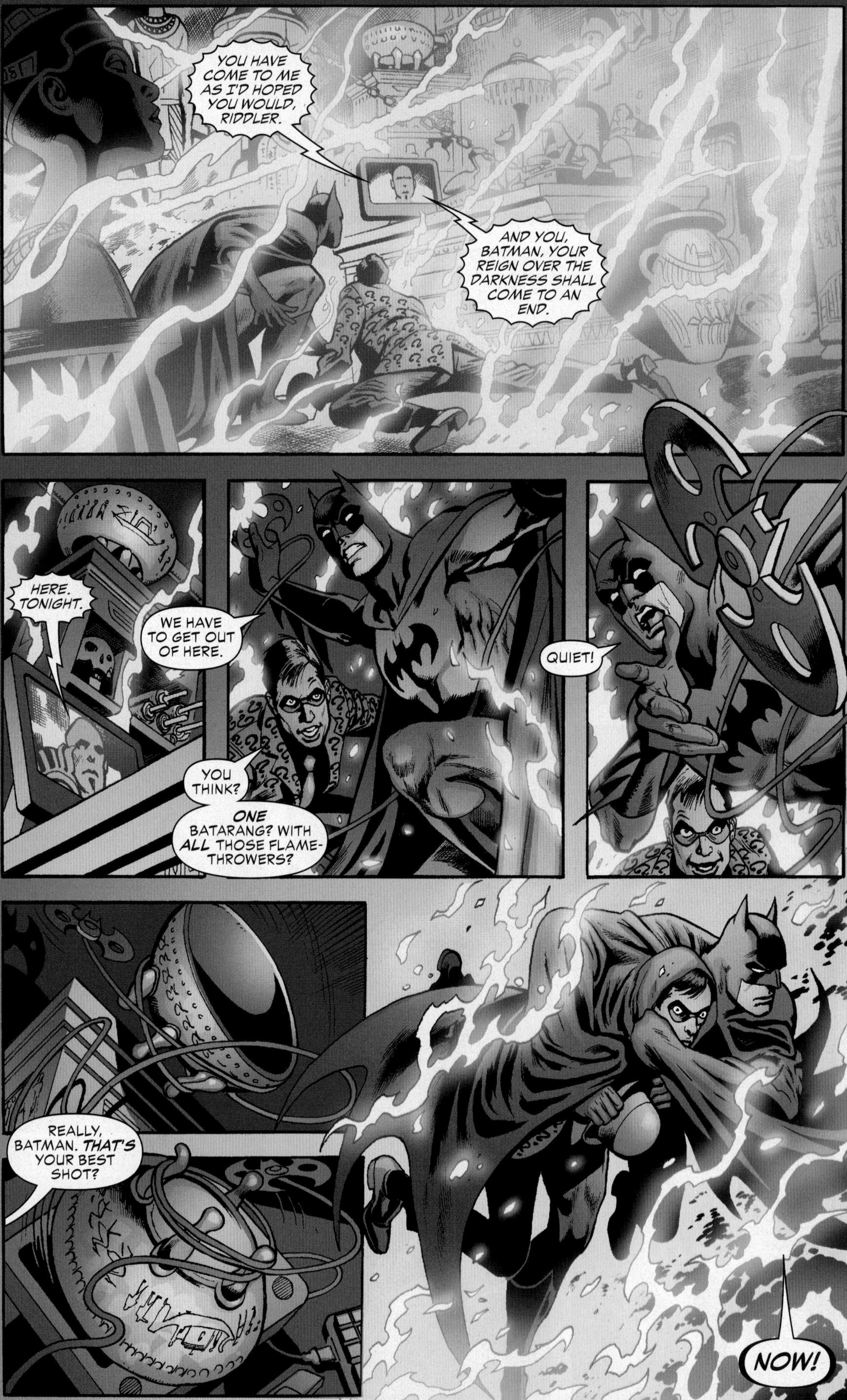
YOU HAVE COME TO ME AS I'D HOPED YOU WOULD, RIDDLER.
AND YOU, BATMAN, YOUR REIGN OVER THE DARKNESS SHALL COME TO AN END.
HERE. TONIGHT.
WE HAVE TO GET OUT OF HERE.
YOU THINK?
ONE BATARANG? WITH ALL THOSE FLAME-THROWERS?
QUIET!
REALLY, BATMAN. THAT'S YOUR BEST SHOT?
NOW!

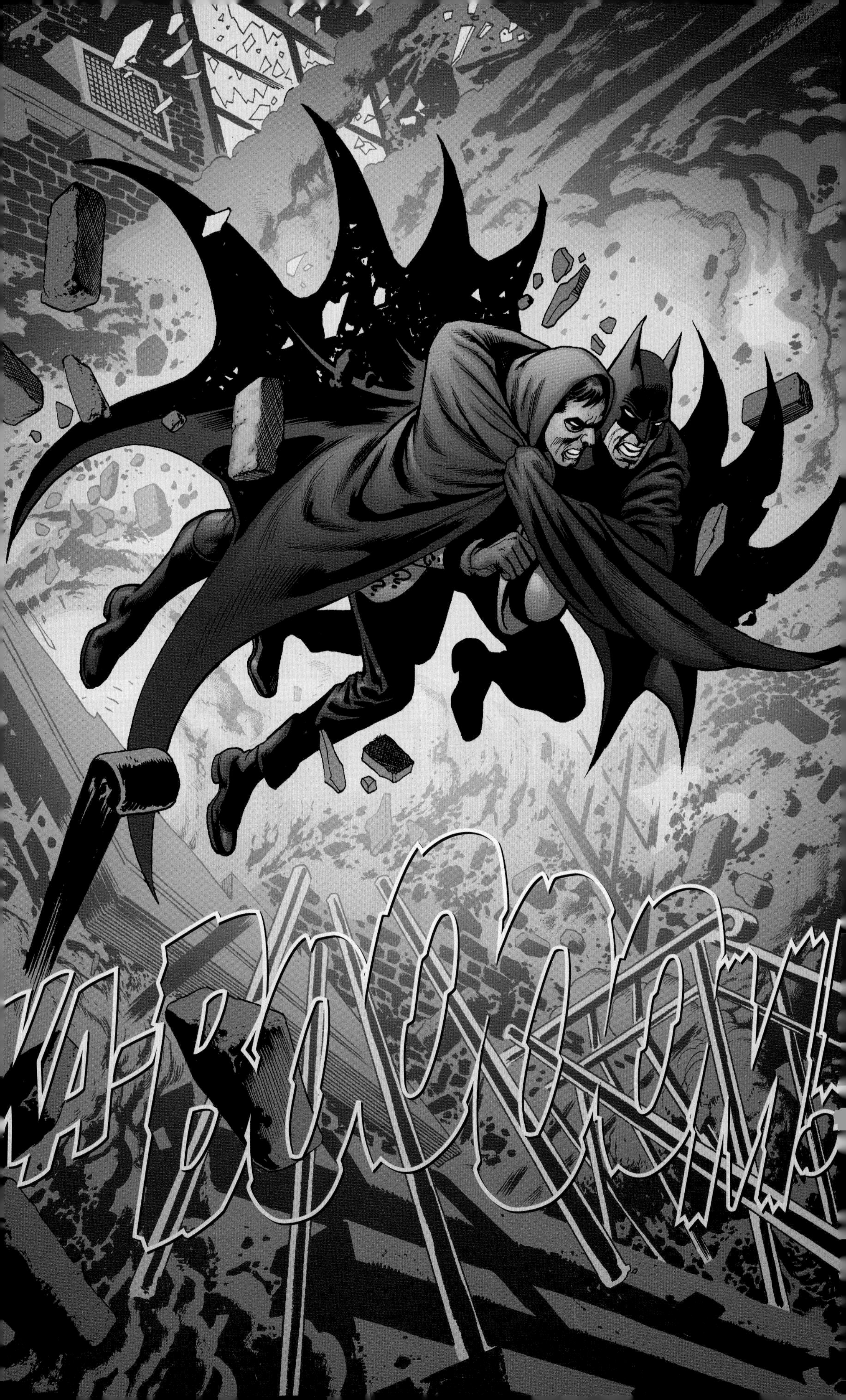
KA-BOOOOM!

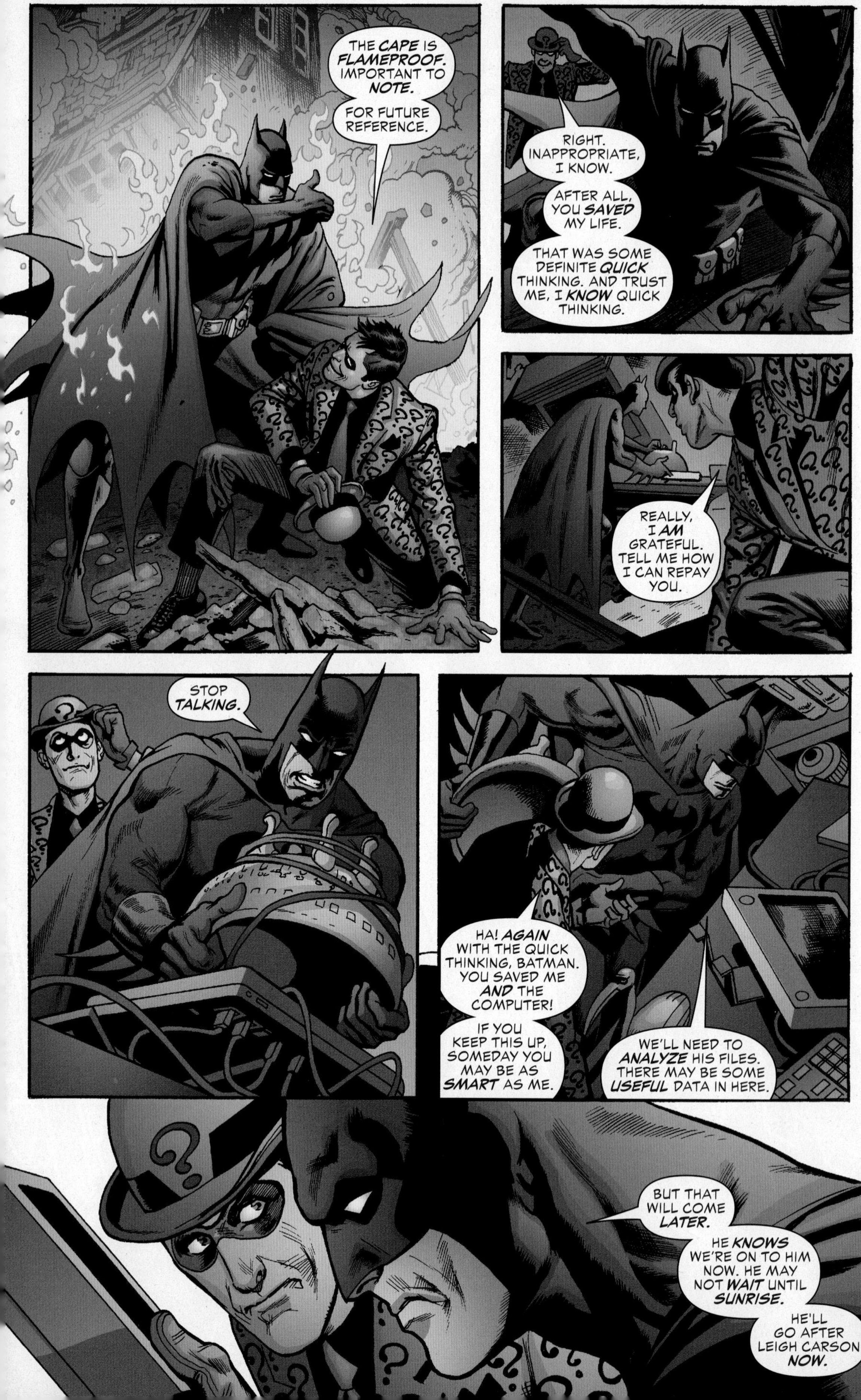
THE CAPE IS FLAMEPROOF. IMPORTANT TO NOTE.
FOR FUTURE REFERENCE.
RIGHT. INAPPROPRIATE, I KNOW.
AFTER ALL, YOU SAVED MY LIFE.
THAT WAS SOME DEFINITE QUICK THINKING. AND TRUST ME, I KNOW QUICK THINKING.
REALLY, I AM GRATEFUL. TELL ME HOW I CAN REPAY YOU.
STOP TALKING.
HA! AGAIN WITH THE QUICK THINKING, BATMAN. YOU SAVED ME AND THE COMPUTER!
IF YOU KEEP THIS UP, SOMEDAY YOU MAY BE AS SMART AS ME.
WE'LL NEED TO ANALYZE HIS FILES. THERE MAY BE SOME USEFUL DATA IN HERE.
BUT THAT WILL COME LATER.
HE KNOWS WE'RE ON TO HIM NOW. HE MAY NOT WAIT UNTIL SUNRISE.
HE'LL GO AFTER LEIGH CARSON NOW.

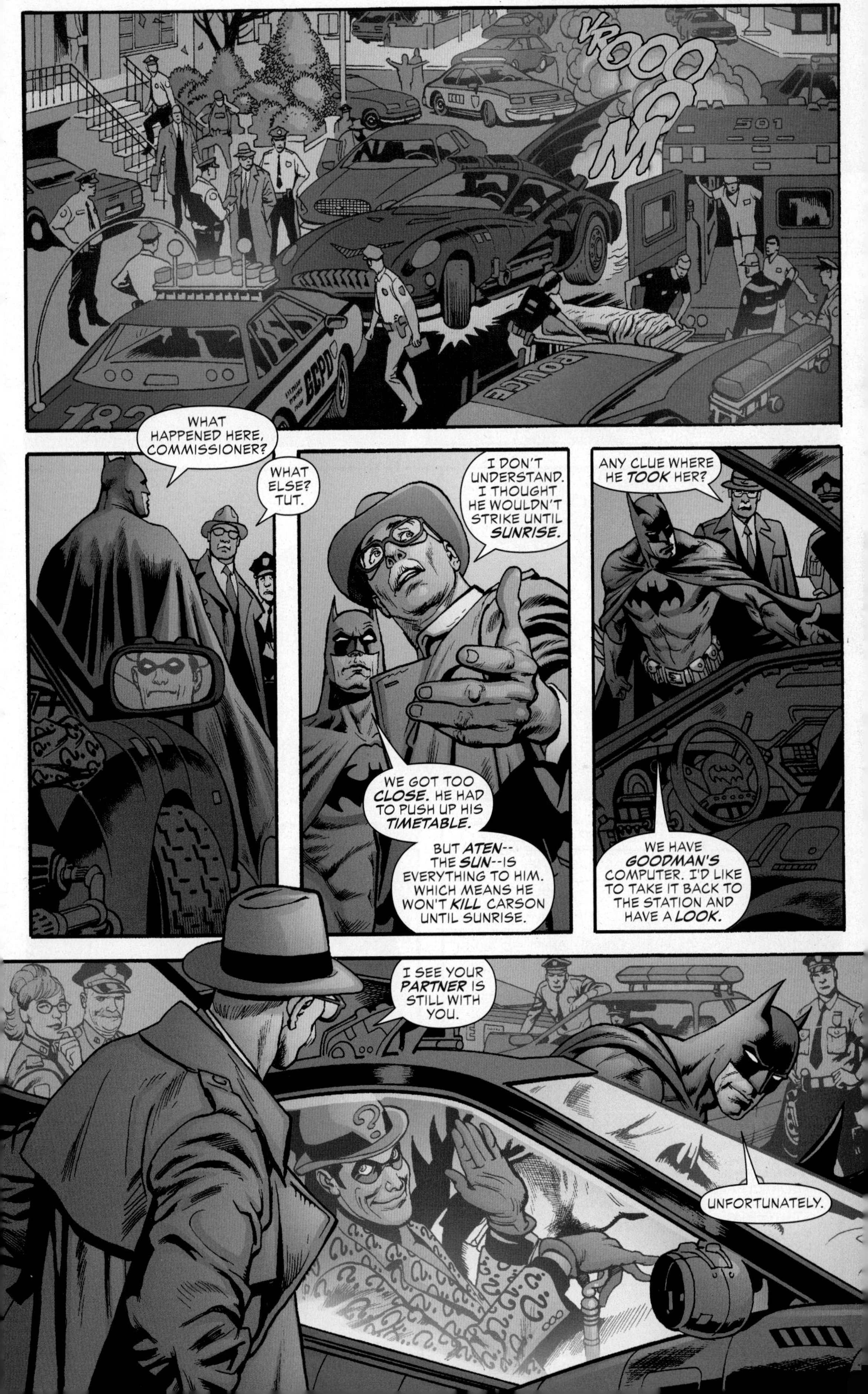
VROOOOOM
182
GCPD
POLICE
501
WHAT HAPPENED HERE, COMMISSIONER?
WHAT ELSE? TUT.
I DON'T UNDERSTAND. I THOUGHT HE WOULDN'T STRIKE UNTIL SUNRISE.
WE GOT TOO CLOSE. HE HAD TO PUSH UP HIS TIMETABLE.
BUT ATEN-- THE SUN--IS EVERYTHING TO HIM. WHICH MEANS HE WON'T KILL CARSON UNTIL SUNRISE.
ANY CLUE WHERE HE TOOK HER?
WE HAVE GOODMAN'S COMPUTER. I'D LIKE TO TAKE IT BACK TO THE STATION AND HAVE A LOOK.
I SEE YOUR PARTNER IS STILL WITH YOU.
UNFORTUNATELY.

Riddler: FIRST HE STEALS MY MOTIF...

Riddler: I MEAN, HONESTLY!

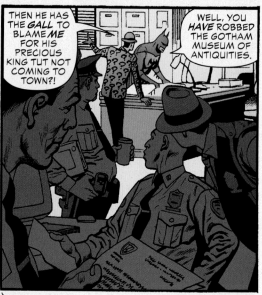

Riddler: THEN HE HAS THE GALL TO BLAME ME FOR HIS PRECIOUS KING TUT NOT COMING TO TOWN?!

Cop: WELL, YOU HAVE ROBBED THE GOTHAM MUSEUM OF ANTIQUITIES.

Riddler: ANYONE WHO'S SPENT ANY TIME IN GOTHAM KNOWS THAT RIDDLES ARE MY THING.

Riddler: SURE... TWO, MAYBE THREE TIMES.

Riddler: BUT I AM NOT RESPONSIBLE FOR THAT MESS LAST FALL. I WAS FALSELY ACCUSED.

Batman: RIGHT. OF COURSE. IT'S NEVER YOUR FAULT.

Batman: HERE WE GO. I CAN ACCESS HIS DRIVE FROM THIS COMPUTER.

Batman: HE DID EMBEZZLE THE MONEY FROM THE MUSEUM'S ACQUISITIONS FUND--

Batman: --BUT THERE'S NO HINT HERE THAT HE KNEW SOMEONE WOULD SHIFT SO MUCH MONEY INTO THAT ACCOUNT.

Riddler: BATMAN, HE KIDNAPPED CARSON. CLEARLY, SHE'S NOT IN ON IT WITH HIM.

Riddler: CLEARLY.

Batman: STILL, IT LEFT HIM MORE MONEY THAN HE'D PLANNED FOR. AND HERE'S HOW HE SPENT IT.

Batman: A WAREHOUSE BY THE RIVER.

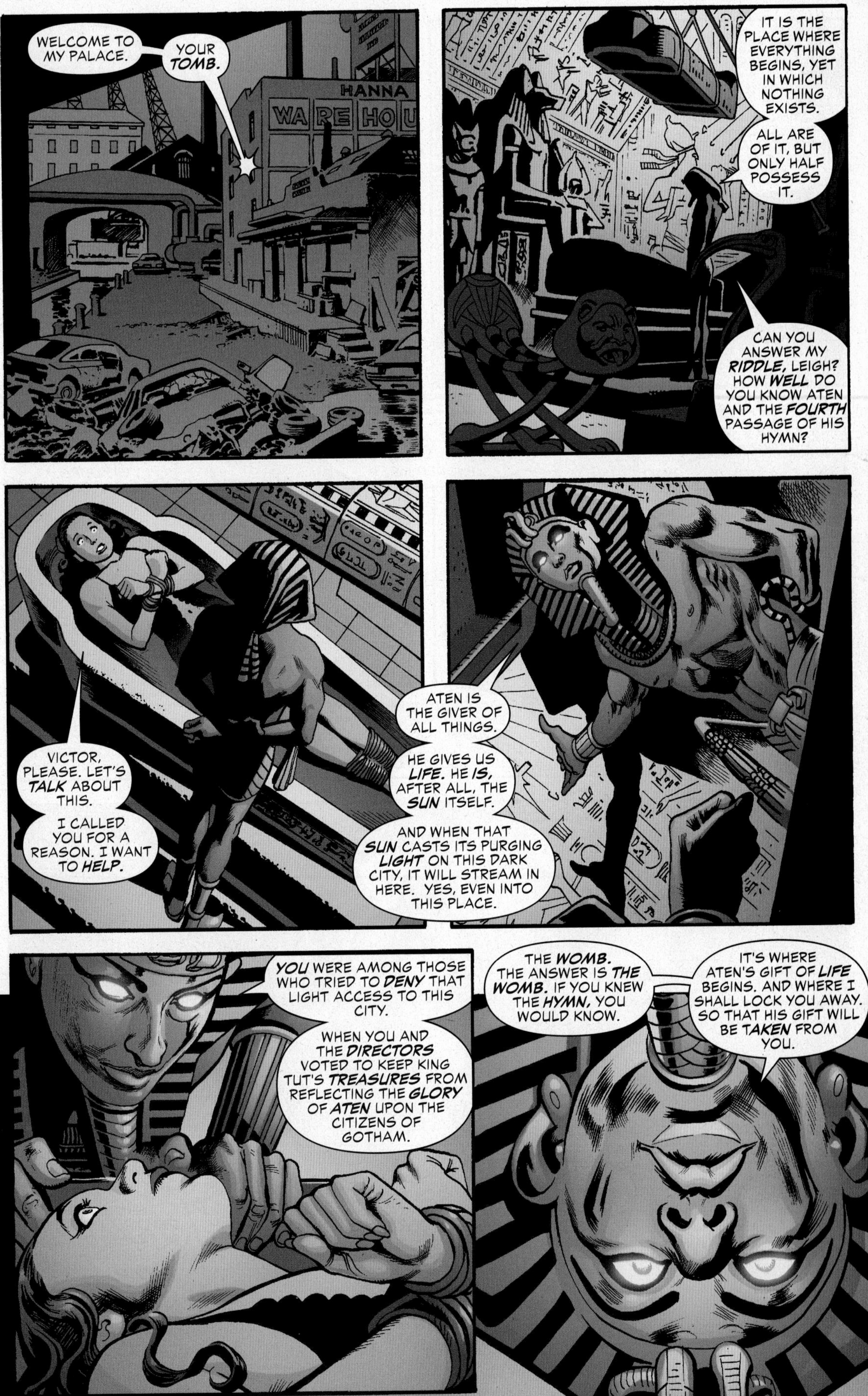
WELCOME TO MY PALACE.
YOUR TOMB.
HANNA
WAREHOU
IT IS THE PLACE WHERE EVERYTHING BEGINS, YET IN WHICH NOTHING EXISTS.
ALL ARE OF IT, BUT ONLY HALF POSSESS IT.
CAN YOU ANSWER MY RIDDLE, LEIGH? HOW WELL DO YOU KNOW ATEN AND THE FOURTH PASSAGE OF HIS HYMN?
VICTOR, PLEASE. LET'S TALK ABOUT THIS.
I CALLED YOU FOR A REASON. I WANT TO HELP.
ATEN IS THE GIVER OF ALL THINGS.
HE GIVES US LIFE. HE IS, AFTER ALL, THE SUN ITSELF.
AND WHEN THAT SUN CASTS ITS PURGING LIGHT ON THIS DARK CITY, IT WILL STREAM IN HERE. YES, EVEN INTO THIS PLACE.
YOU WERE AMONG THOSE WHO TRIED TO DENY THAT LIGHT ACCESS TO THIS CITY.
WHEN YOU AND THE DIRECTORS VOTED TO KEEP KING TUT'S TREASURES FROM REFLECTING THE GLORY OF ATEN UPON THE CITIZENS OF GOTHAM.
THE WOMB. THE ANSWER IS THE WOMB. IF YOU KNEW THE HYMN, YOU WOULD KNOW.
IT'S WHERE ATEN'S GIFT OF LIFE BEGINS. AND WHERE I SHALL LOCK YOU AWAY. SO THAT HIS GIFT WILL BE TAKEN FROM YOU.

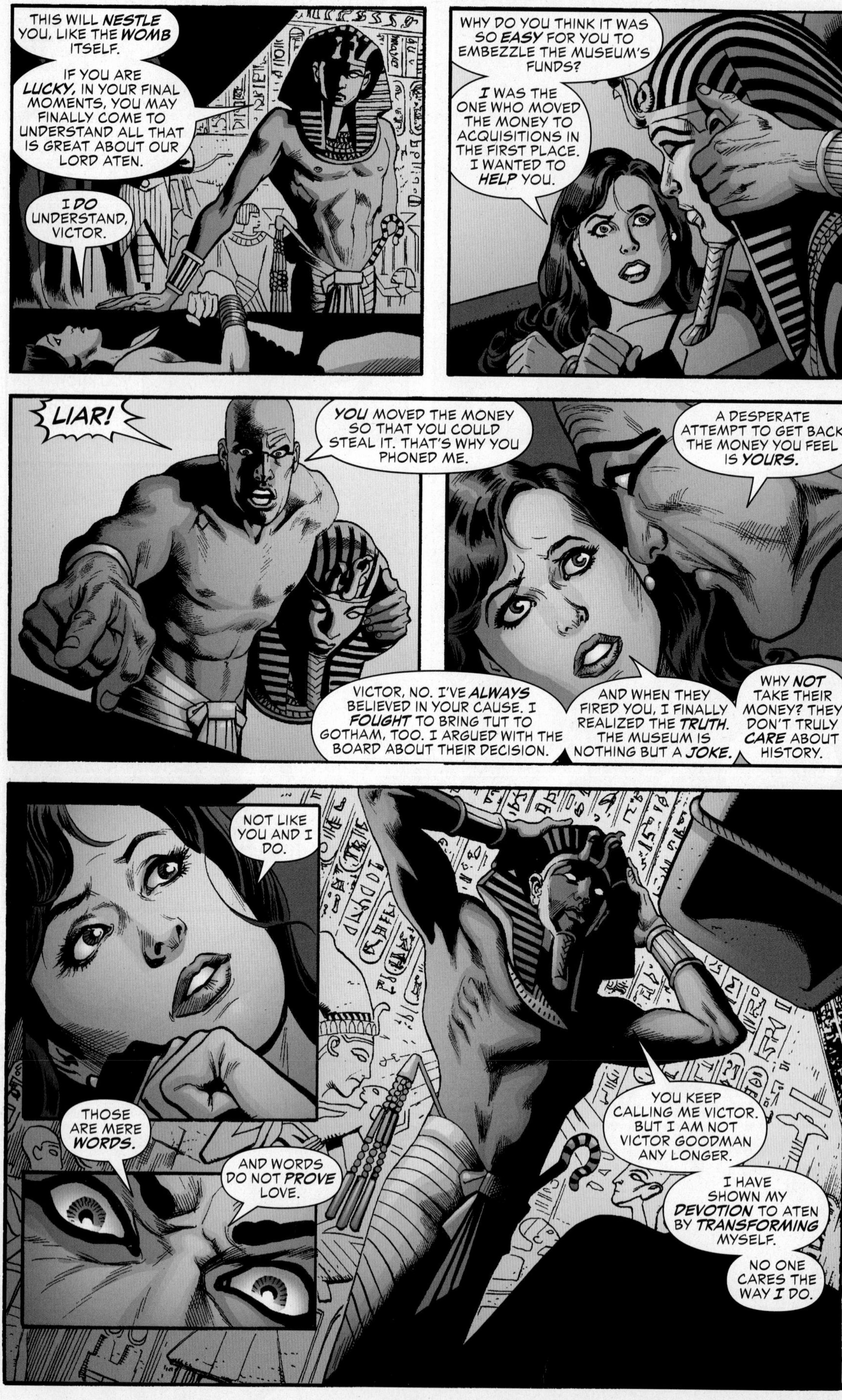
THIS WILL NESTLE YOU, LIKE THE WOMB ITSELF.
IF YOU ARE LUCKY, IN YOUR FINAL MOMENTS, YOU MAY FINALLY COME TO UNDERSTAND ALL THAT IS GREAT ABOUT OUR LORD ATEN.
I DO UNDERSTAND, VICTOR.
WHY DO YOU THINK IT WAS SO EASY FOR YOU TO EMBEZZLE THE MUSEUM'S FUNDS?
I WAS THE ONE WHO MOVED THE MONEY TO ACQUISITIONS IN THE FIRST PLACE. I WANTED TO HELP YOU.
LIAR!
YOU MOVED THE MONEY SO THAT YOU COULD STEAL IT. THAT'S WHY YOU PHONED ME.
A DESPERATE ATTEMPT TO GET BACK THE MONEY YOU FEEL IS YOURS.
VICTOR, NO. I'VE ALWAYS BELIEVED IN YOUR CAUSE. I FOUGHT TO BRING TUT TO GOTHAM, TOO. I ARGUED WITH THE BOARD ABOUT THEIR DECISION.
AND WHEN THEY FIRED YOU, I FINALLY REALIZED THE TRUTH. THE MUSEUM IS NOTHING BUT A JOKE.
WHY NOT TAKE THEIR MONEY? THEY DON'T TRULY CARE ABOUT HISTORY.
NOT LIKE YOU AND I DO.
THOSE ARE MERE WORDS.
AND WORDS DO NOT PROVE LOVE.
YOU KEEP CALLING ME VICTOR. BUT I AM NOT VICTOR GOODMAN ANY LONGER.
I HAVE SHOWN MY DEVOTION TO ATEN BY TRANSFORMING MYSELF.
NO ONE CARES THE WAY I DO.

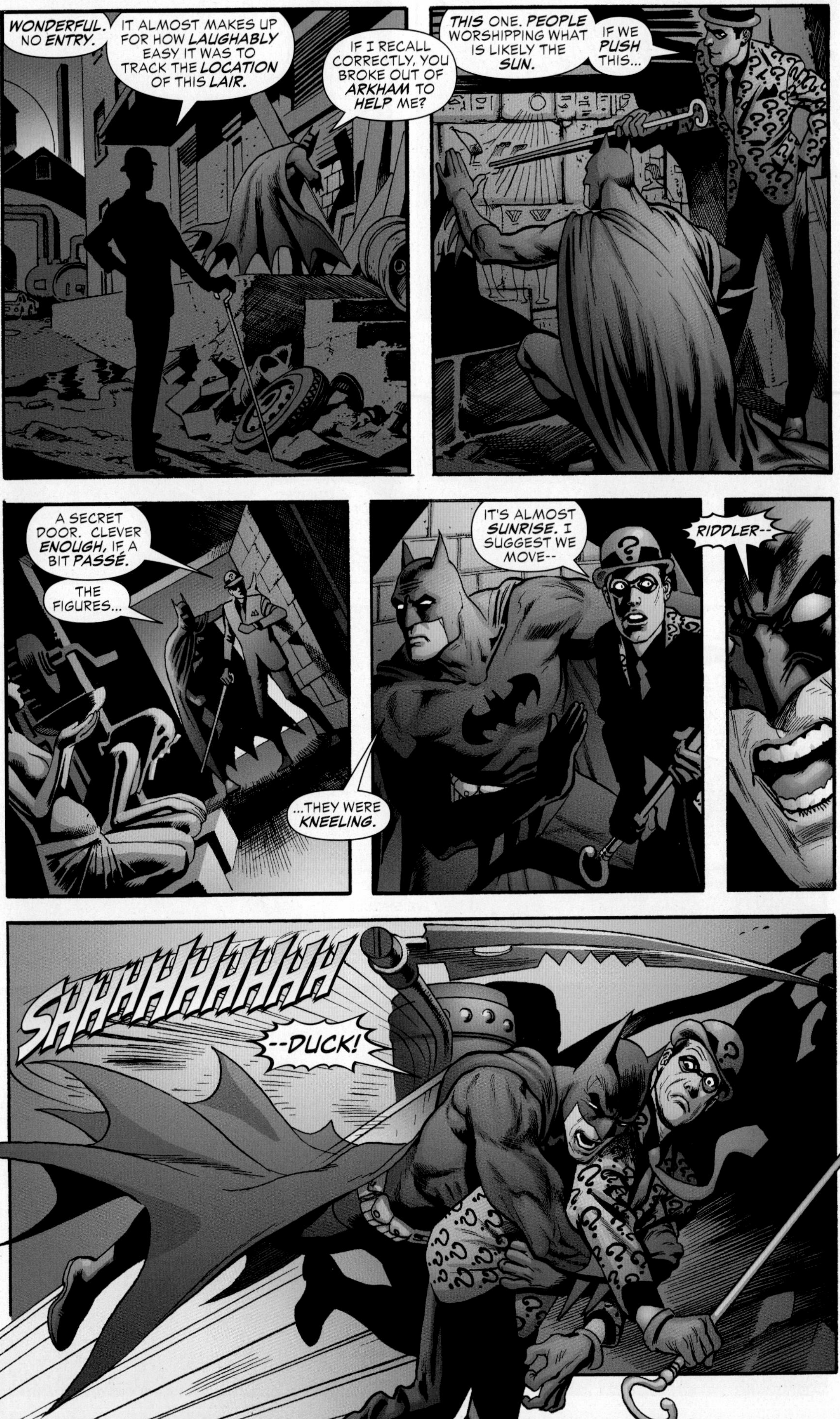
WONDERFUL. NO ENTRY.
IT ALMOST MAKES UP FOR HOW LAUGHABLY EASY IT WAS TO TRACK THE LOCATION OF THIS LAIR.
IF I RECALL CORRECTLY, YOU BROKE OUT OF ARKHAM TO HELP ME?
THIS ONE. PEOPLE WORSHIPPING WHAT IS LIKELY THE SUN.
IF WE PUSH THIS...
A SECRET DOOR. CLEVER ENOUGH, IF A BIT PASSÉ.
THE FIGURES...
...THEY WERE KNEELING.
IT'S ALMOST SUNRISE. I SUGGEST WE MOVE--
RIDDLER--
SHHHHHHHHHH
--DUCK!

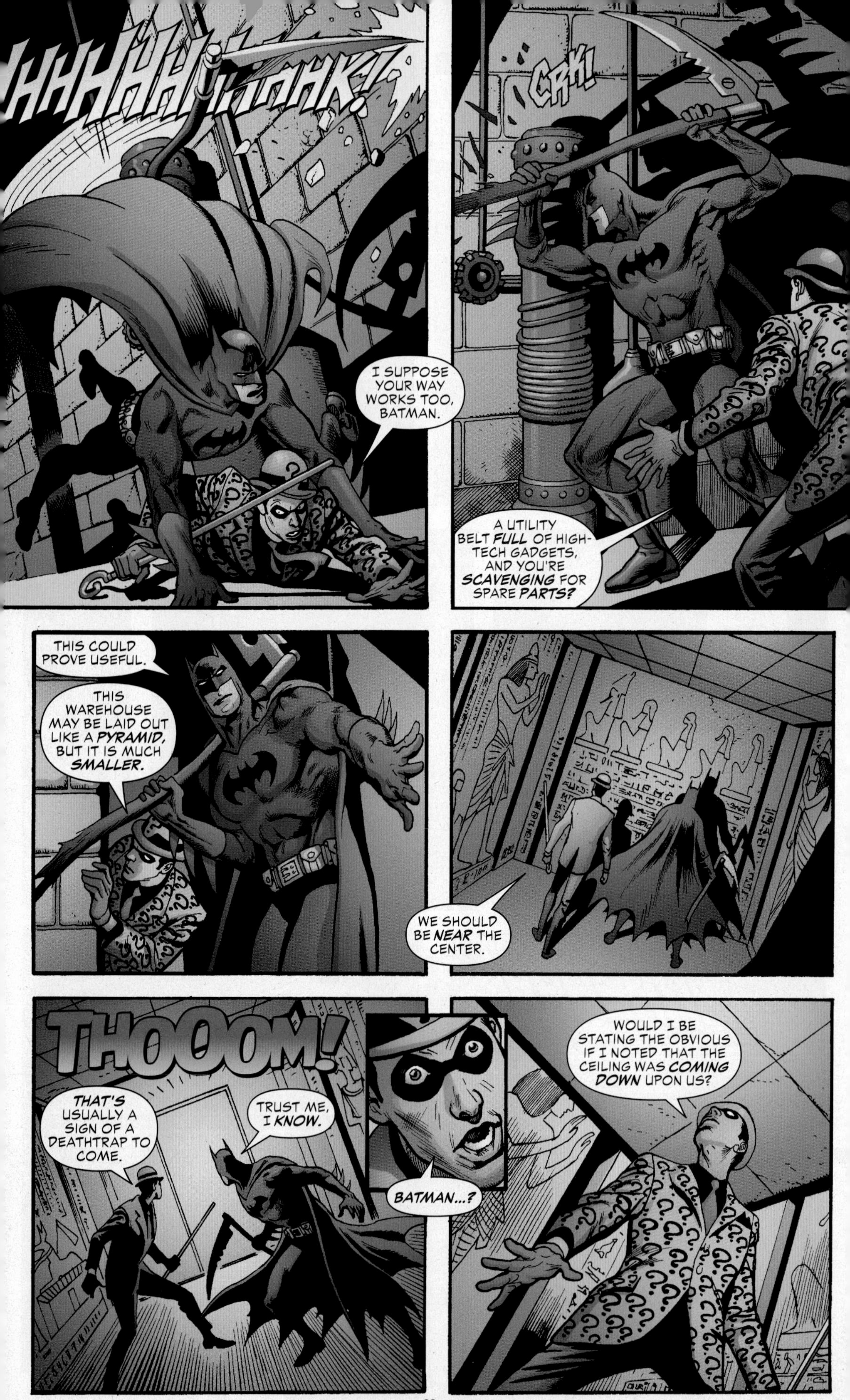

HHHHHHHHNNNK!
I SUPPOSE YOUR WAY WORKS TOO, BATMAN.
CRK!
A UTILITY BELT FULL OF HIGH-TECH GADGETS, AND YOU'RE SCAVENGING FOR SPARE PARTS?
THIS COULD PROVE USEFUL.
THIS WAREHOUSE MAY BE LAID OUT LIKE A PYRAMID, BUT IT IS MUCH SMALLER.
WE SHOULD BE NEAR THE CENTER.
THOOOM!
THAT'S USUALLY A SIGN OF A DEATHTRAP TO COME.
TRUST ME, I KNOW.
BATMAN...?
WOULD I BE STATING THE OBVIOUS IF I NOTED THAT THE CEILING WAS COMING DOWN UPON US?

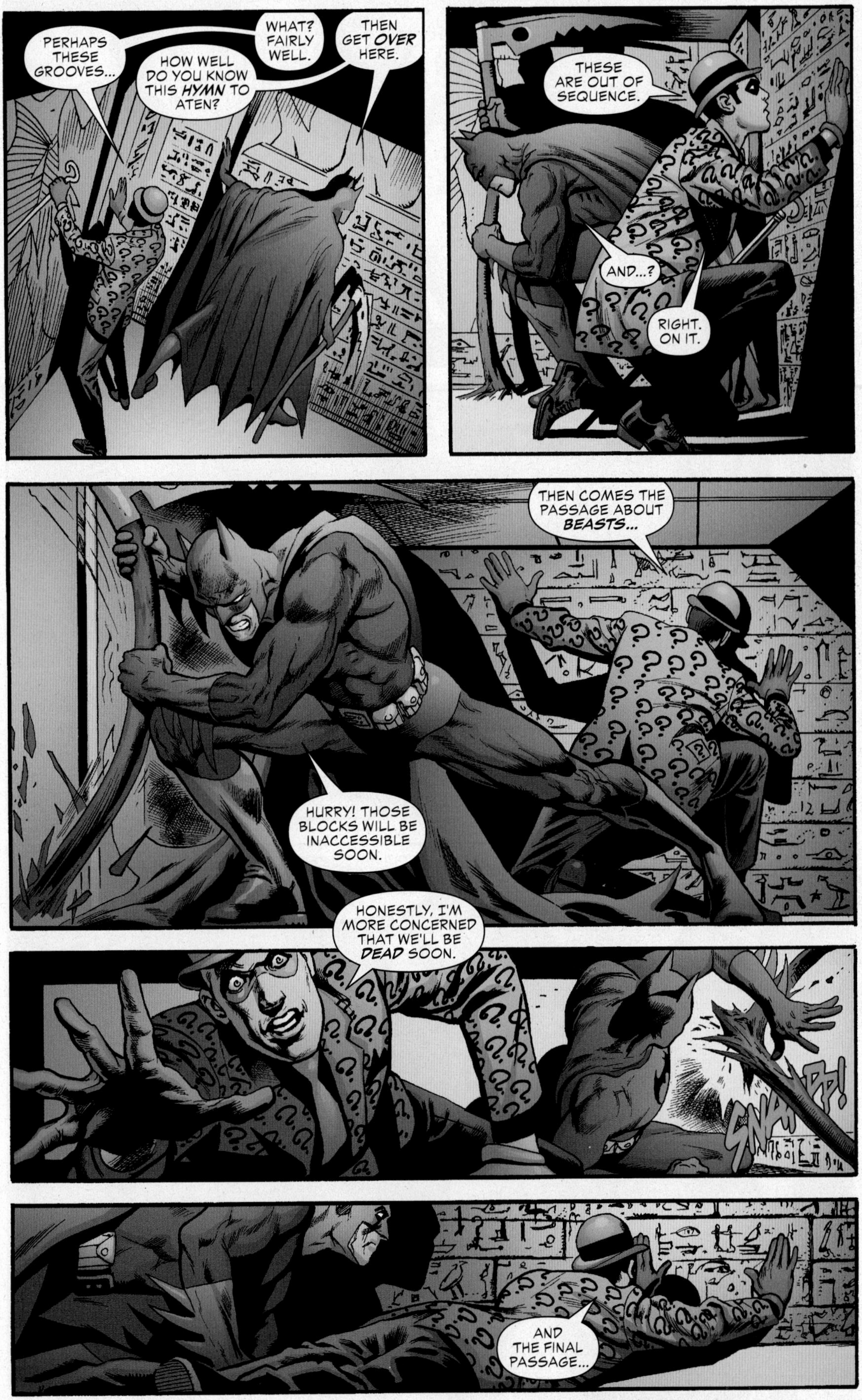
PERHAPS THESE GROOVES...
HOW WELL DO YOU KNOW THIS *HYMN* TO ATEN?
WHAT? FAIRLY WELL.
THEN GET *OVER* HERE.
THESE ARE OUT OF SEQUENCE.
AND...?
RIGHT. ON IT.
THEN COMES THE PASSAGE ABOUT *BEASTS*...
HURRY! THOSE BLOCKS WILL BE INACCESSIBLE SOON.
HONESTLY, I'M MORE CONCERNED THAT WE'LL BE *DEAD* SOON.
AND THE FINAL PASSAGE...

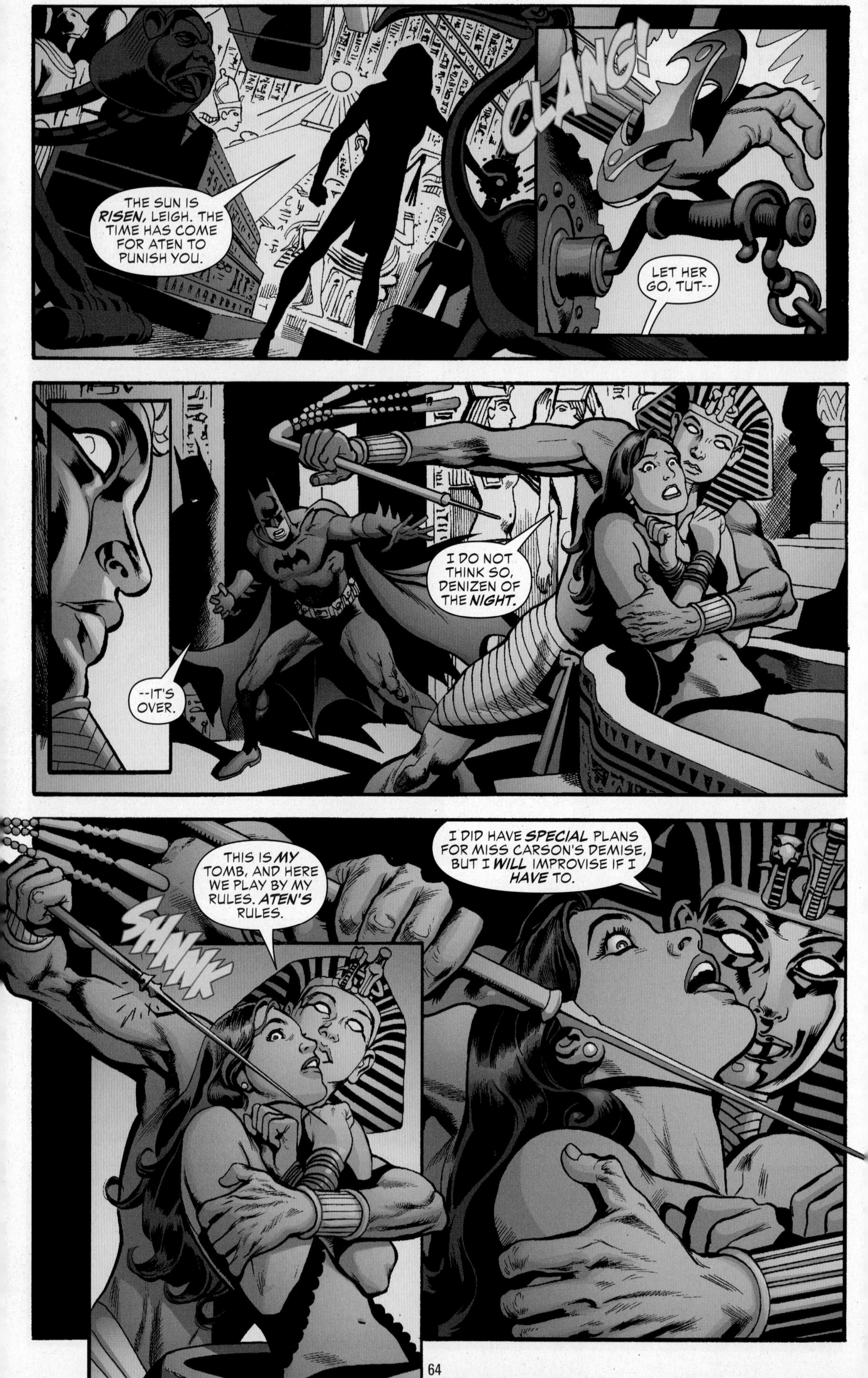

THE SUN IS RISEN, LEIGH. THE TIME HAS COME FOR ATEN TO PUNISH YOU.
CLANG!
LET HER GO, TUT--
--IT'S OVER.
I DO NOT THINK SO, DENIZEN OF THE NIGHT.
THIS IS MY TOMB, AND HERE WE PLAY BY MY RULES. ATEN'S RULES.
SHNNK
I DID HAVE SPECIAL PLANS FOR MISS CARSON'S DEMISE, BUT I WILL IMPROVISE IF I HAVE TO.

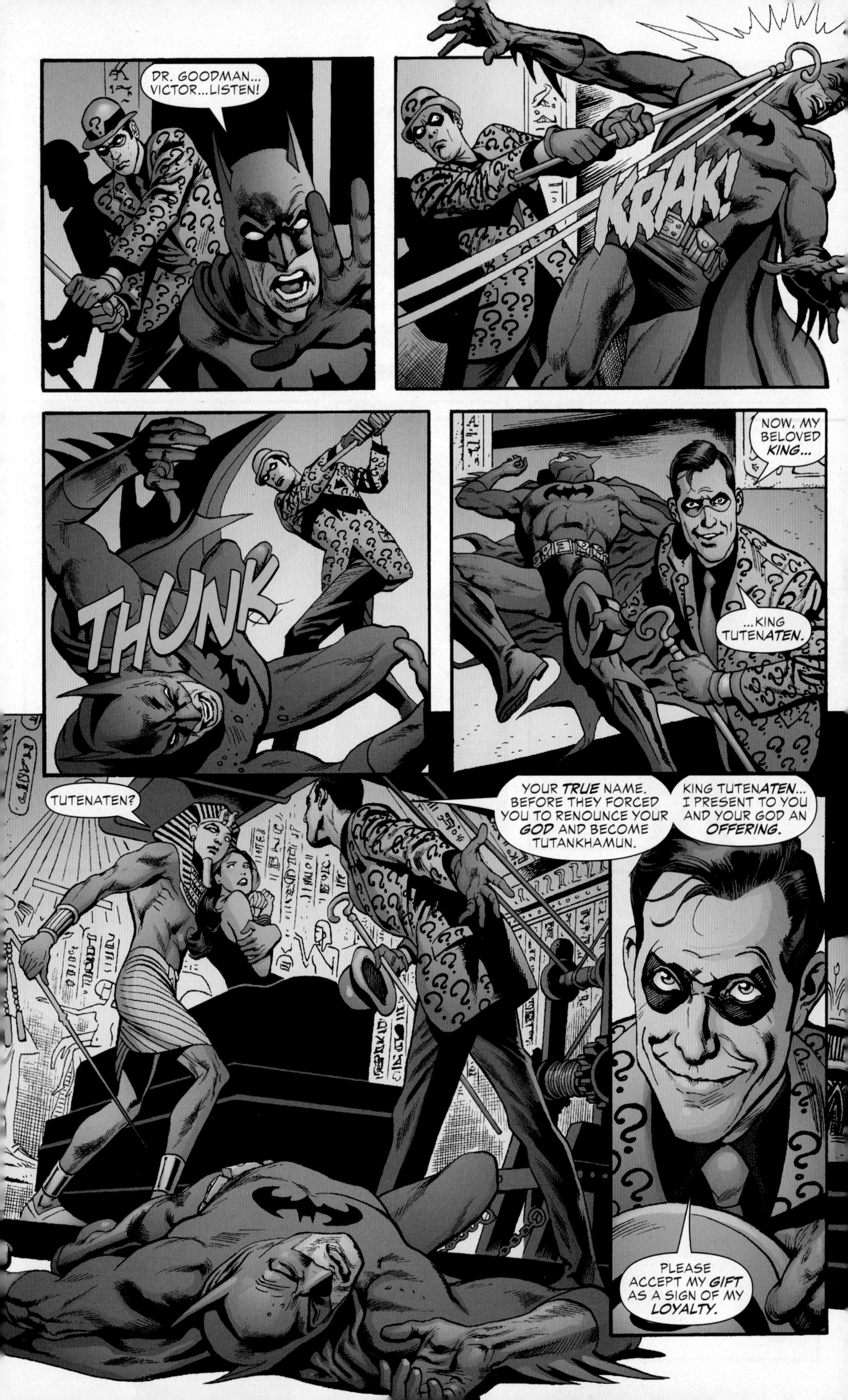
DR. GOODMAN... VICTOR...LISTEN!
KRAK!
THUNK
NOW, MY BELOVED KING...
...KING TUTENATEN.
TUTENATEN?
YOUR TRUE NAME. BEFORE THEY FORCED YOU TO RENOUNCE YOUR GOD AND BECOME TUTANKHAMUN.
KING TUTENATEN... I PRESENT TO YOU AND YOUR GOD AN OFFERING.
PLEASE ACCEPT MY GIFT AS A SIGN OF MY LOYALTY.

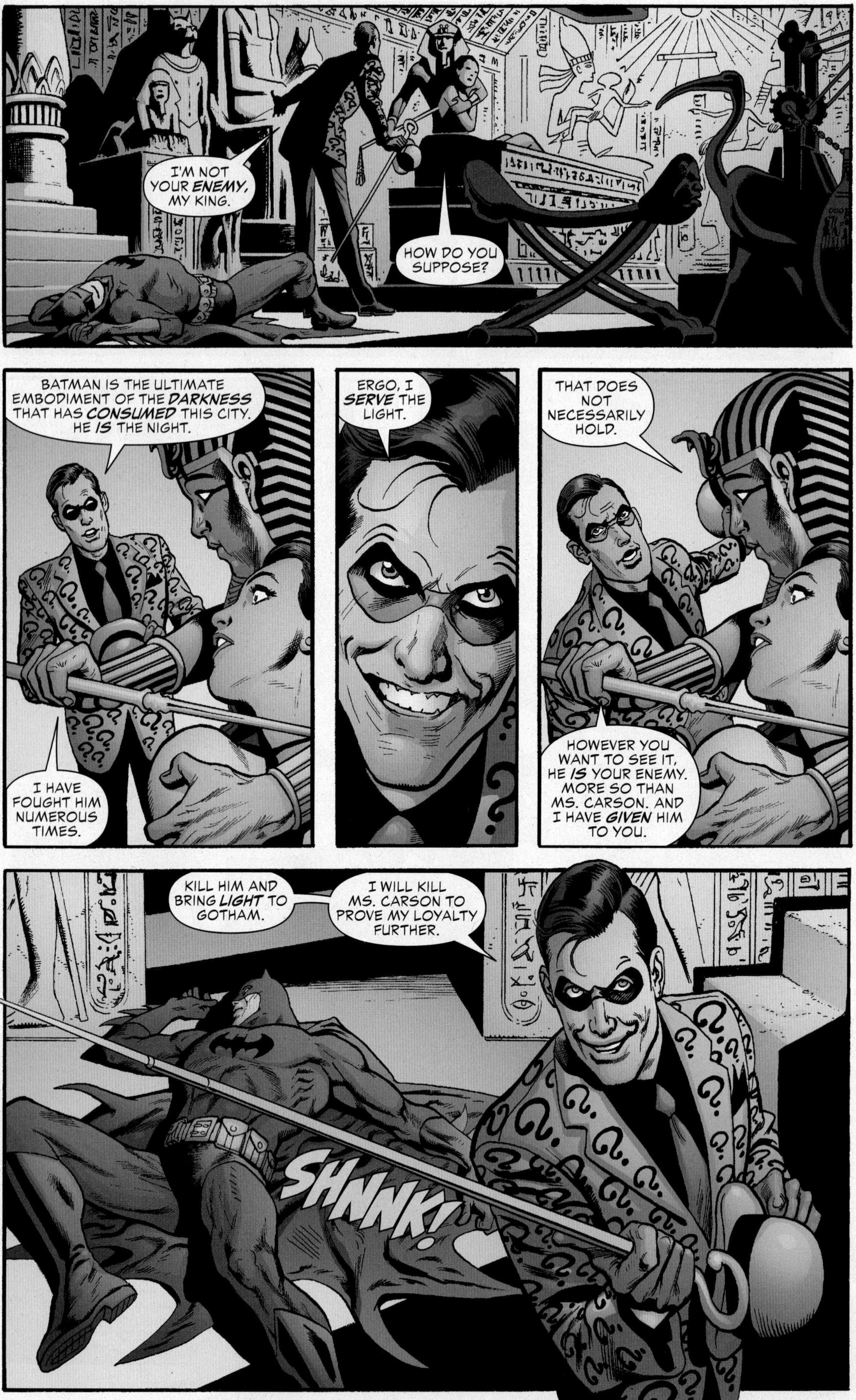

I'M NOT YOUR *ENEMY,* MY KING.
HOW DO YOU SUPPOSE?
BATMAN IS THE ULTIMATE EMBODIMENT OF THE *DARKNESS* THAT HAS *CONSUMED* THIS CITY. HE *IS* THE NIGHT.
I HAVE FOUGHT HIM NUMEROUS TIMES.
ERGO, I *SERVE* THE LIGHT.
THAT DOES NOT NECESSARILY HOLD.
HOWEVER YOU WANT TO SEE IT, HE *IS* YOUR ENEMY. MORE SO THAN MS. CARSON. AND I HAVE *GIVEN* HIM TO YOU.
KILL HIM AND BRING *LIGHT* TO GOTHAM.
I WILL KILL MS. CARSON TO PROVE MY LOYALTY FURTHER.
SHNNK!

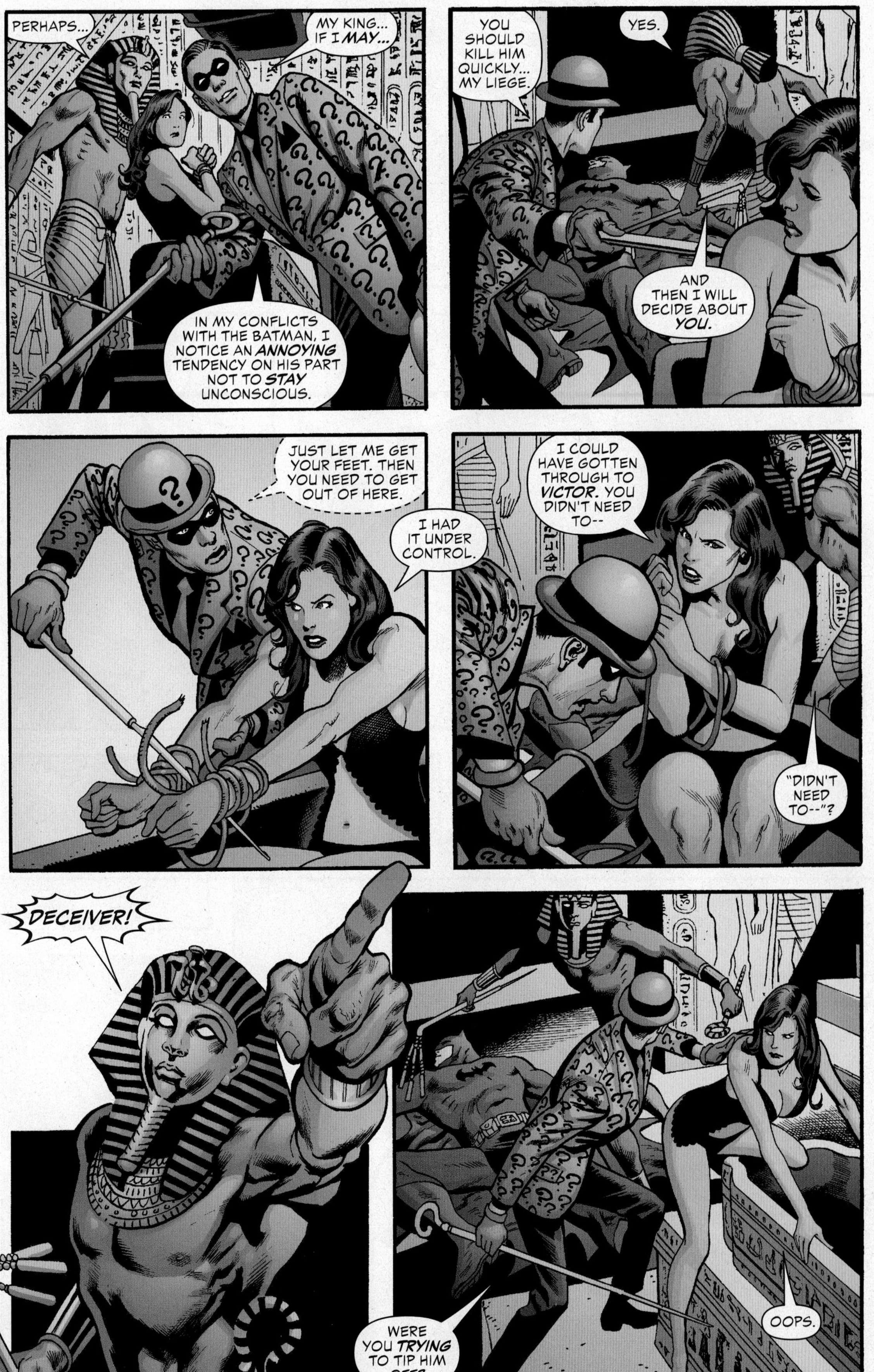
PERHAPS...
MY KING... IF I MAY...
IN MY CONFLICTS WITH THE BATMAN, I NOTICE AN ANNOYING TENDENCY ON HIS PART NOT TO STAY UNCONSCIOUS.
YOU SHOULD KILL HIM QUICKLY... MY LIEGE.
YES.
AND THEN I WILL DECIDE ABOUT YOU.
JUST LET ME GET YOUR FEET. THEN YOU NEED TO GET OUT OF HERE.
I HAD IT UNDER CONTROL.
I COULD HAVE GOTTEN THROUGH TO VICTOR. YOU DIDN'T NEED TO--
"DIDN'T NEED TO--"?
DECEIVER!
WERE YOU TRYING TO TIP HIM OFF?
OOPS.

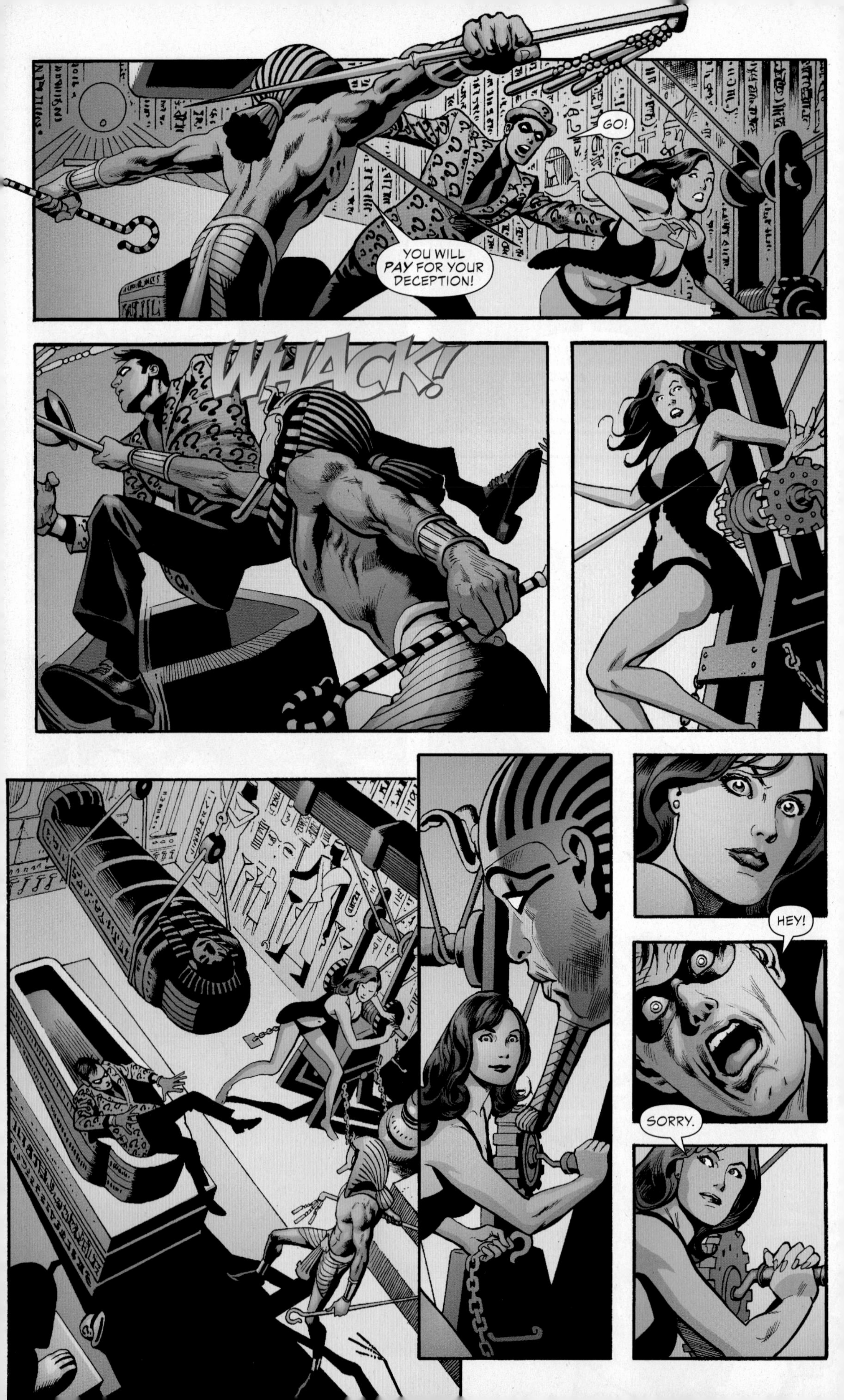
GO!
YOU WILL PAY FOR YOUR DECEPTION!
WHACK!
HEY!
SORRY.

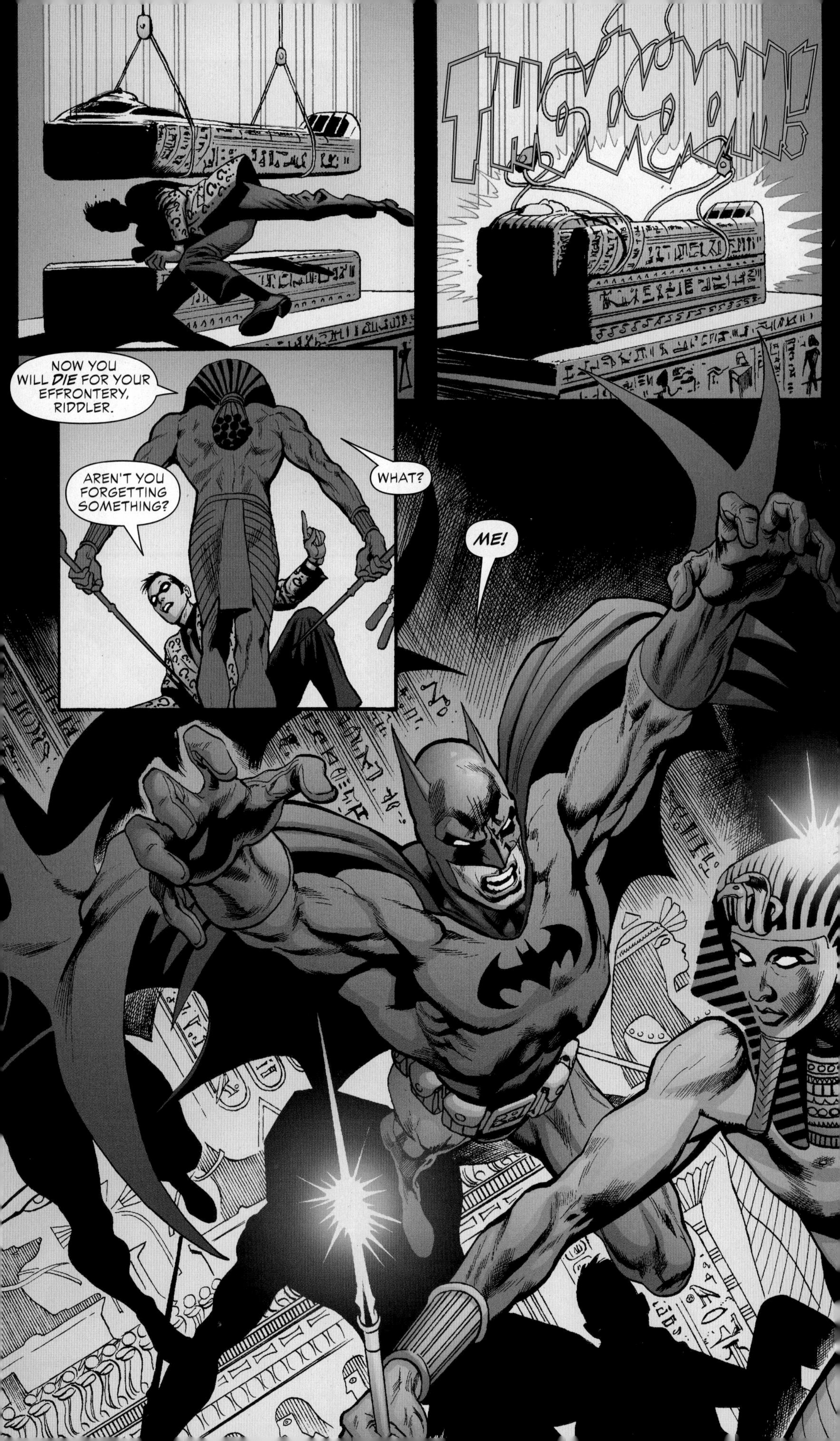
NOW YOU WILL DIE FOR YOUR EFFRONTERY, RIDDLER.
AREN'T YOU FORGETTING SOMETHING?
WHAT?
ME!

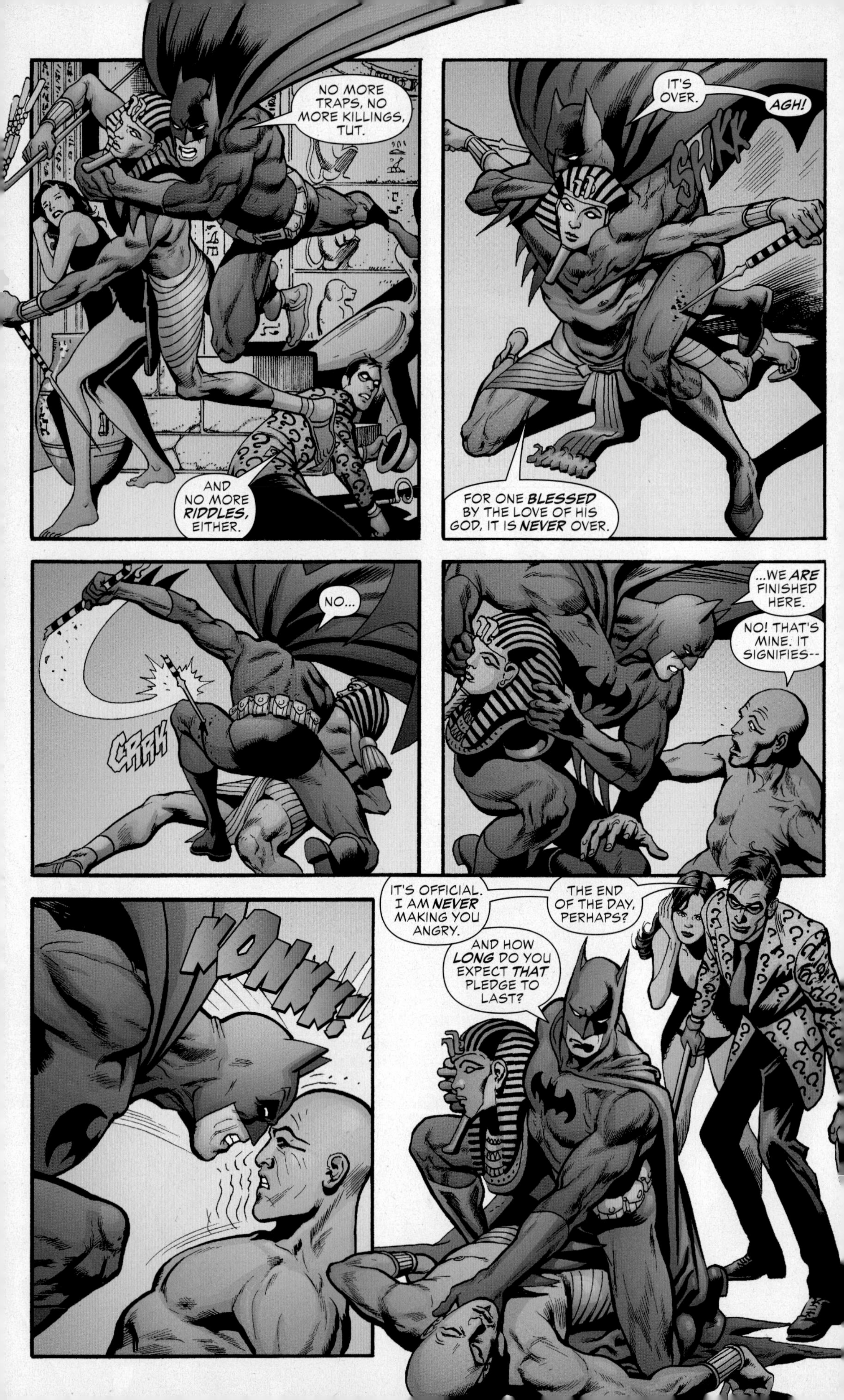
NO MORE TRAPS, NO MORE KILLINGS, TUT.
AND NO MORE RIDDLES, EITHER.
IT'S OVER.
AGH!
SHKK
FOR ONE BLESSED BY THE LOVE OF HIS GOD, IT IS NEVER OVER.
NO...
CRAK
...WE ARE FINISHED HERE.
NO! THAT'S MINE. IT SIGNIFIES--
KONKK!
IT'S OFFICIAL. I AM NEVER MAKING YOU ANGRY.
THE END OF THE DAY, PERHAPS?
AND HOW LONG DO YOU EXPECT THAT PLEDGE TO LAST?

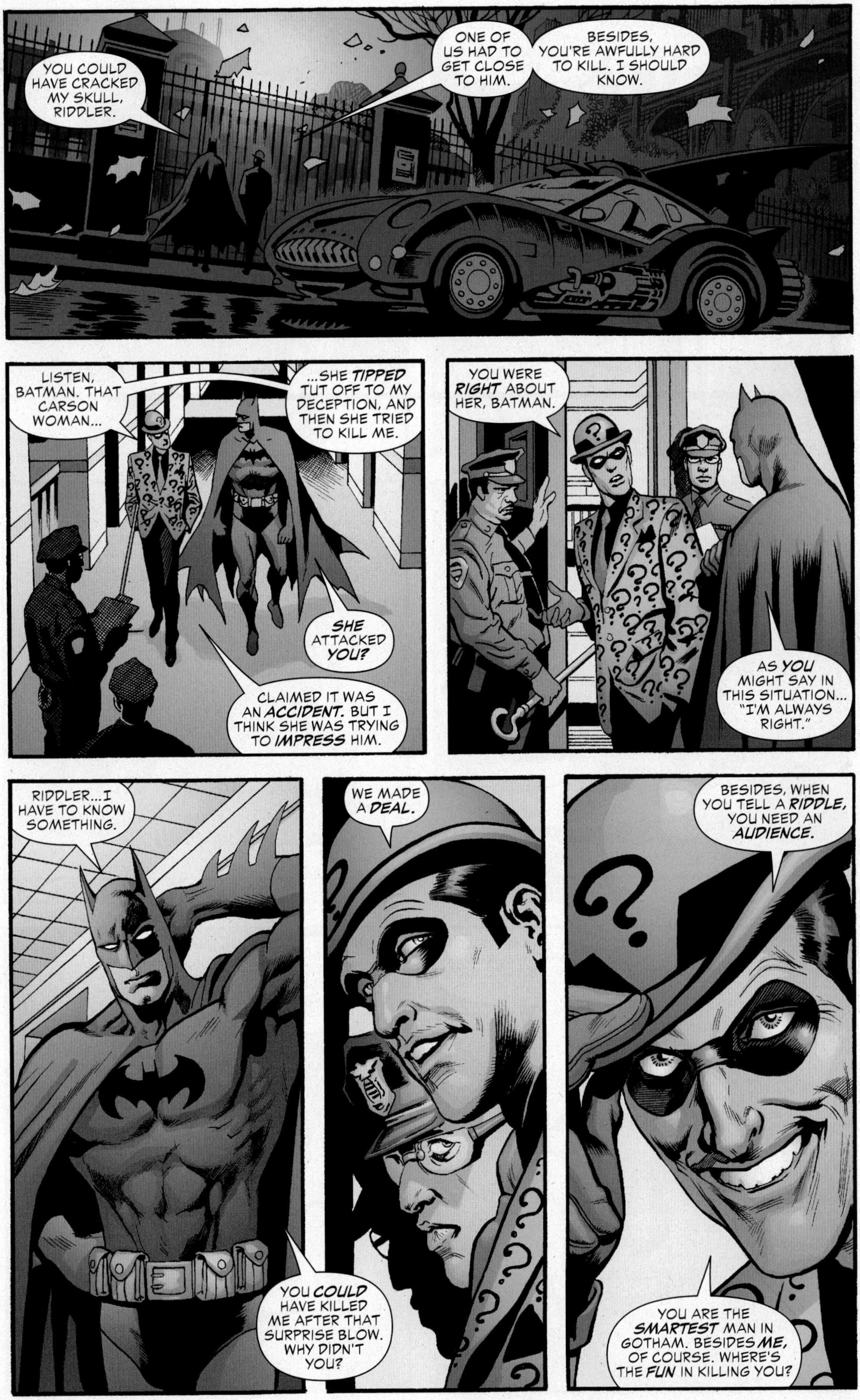
YOU COULD HAVE CRACKED MY SKULL, RIDDLER.
ONE OF US HAD TO GET CLOSE TO HIM.
BESIDES, YOU'RE AWFULLY HARD TO KILL. I SHOULD KNOW.
LISTEN, BATMAN. THAT CARSON WOMAN...
...SHE TIPPED TUT OFF TO MY DECEPTION, AND THEN SHE TRIED TO KILL ME.
SHE ATTACKED YOU?
CLAIMED IT WAS AN ACCIDENT. BUT I THINK SHE WAS TRYING TO IMPRESS HIM.
YOU WERE RIGHT ABOUT HER, BATMAN.
AS YOU MIGHT SAY IN THIS SITUATION... "I'M ALWAYS RIGHT."
RIDDLER...I HAVE TO KNOW SOMETHING.
YOU COULD HAVE KILLED ME AFTER THAT SURPRISE BLOW. WHY DIDN'T YOU?
WE MADE A DEAL.
BESIDES, WHEN YOU TELL A RIDDLE, YOU NEED AN AUDIENCE.
YOU ARE THE SMARTEST MAN IN GOTHAM. BESIDES ME, OF COURSE. WHERE'S THE FUN IN KILLING YOU?

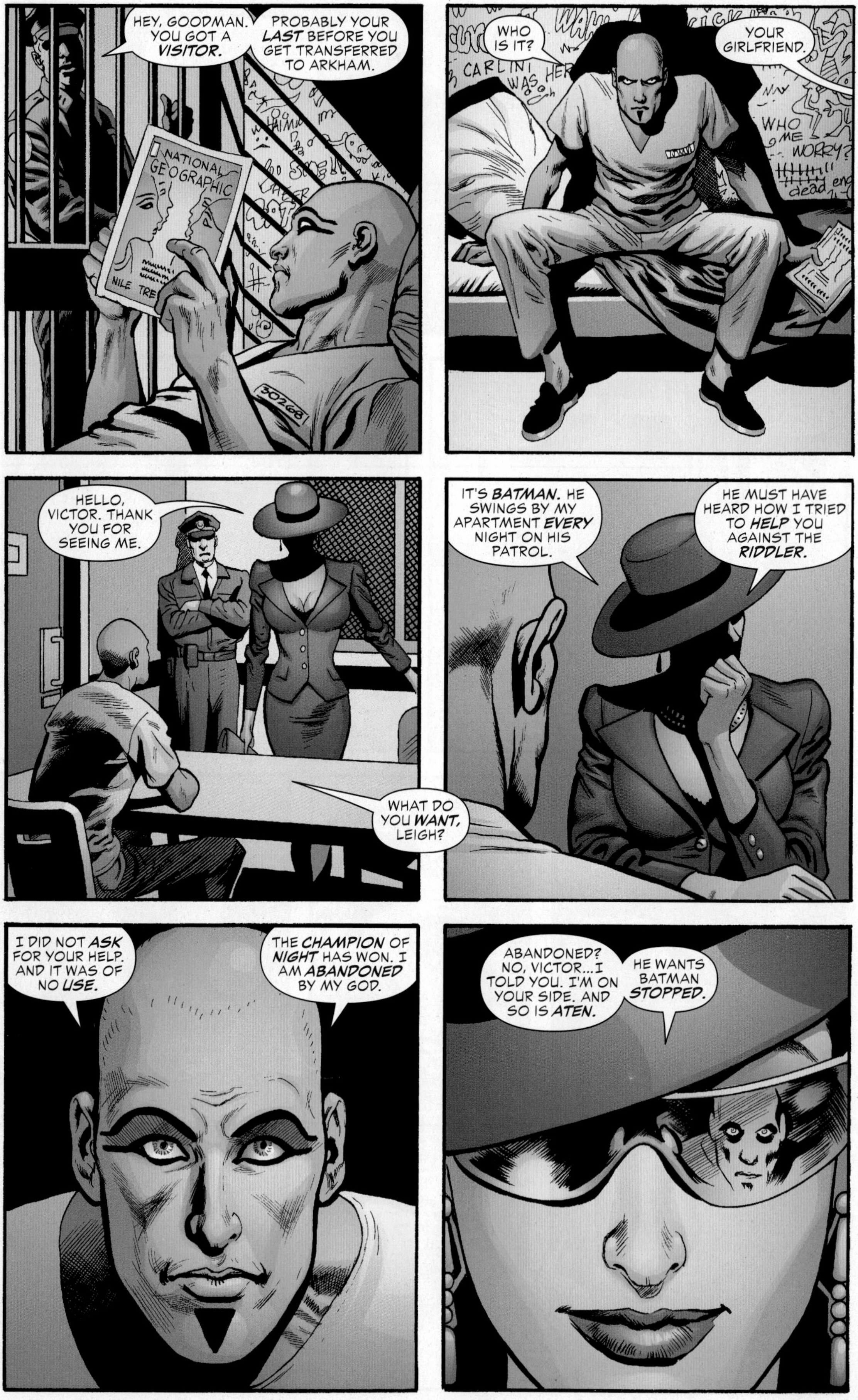
HEY, GOODMAN. YOU GOT A VISITOR.
PROBABLY YOUR LAST BEFORE YOU GET TRANSFERRED TO ARKHAM.
NATIONAL GEOGRAPHIC
WHO IS IT?
YOUR GIRLFRIEND.
WHO ME WORRY?
HELLO, VICTOR. THANK YOU FOR SEEING ME.
WHAT DO YOU WANT, LEIGH?
IT'S BATMAN. HE SWINGS BY MY APARTMENT EVERY NIGHT ON HIS PATROL.
HE MUST HAVE HEARD HOW I TRIED TO HELP YOU AGAINST THE RIDDLER.
I DID NOT ASK FOR YOUR HELP. AND IT WAS OF NO USE.
THE CHAMPION OF NIGHT HAS WON. I AM ABANDONED BY MY GOD.
ABANDONED? NO, VICTOR...I TOLD YOU. I'M ON YOUR SIDE. AND SO IS ATEN.
HE WANTS BATMAN STOPPED.

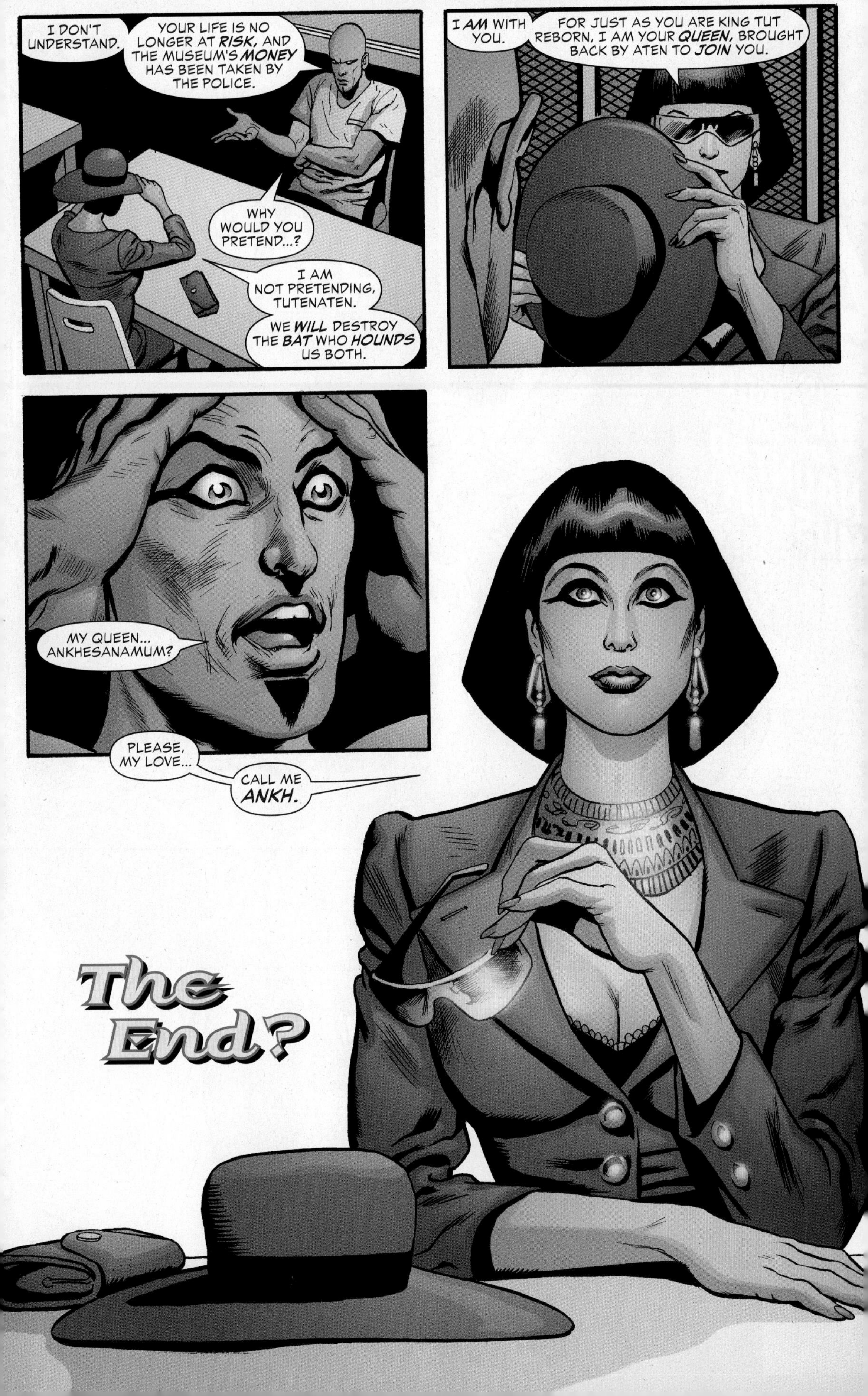
I DON'T UNDERSTAND.
YOUR LIFE IS NO LONGER AT RISK, AND THE MUSEUM'S MONEY HAS BEEN TAKEN BY THE POLICE.
WHY WOULD YOU PRETEND...?
I AM NOT PRETENDING, TUTENATEN.
WE WILL DESTROY THE BAT WHO HOUNDS US BOTH.
I AM WITH YOU.
FOR JUST AS YOU ARE KING TUT REBORN, I AM YOUR QUEEN, BROUGHT BACK BY ATEN TO JOIN YOU.
MY QUEEN... ANKHESANAMUM?
PLEASE, MY LOVE...
CALL ME ANKH.
The End?

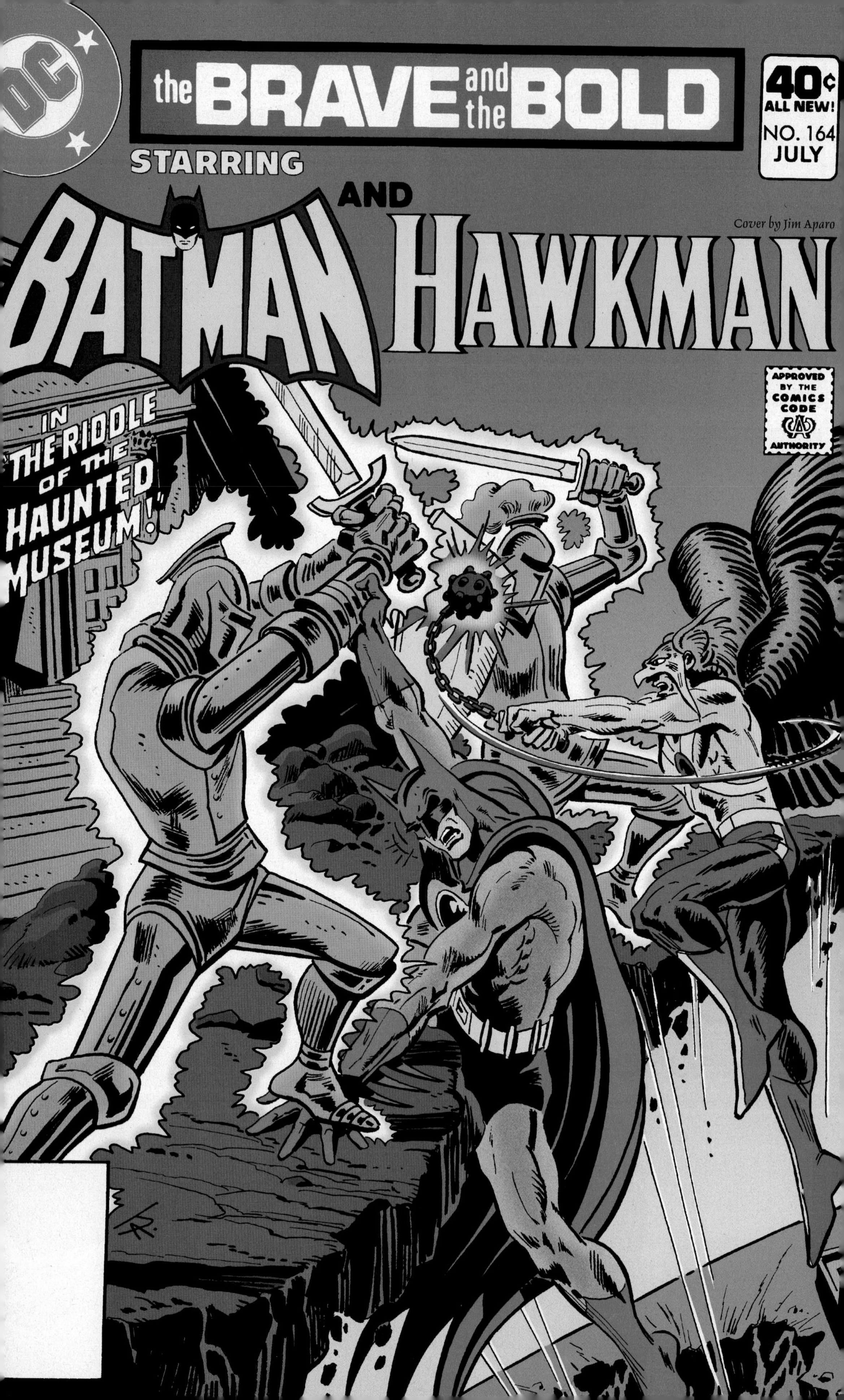

DC
the BRAVE and the BOLD
40¢
ALL NEW!
NO. 164
JULY
STARRING
BATMAN
AND
HAWKMAN
Cover by Jim Aparo
APPROVED BY THE COMICS CODE AUTHORITY
IN "THE RIDDLE OF THE HAUNTED MUSEUM!"

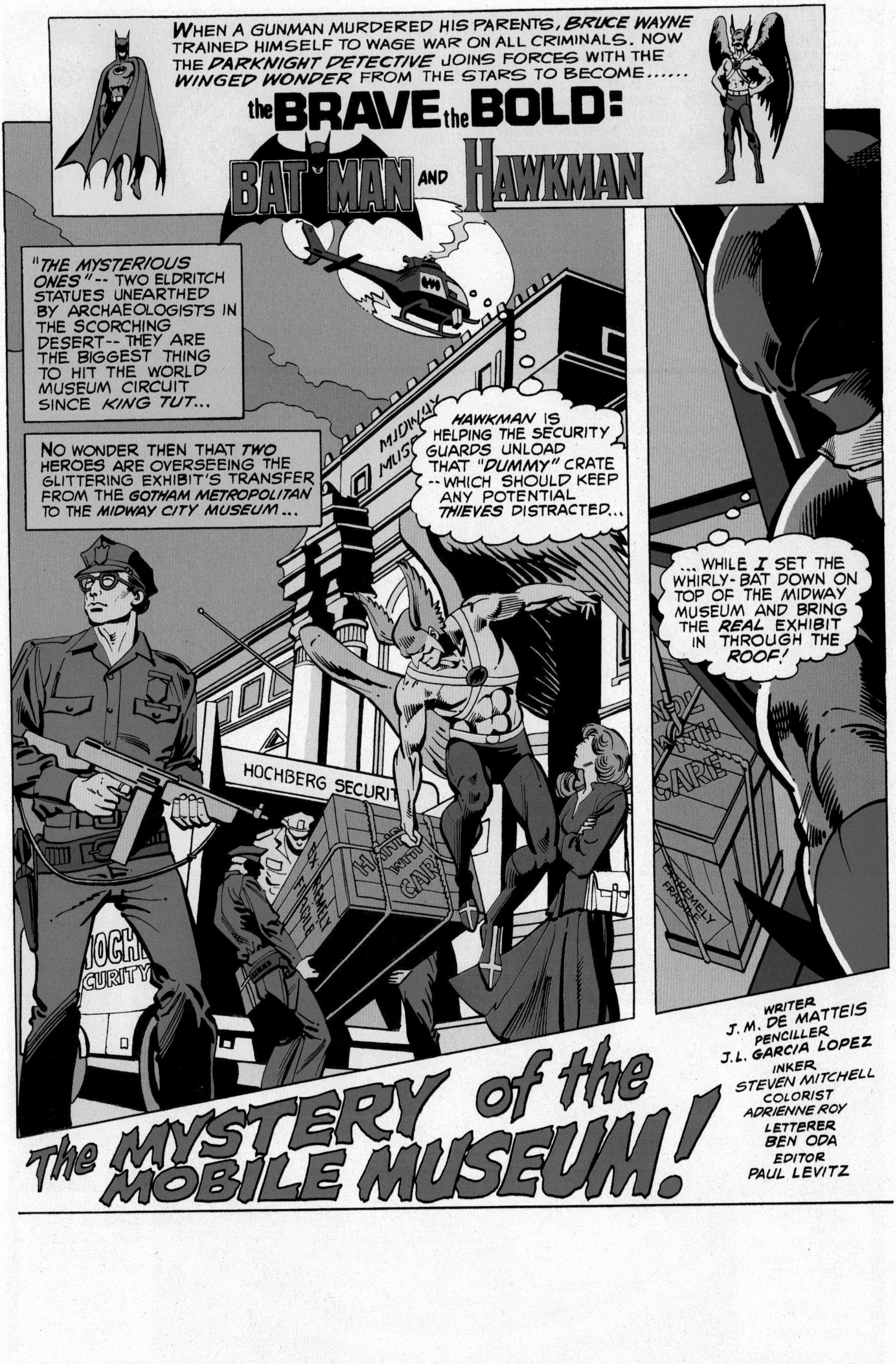

WHEN A GUNMAN MURDERED HIS PARENTS, BRUCE WAYNE TRAINED HIMSELF TO WAGE WAR ON ALL CRIMINALS. NOW THE DARKNIGHT DETECTIVE JOINS FORCES WITH THE WINGED WONDER FROM THE STARS TO BECOME......
the BRAVE the BOLD: BATMAN AND HAWKMAN
"THE MYSTERIOUS ONES" -- TWO ELDRITCH STATUES UNEARTHED BY ARCHAEOLOGISTS IN THE SCORCHING DESERT-- THEY ARE THE BIGGEST THING TO HIT THE WORLD MUSEUM CIRCUIT SINCE KING TUT...
NO WONDER THEN THAT TWO HEROES ARE OVERSEEING THE GLITTERING EXHIBIT'S TRANSFER FROM THE GOTHAM METROPOLITAN TO THE MIDWAY CITY MUSEUM...
HAWKMAN IS HELPING THE SECURITY GUARDS UNLOAD THAT "DUMMY" CRATE --WHICH SHOULD KEEP ANY POTENTIAL THIEVES DISTRACTED...
...WHILE I SET THE WHIRLY-BAT DOWN ON TOP OF THE MIDWAY MUSEUM AND BRING THE REAL EXHIBIT IN THROUGH THE ROOF!
HOCHBERG SECURIT
The MYSTERY of the MOBILE MUSEUM!
WRITER J. M. DE MATTEIS
PENCILLER J.L. GARCIA LOPEZ
INKER STEVEN MITCHELL
COLORIST ADRIENNE ROY
LETTERER BEN ODA
EDITOR PAUL LEVITZ

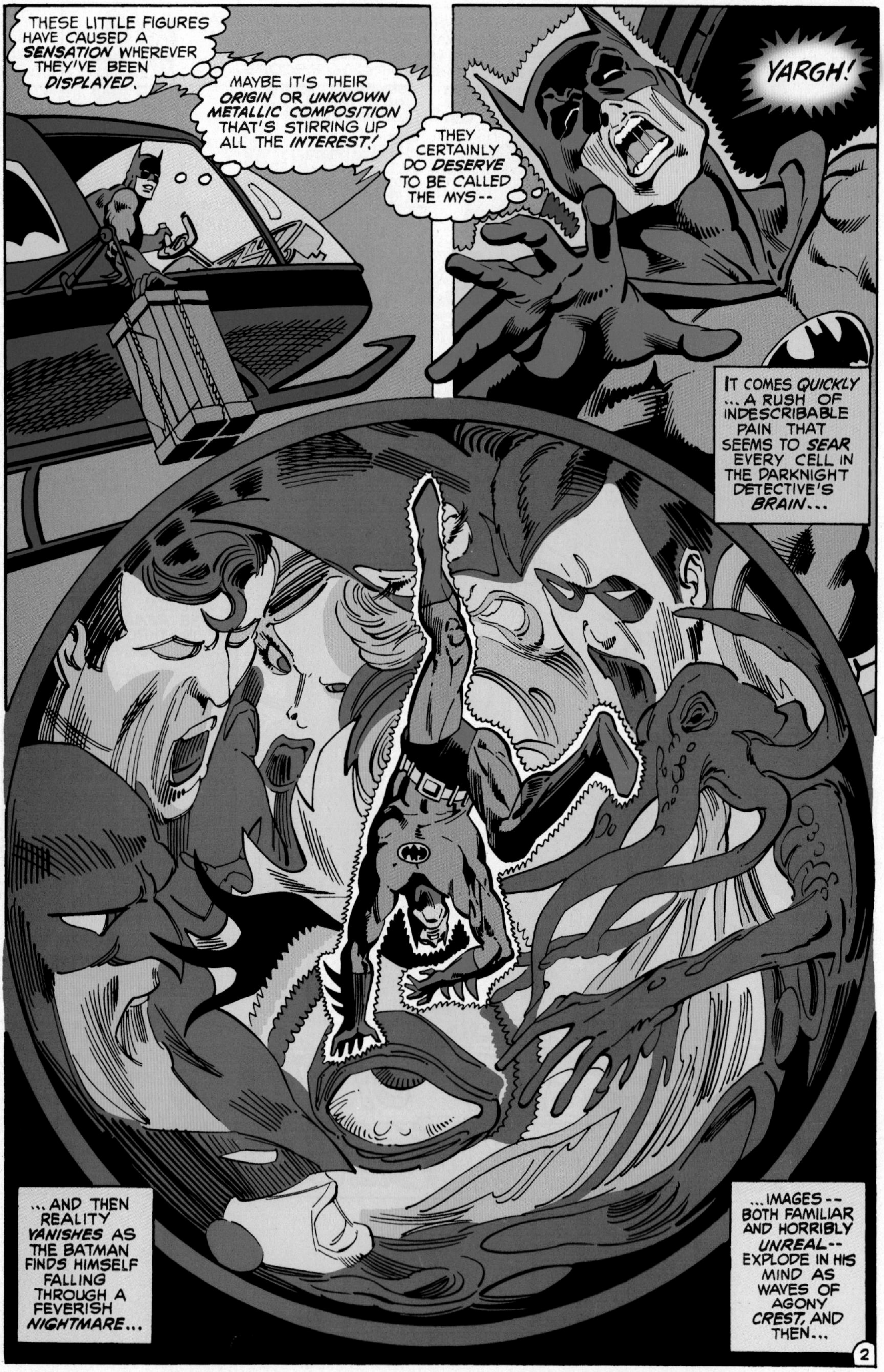
THESE LITTLE FIGURES HAVE CAUSED A SENSATION WHEREVER THEY'VE BEEN DISPLAYED.
MAYBE IT'S THEIR ORIGIN OR UNKNOWN METALLIC COMPOSITION THAT'S STIRRING UP ALL THE INTEREST!
THEY CERTAINLY DO DESERVE TO BE CALLED THE MYS--
YARGH!
IT COMES QUICKLY ...A RUSH OF INDESCRIBABLE PAIN THAT SEEMS TO SEAR EVERY CELL IN THE DARKNIGHT DETECTIVE'S BRAIN...
...AND THEN REALITY VANISHES AS THE BATMAN FINDS HIMSELF FALLING THROUGH A FEVERISH NIGHTMARE...
...IMAGES -- BOTH FAMILIAR AND HORRIBLY UNREAL-- EXPLODE IN HIS MIND AS WAVES OF AGONY CREST, AND THEN...
2

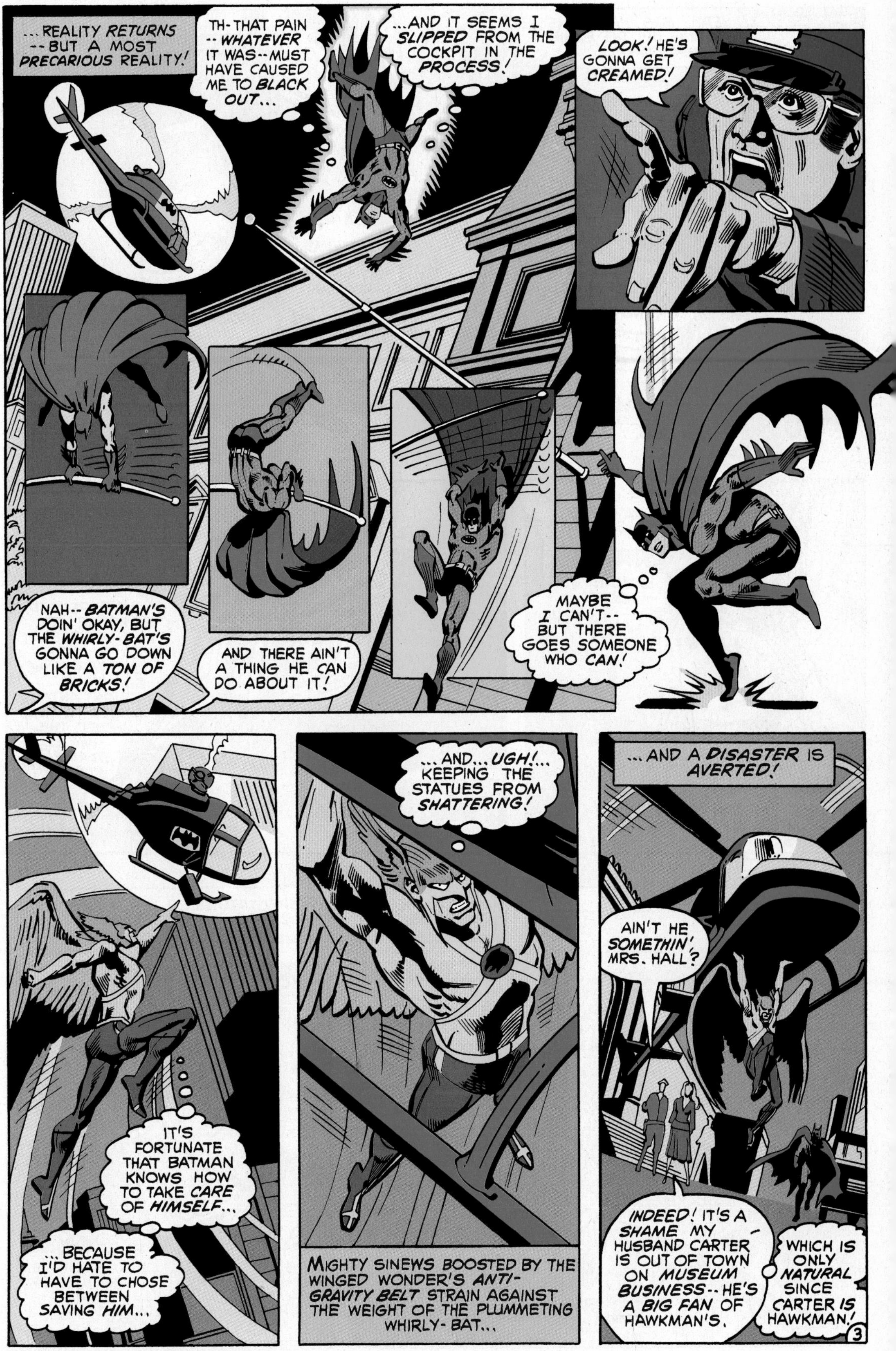

...REALITY RETURNS --BUT A MOST PRECARIOUS REALITY!
TH-THAT PAIN --WHATEVER IT WAS--MUST HAVE CAUSED ME TO BLACK OUT...
...AND IT SEEMS I SLIPPED FROM THE COCKPIT IN THE PROCESS!
LOOK! HE'S GONNA GET CREAMED!
NAH--BATMAN'S DOIN' OKAY, BUT THE WHIRLY-BAT'S GONNA GO DOWN LIKE A TON OF BRICKS!
AND THERE AIN'T A THING HE CAN DO ABOUT IT!
MAYBE I CAN'T-- BUT THERE GOES SOMEONE WHO CAN!
IT'S FORTUNATE THAT BATMAN KNOWS HOW TO TAKE CARE OF HIMSELF...
...BECAUSE I'D HATE TO HAVE TO CHOSE BETWEEN SAVING HIM...
...AND...UGH!...KEEPING THE STATUES FROM SHATTERING!
MIGHTY SINEWS BOOSTED BY THE WINGED WONDER'S ANTI-GRAVITY BELT STRAIN AGAINST THE WEIGHT OF THE PLUMMETING WHIRLY-BAT...
...AND A DISASTER IS AVERTED!
AIN'T HE SOMETHIN' MRS. HALL?
INDEED! IT'S A SHAME MY HUSBAND CARTER IS OUT OF TOWN ON MUSEUM BUSINESS--HE'S A BIG FAN OF HAWKMAN'S.
WHICH IS ONLY NATURAL SINCE CARTER IS HAWKMAN!
3

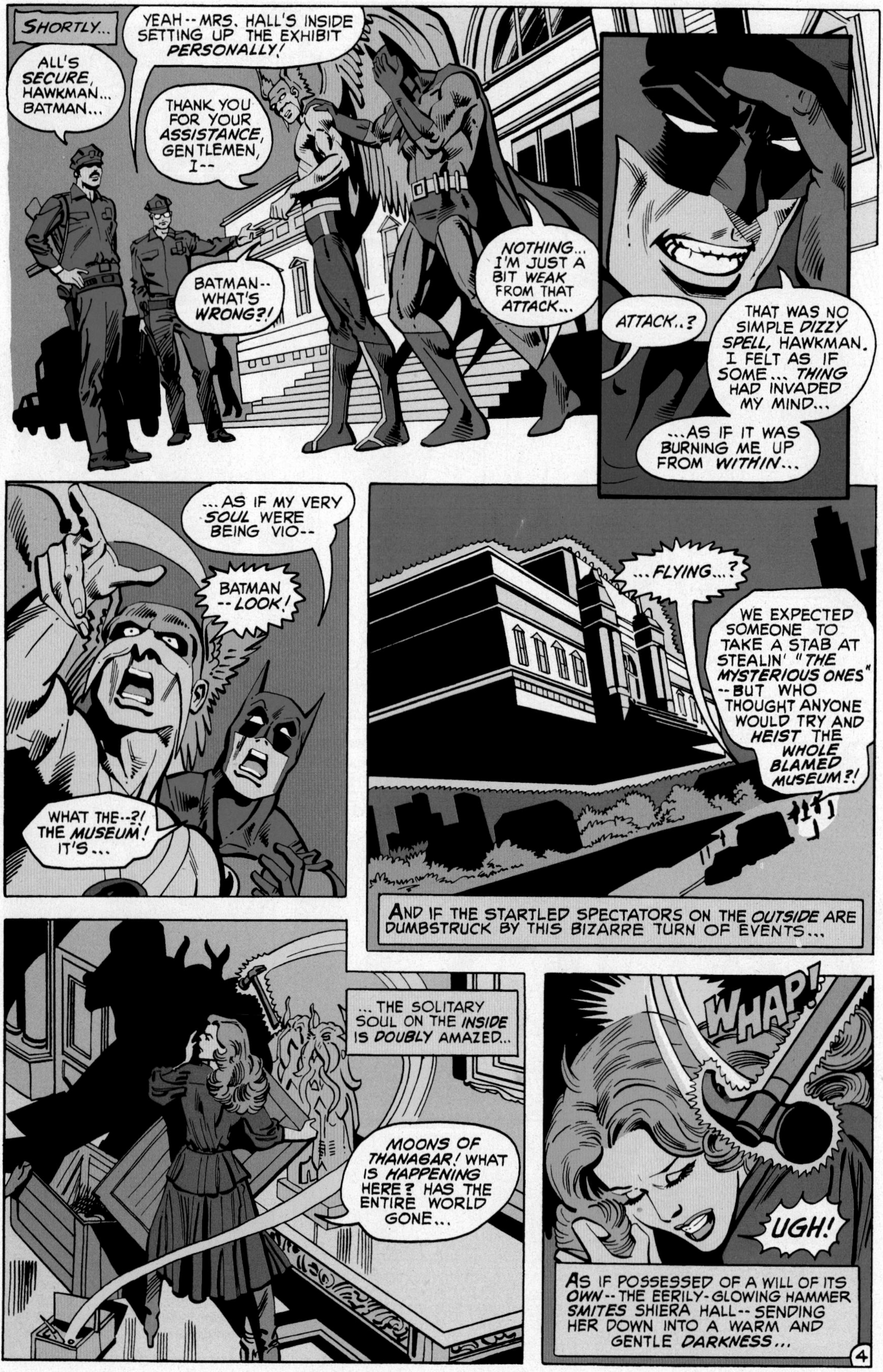
SHORTLY...
ALL'S SECURE, HAWKMAN... BATMAN...
YEAH -- MRS. HALL'S INSIDE SETTING UP THE EXHIBIT PERSONALLY!
THANK YOU FOR YOUR ASSISTANCE, GENTLEMEN, I--
BATMAN-- WHAT'S WRONG?!
NOTHING... I'M JUST A BIT WEAK FROM THAT ATTACK...
ATTACK..?
THAT WAS NO SIMPLE DIZZY SPELL, HAWKMAN. I FELT AS IF SOME... THING HAD INVADED MY MIND...
...AS IF IT WAS BURNING ME UP FROM WITHIN...
...AS IF MY VERY SOUL WERE BEING VIO--
BATMAN --LOOK!
WHAT THE--?! THE MUSEUM! IT'S...
...FLYING...?
WE EXPECTED SOMEONE TO TAKE A STAB AT STEALIN' "THE MYSTERIOUS ONES" --BUT WHO THOUGHT ANYONE WOULD TRY AND HEIST THE WHOLE BLAMED MUSEUM?!
AND IF THE STARTLED SPECTATORS ON THE OUTSIDE ARE DUMBSTRUCK BY THIS BIZARRE TURN OF EVENTS...
...THE SOLITARY SOUL ON THE INSIDE IS DOUBLY AMAZED...
MOONS OF THANAGAR! WHAT IS HAPPENING HERE? HAS THE ENTIRE WORLD GONE...
WHAP!
UGH!
AS IF POSSESSED OF A WILL OF ITS OWN -- THE EERILY-GLOWING HAMMER SMITES SHIERA HALL -- SENDING HER DOWN INTO A WARM AND GENTLE DARKNESS...
4

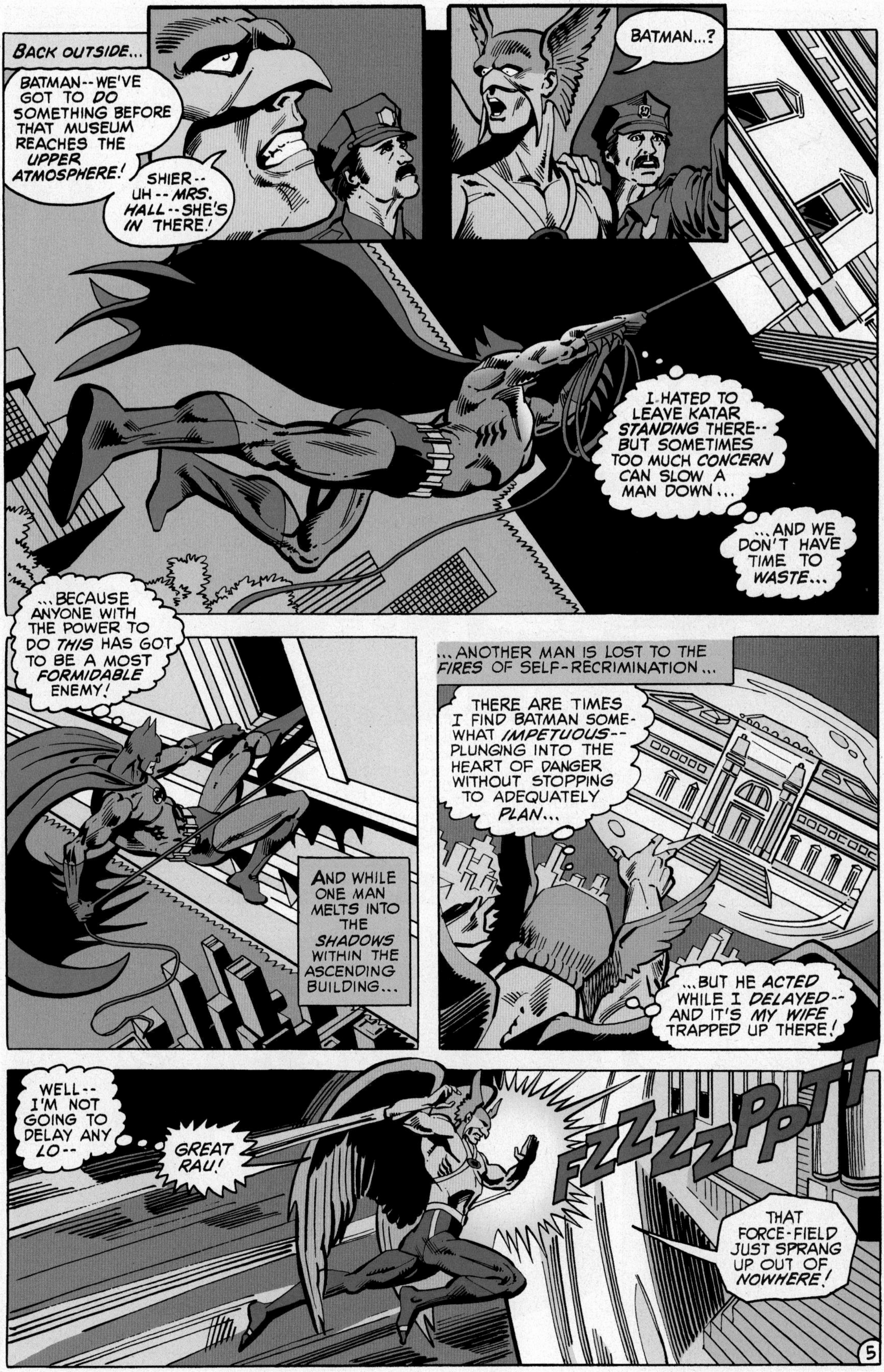
BACK OUTSIDE...
BATMAN--WE'VE GOT TO DO SOMETHING BEFORE THAT MUSEUM REACHES THE UPPER ATMOSPHERE!
SHIER--UH--MRS. HALL--SHE'S IN THERE!
BATMAN...?
I HATED TO LEAVE KATAR STANDING THERE--BUT SOMETIMES TOO MUCH CONCERN CAN SLOW A MAN DOWN...
...AND WE DON'T HAVE TIME TO WASTE...
...BECAUSE ANYONE WITH THE POWER TO DO THIS HAS GOT TO BE A MOST FORMIDABLE ENEMY!
AND WHILE ONE MAN MELTS INTO THE SHADOWS WITHIN THE ASCENDING BUILDING...
...ANOTHER MAN IS LOST TO THE FIRES OF SELF-RECRIMINATION...
THERE ARE TIMES I FIND BATMAN SOMEWHAT IMPETUOUS--PLUNGING INTO THE HEART OF DANGER WITHOUT STOPPING TO ADEQUATELY PLAN...
...BUT HE ACTED WHILE I DELAYED--AND IT'S MY WIFE TRAPPED UP THERE!
WELL--I'M NOT GOING TO DELAY ANY LO--
GREAT RAU!
FZZZZZPPTT
THAT FORCE-FIELD JUST SPRANG UP OUT OF NOWHERE!
5

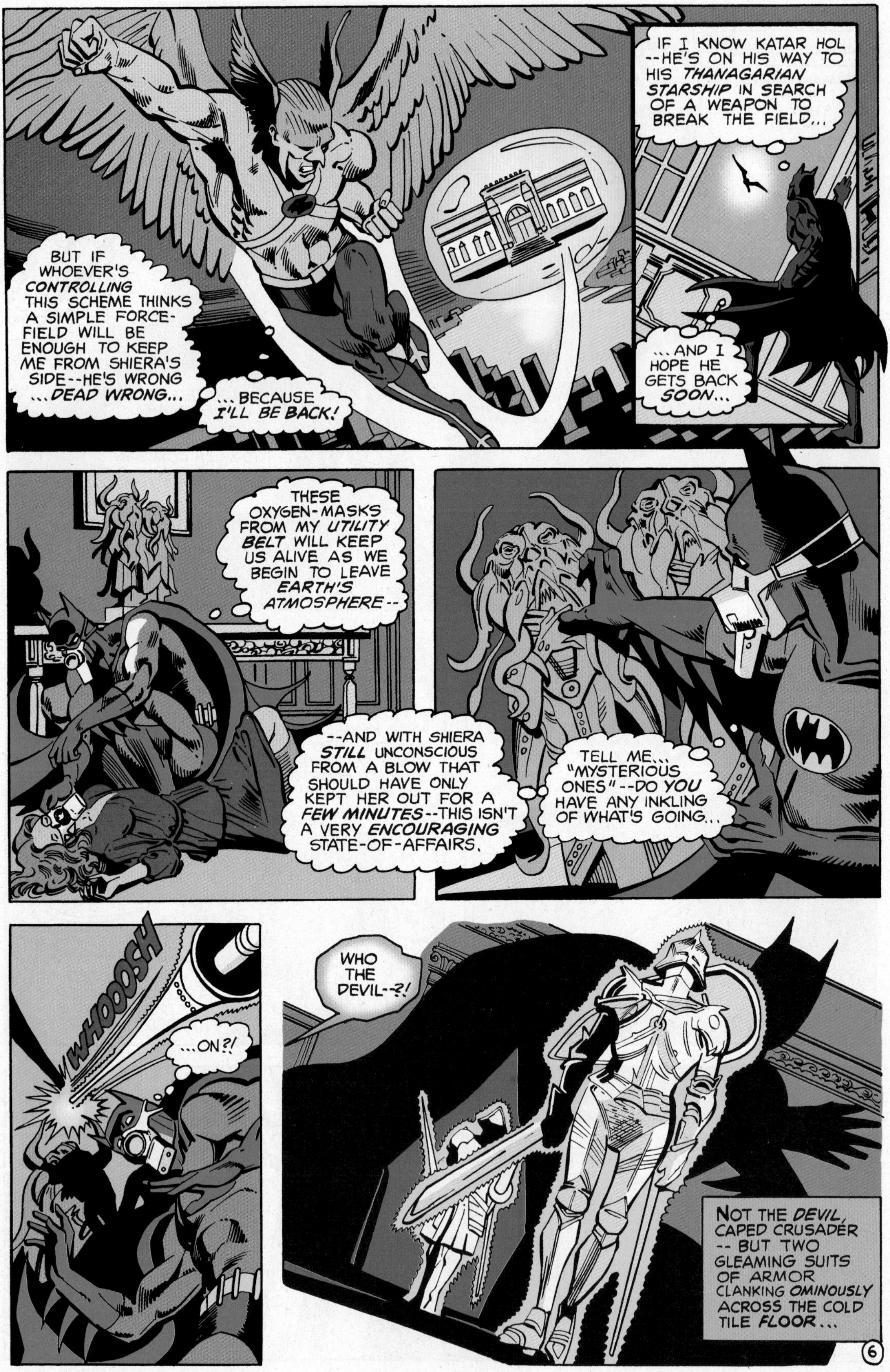
BUT IF WHOEVER'S CONTROLLING THIS SCHEME THINKS A SIMPLE FORCE-FIELD WILL BE ENOUGH TO KEEP ME FROM SHIERA'S SIDE--HE'S WRONG ...DEAD WRONG...
...BECAUSE I'LL BE BACK!
IF I KNOW KATAR HOL --HE'S ON HIS WAY TO HIS THANAGARIAN STARSHIP IN SEARCH OF A WEAPON TO BREAK THE FIELD...
...AND I HOPE HE GETS BACK SOON...
THESE OXYGEN-MASKS FROM MY UTILITY BELT WILL KEEP US ALIVE AS WE BEGIN TO LEAVE EARTH'S ATMOSPHERE--
--AND WITH SHIERA STILL UNCONSCIOUS FROM A BLOW THAT SHOULD HAVE ONLY KEPT HER OUT FOR A FEW MINUTES--THIS ISN'T A VERY ENCOURAGING STATE-OF-AFFAIRS.
TELL ME... "MYSTERIOUS ONES"--DO YOU HAVE ANY INKLING OF WHAT'S GOING...
WHOOOSH
...ON?!
WHO THE DEVIL--?!
NOT THE DEVIL, CAPED CRUSADER -- BUT TWO GLEAMING SUITS OF ARMOR CLANKING OMINOUSLY ACROSS THE COLD TILE FLOOR...
6

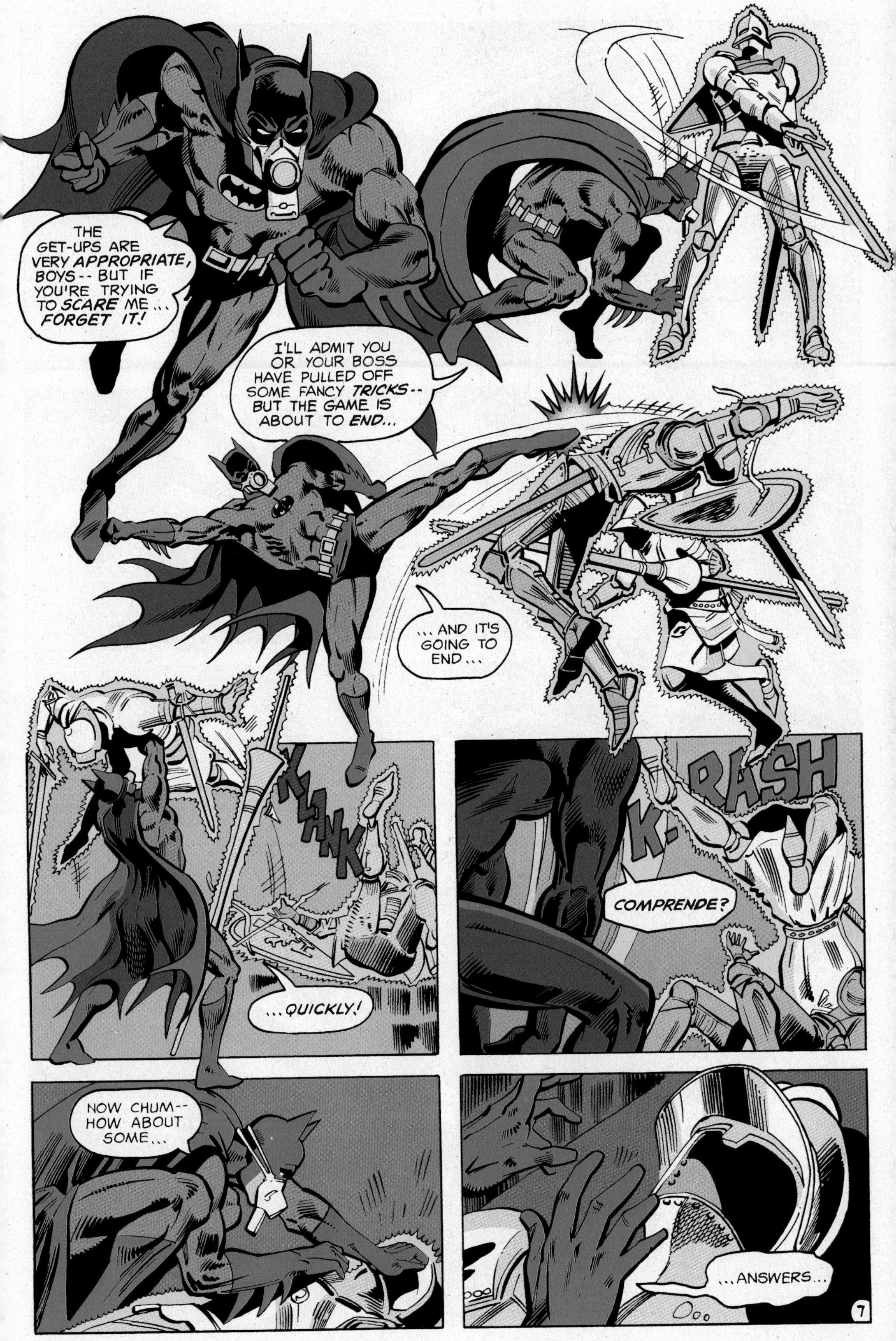

THE GET-UPS ARE VERY APPROPRIATE, BOYS -- BUT IF YOU'RE TRYING TO SCARE ME... FORGET IT!
I'LL ADMIT YOU OR YOUR BOSS HAVE PULLED OFF SOME FANCY TRICKS -- BUT THE GAME IS ABOUT TO END...
...AND IT'S GOING TO END...
KLANK
...QUICKLY!
K-RASH
COMPRENDE?
NOW CHUM -- HOW ABOUT SOME...
...ANSWERS...
7

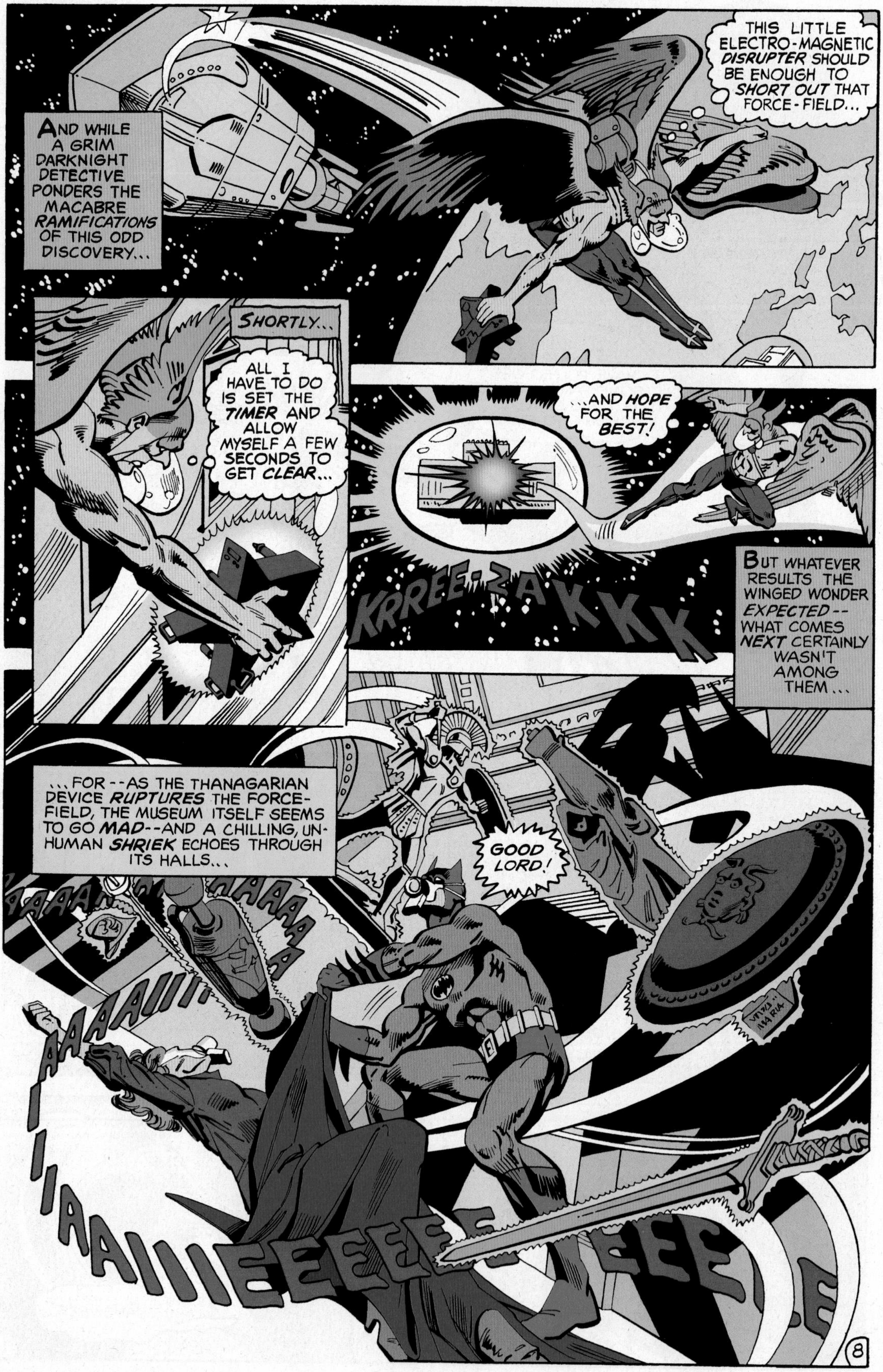
AND WHILE A GRIM DARKNIGHT DETECTIVE PONDERS THE MACABRE RAMIFICATIONS OF THIS ODD DISCOVERY...
THIS LITTLE ELECTRO-MAGNETIC DISRUPTER SHOULD BE ENOUGH TO SHORT OUT THAT FORCE-FIELD...
SHORTLY...
ALL I HAVE TO DO IS SET THE TIMER AND ALLOW MYSELF A FEW SECONDS TO GET CLEAR...
...AND HOPE FOR THE BEST!
KRREE-ZAKKKK
BUT WHATEVER RESULTS THE WINGED WONDER EXPECTED -- WHAT COMES NEXT CERTAINLY WASN'T AMONG THEM...
...FOR--AS THE THANAGARIAN DEVICE RUPTURES THE FORCE-FIELD, THE MUSEUM ITSELF SEEMS TO GO MAD--AND A CHILLING, UN-HUMAN SHRIEK ECHOES THROUGH ITS HALLS...
GOOD LORD!
AAAAIIIIEEEEEEEEEEE
8

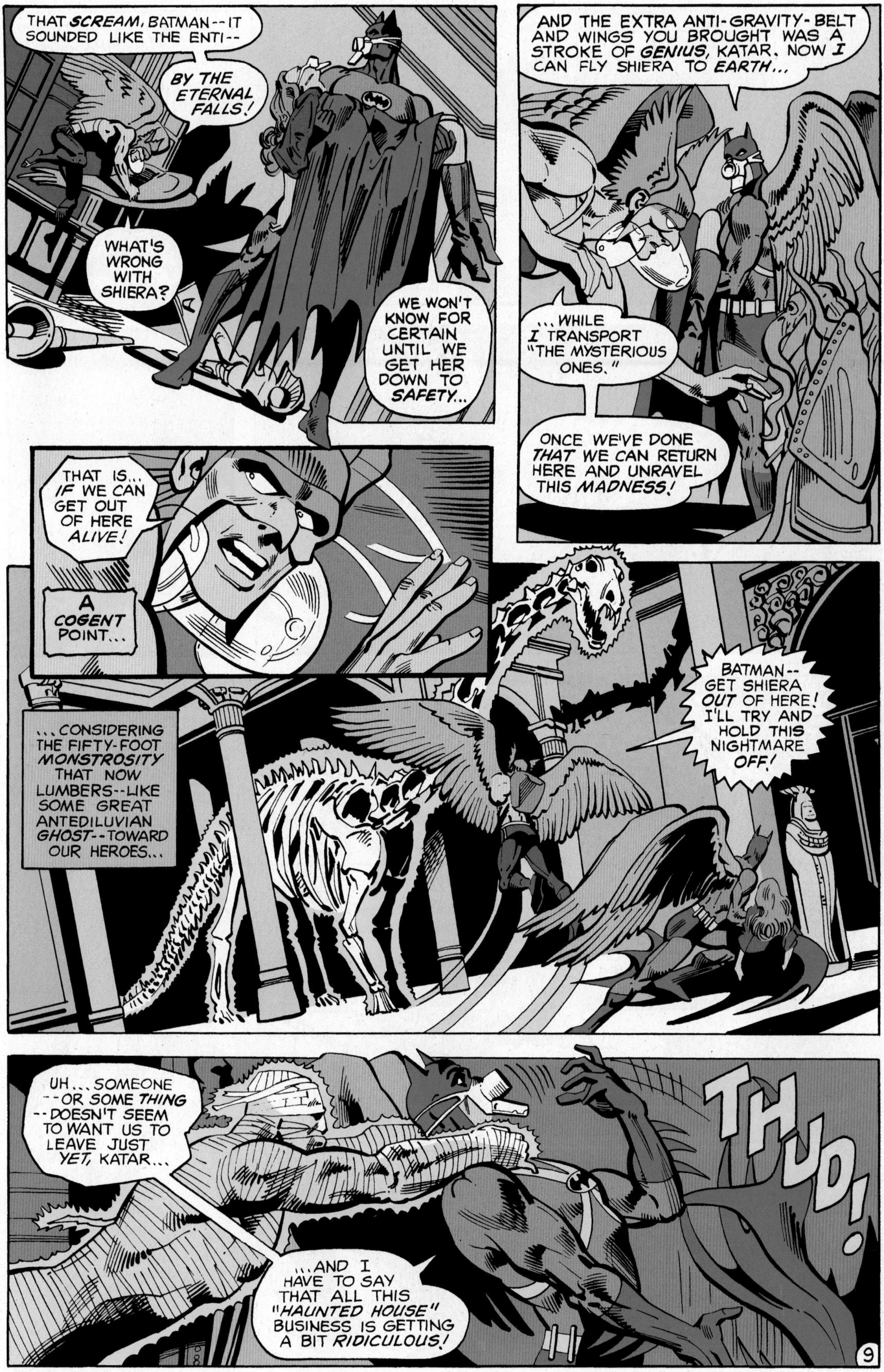
THAT SCREAM, BATMAN--IT SOUNDED LIKE THE ENTI--
BY THE ETERNAL FALLS!
WHAT'S WRONG WITH SHIERA?
WE WON'T KNOW FOR CERTAIN UNTIL WE GET HER DOWN TO SAFETY...
AND THE EXTRA ANTI-GRAVITY-BELT AND WINGS YOU BROUGHT WAS A STROKE OF GENIUS, KATAR. NOW I CAN FLY SHIERA TO EARTH...
...WHILE I TRANSPORT "THE MYSTERIOUS ONES."
ONCE WE'VE DONE THAT WE CAN RETURN HERE AND UNRAVEL THIS MADNESS!
THAT IS... IF WE CAN GET OUT OF HERE ALIVE!
A COGENT POINT...
...CONSIDERING THE FIFTY-FOOT MONSTROSITY THAT NOW LUMBERS--LIKE SOME GREAT ANTEDILUVIAN GHOST--TOWARD OUR HEROES...
BATMAN--GET SHIERA OUT OF HERE! I'LL TRY AND HOLD THIS NIGHTMARE OFF!
UH... SOMEONE --OR SOME THING --DOESN'T SEEM TO WANT US TO LEAVE JUST YET, KATAR...
THUD!
...AND I HAVE TO SAY THAT ALL THIS "HAUNTED HOUSE" BUSINESS IS GETTING A BIT RIDICULOUS!
9

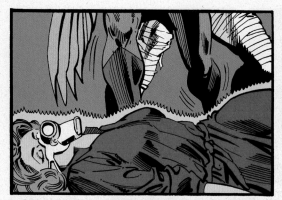

I DON'T KNOW IF *"RIDICULOUS"* IS THE PROPER WORD TO *DESCRIBE* OUR CURRENT PREDICAMENT, BATMAN...

...THIS IS HARDLY A *LAUGHING* MATTER!

THEN AGAIN-- PERHAPS *"RIDICULOUS" IS* CORRECT!

DESPITE ITS MAMMOTH PROPORTIONS, THIS BEHEMOTH MOVES *CLUMSILY*...

...AND IT CAN *HARDLY* BE VIEWED AS A *SERIOUS* THREAT!

KEE- RASH!

KATAR'S *RIGHT!* THE PHANTOM KNIGHTS -- THE DINOSAUR -- THIS *MUMMY*...

...ALL OF THEM HAVE BEEN *EXTREMELY* EASY TO DISPATCH!

BOOPP!

⑩

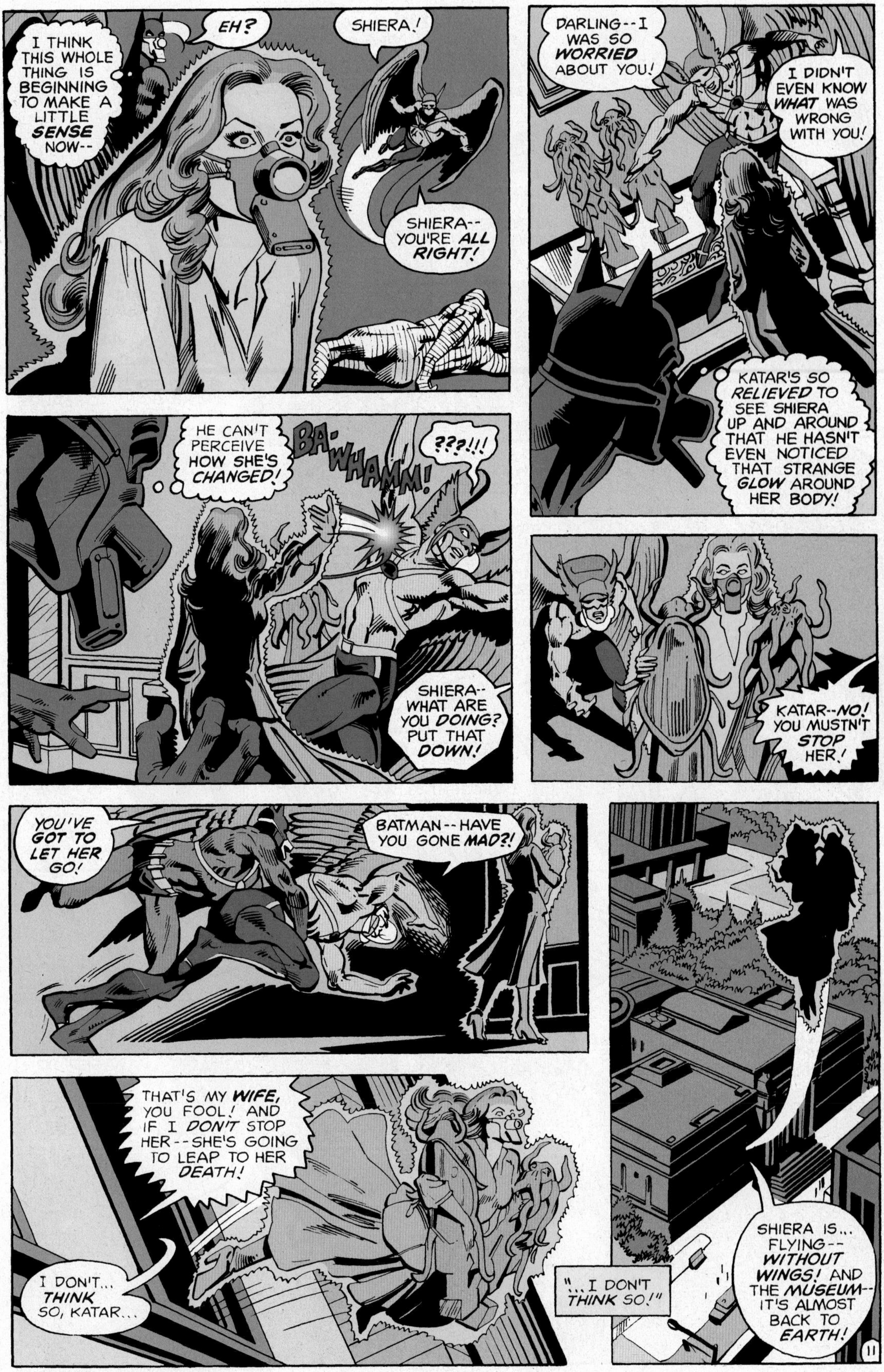
I THINK THIS WHOLE THING IS BEGINNING TO MAKE A LITTLE SENSE NOW--
EH?
SHIERA!
SHIERA-- YOU'RE ALL RIGHT!
DARLING--I WAS SO WORRIED ABOUT YOU!
I DIDN'T EVEN KNOW WHAT WAS WRONG WITH YOU!
KATAR'S SO RELIEVED TO SEE SHIERA UP AND AROUND THAT HE HASN'T EVEN NOTICED THAT STRANGE GLOW AROUND HER BODY!
HE CAN'T PERCEIVE HOW SHE'S CHANGED!
BA-WHAMM!
???!!!
SHIERA-- WHAT ARE YOU DOING? PUT THAT DOWN!
KATAR--NO! YOU MUSTN'T STOP HER!
YOU'VE GOT TO LET HER GO!
BATMAN--HAVE YOU GONE MAD?!
THAT'S MY WIFE, YOU FOOL! AND IF I DON'T STOP HER--SHE'S GOING TO LEAP TO HER DEATH!
I DON'T... THINK SO, KATAR...
"...I DON'T THINK SO!"
SHIERA IS... FLYING-- WITHOUT WINGS! AND THE MUSEUM-- IT'S ALMOST BACK TO EARTH!
11

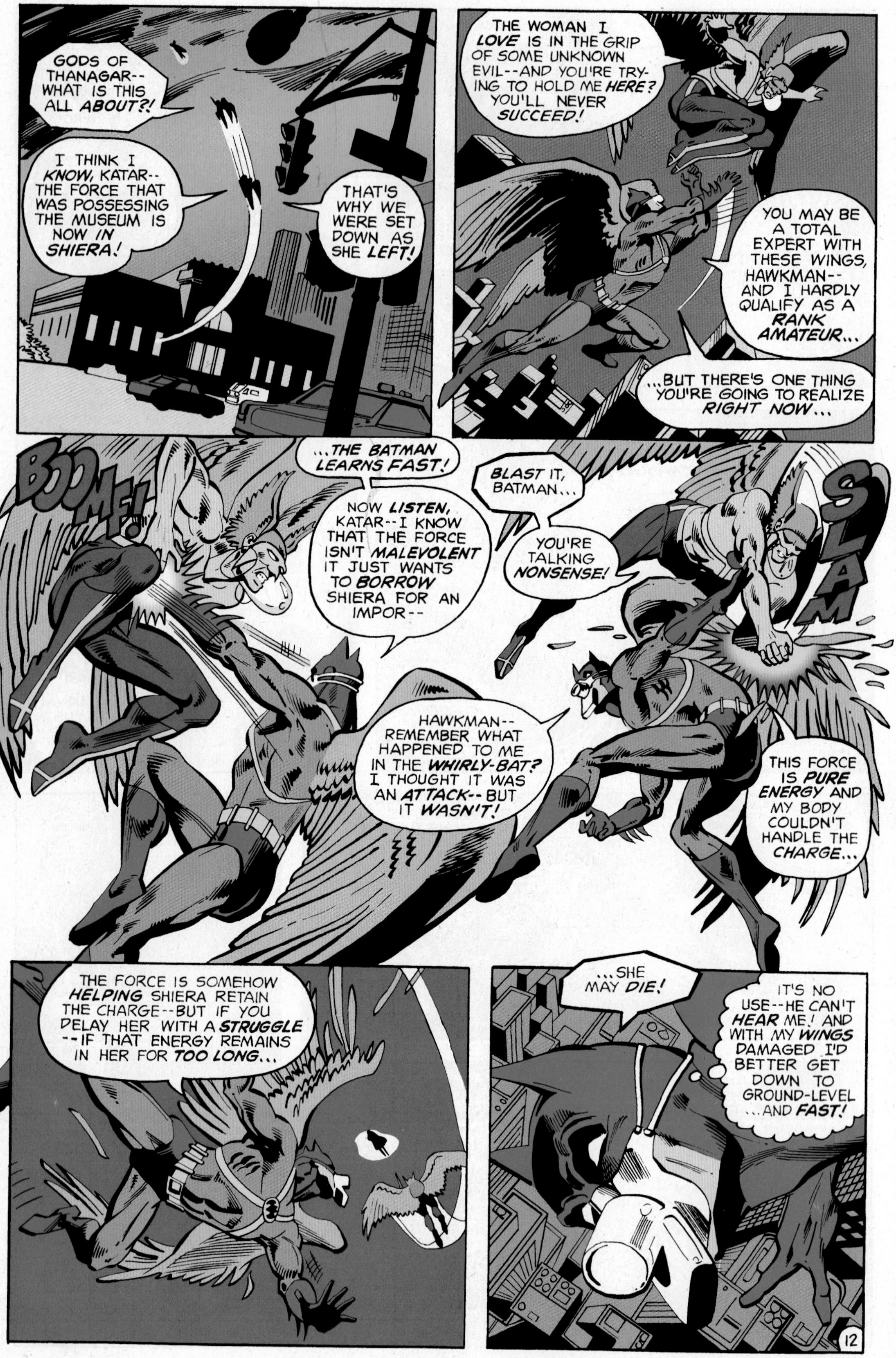
GODS OF THANAGAR-- WHAT IS THIS ALL ABOUT?!
I THINK I KNOW, KATAR-- THE FORCE THAT WAS POSSESSING THE MUSEUM IS NOW IN SHIERA!
THAT'S WHY WE WERE SET DOWN AS SHE LEFT!
THE WOMAN I LOVE IS IN THE GRIP OF SOME UNKNOWN EVIL--AND YOU'RE TRYING TO HOLD ME HERE? YOU'LL NEVER SUCCEED!
YOU MAY BE A TOTAL EXPERT WITH THESE WINGS, HAWKMAN-- AND I HARDLY QUALIFY AS A RANK AMATEUR...
...BUT THERE'S ONE THING YOU'RE GOING TO REALIZE RIGHT NOW...
BOOMF!
...THE BATMAN LEARNS FAST!
NOW LISTEN, KATAR--I KNOW THAT THE FORCE ISN'T MALEVOLENT IT JUST WANTS TO BORROW SHIERA FOR AN IMPOR--
BLAST IT, BATMAN...
YOU'RE TALKING NONSENSE!
SLAM
HAWKMAN-- REMEMBER WHAT HAPPENED TO ME IN THE WHIRLY-BAT? I THOUGHT IT WAS AN ATTACK--BUT IT WASN'T!
THIS FORCE IS PURE ENERGY AND MY BODY COULDN'T HANDLE THE CHARGE...
THE FORCE IS SOMEHOW HELPING SHIERA RETAIN THE CHARGE--BUT IF YOU DELAY HER WITH A STRUGGLE --IF THAT ENERGY REMAINS IN HER FOR TOO LONG...
...SHE MAY DIE!
IT'S NO USE--HE CAN'T HEAR ME! AND WITH MY WINGS DAMAGED I'D BETTER GET DOWN TO GROUND-LEVEL ...AND FAST!
12

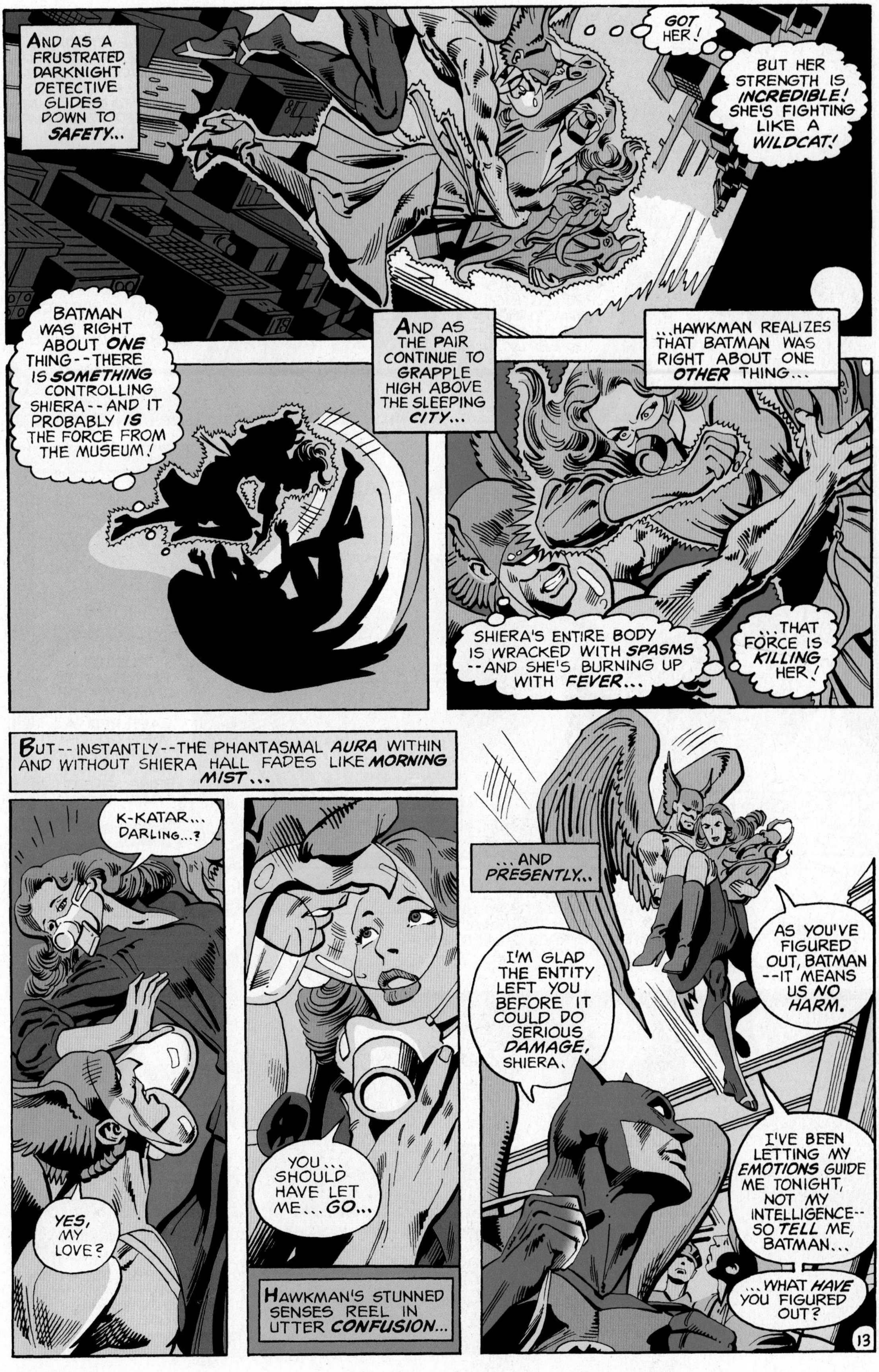
AND AS A FRUSTRATED DARKNIGHT DETECTIVE GLIDES DOWN TO SAFETY...
GOT HER!
BUT HER STRENGTH IS INCREDIBLE! SHE'S FIGHTING LIKE A WILDCAT!
BATMAN WAS RIGHT ABOUT ONE THING--THERE IS SOMETHING CONTROLLING SHIERA--AND IT PROBABLY IS THE FORCE FROM THE MUSEUM!
AND AS THE PAIR CONTINUE TO GRAPPLE HIGH ABOVE THE SLEEPING CITY...
...HAWKMAN REALIZES THAT BATMAN WAS RIGHT ABOUT ONE OTHER THING...
SHIERA'S ENTIRE BODY IS WRACKED WITH SPASMS --AND SHE'S BURNING UP WITH FEVER...
...THAT FORCE IS KILLING HER!
BUT--INSTANTLY--THE PHANTASMAL AURA WITHIN AND WITHOUT SHIERA HALL FADES LIKE MORNING MIST...
K-KATAR... DARLING...?
YES, MY LOVE?
YOU... SHOULD HAVE LET ME... GO...
HAWKMAN'S STUNNED SENSES REEL IN UTTER CONFUSION...
...AND PRESENTLY...
I'M GLAD THE ENTITY LEFT YOU BEFORE IT COULD DO SERIOUS DAMAGE, SHIERA.
AS YOU'VE FIGURED OUT, BATMAN --IT MEANS US NO HARM.
I'VE BEEN LETTING MY EMOTIONS GUIDE ME TONIGHT, NOT MY INTELLIGENCE-- SO TELL ME, BATMAN...
...WHAT HAVE YOU FIGURED OUT?
13

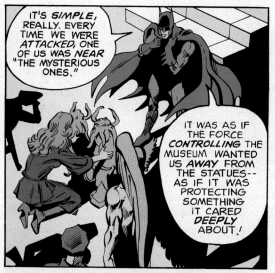

IT'S *SIMPLE*, REALLY. EVERY TIME WE WERE *ATTACKED*, ONE OF US WAS *NEAR* "THE MYSTERIOUS ONES."

IT WAS AS IF THE FORCE *CONTROLLING* THE MUSEUM WANTED US *AWAY* FROM THE STATUES-- AS IF IT WAS PROTECTING SOMETHING IT CARED *DEEPLY* ABOUT!

BUT NEVER *ONCE* WERE WE THREATENED *SERIOUSLY*, YOU SAID *YOURSELF* HOW EASY IT WAS TO BEAT THAT ANIMATED *DINOSAUR SKELETON!*

THE ENTITY WANTED TO PROTECT THE STATUES *AND* DISTRACT US WHILE IT FINISHED ITS *REAL* TASK...

...MAKING CONTACT WITH *SHIERA'S* MIND! IT WA--*EH?*

YOUR DEDUCTIVE POWERS ARE *UNCOMMON*, BATMAN.

...AND IT *CALLS* TO THEM FROM A SPARKLING, SCINTILLANT FORM THAT *BEGGARS DESCRIPTION!*

THE LILTING TELEPATHIC *VOICE* BRUSHES THE TRIO'S THOUGHTS WITH A SOFT *REVERENCE*...

PLEASE PERMIT ME TO *CLARIFY*-- NOW THAT I HAVE MASTERED A METHOD OF *COMMUNICATION* THAT WILL NOT BRING GREAT *PAIN* TO YOU.

WHO... *ARE* YOU?

"MY NAME IS UNIMPORTANT, I COME FROM A WORLD *FAR* FROM HERE-- A WORLD ON WHICH ONCE WALKED A PROUD, LOVING RACE CALLED *THE MA-PRUSHA*."

"A RACE THAT TREASURED ITS GODS--*MERR* AND *WANN*--ABOVE ALL *ELSE*...

14

"AS THE EONS PASSED--OUR PEOPLE LEFT OUR PHYSICAL FORMS *BEHIND*--EVOLVED INTO THE STATE OF *PURE ENERGY* THAT YOU SEE HERE BEFORE YOU...

"...BUT WE DID NOT ABANDON OUR *GODS*--WHO BROUGHT US *TRUTH, LIGHT,* AND *LIFE...*

"THEN *TRAGEDY* STRUCK! A COSMIC STORM SWEPT OVER OUR WORLD--TORE OPEN THE VERY *FABRIC* OF TIME AND SPACE--AND CARRIED OUR GODS HERE.

"I WAS DISPATCHED TO *RETRIEVE* THE BLESSED ONES --AND SO FOLLOWED THROUGH THE *HOLE* IN THE *COSMOS* LEFT BY THE STORM...

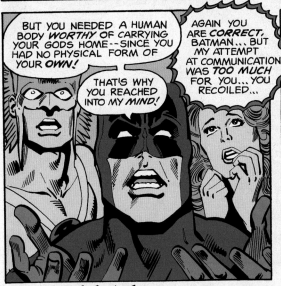

BUT YOU NEEDED A HUMAN BODY *WORTHY* OF CARRYING YOUR GODS HOME-- SINCE YOU HAD NO PHYSICAL FORM OF YOUR *OWN!*

THAT'S WHY YOU REACHED INTO MY *MIND!*

AGAIN YOU ARE *CORRECT,* BATMAN... BUT MY ATTEMPT AT COMMUNICATION WAS *TOO MUCH* FOR YOU... YOU RECOILED...

I *UNDERSTAND!* YOUR PROBE OF BATMAN'S MIND LED YOU TO *SHIERA!*

YES, BOTH YOU AND YOUR WIFE HAVE MINDS MORE ...*RECEPTIVE* DUE TO EXPOSURE TO THE DEVICE YOU CALL THE *ABSORBASCON* *

I SWEPT HER OFF IN THE MUSEUM, RENDERED HER UNCONSCIOUS-- HOPING TO MAKE THE MIND MELD *LESS* PAINFUL.

* A THANAGARIAN DEVICE THAT TAUGHT HAWKMAN AND HAWKGIRL EARTH KNOWLEDGE AND CUSTOMS.

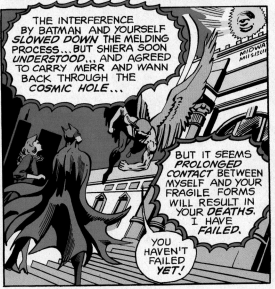

THE INTERFERENCE BY BATMAN AND YOURSELF *SLOWED DOWN* THE MELDING PROCESS... BUT SHIERA SOON *UNDERSTOOD...* AND AGREED TO CARRY MERR AND WANN BACK THROUGH THE *COSMIC HOLE...*

BUT IT SEEMS *PROLONGED CONTACT* BETWEEN MYSELF AND YOUR *FRAGILE* FORMS WILL RESULT IN YOUR *DEATHS.* I HAVE *FAILED.*

YOU HAVEN'T FAILED *YET!*

MAYBE WHAT *ONE* BODY COULDN'T HANDLE--*TWO* COULD!

SHIERA'S BODY COULDN'T TAKE ANOTHER *JOLT*-- BUT WHAT DO *YOU* SAY, BATMAN!

I SAY-- LET'S *TRY* IT!

15

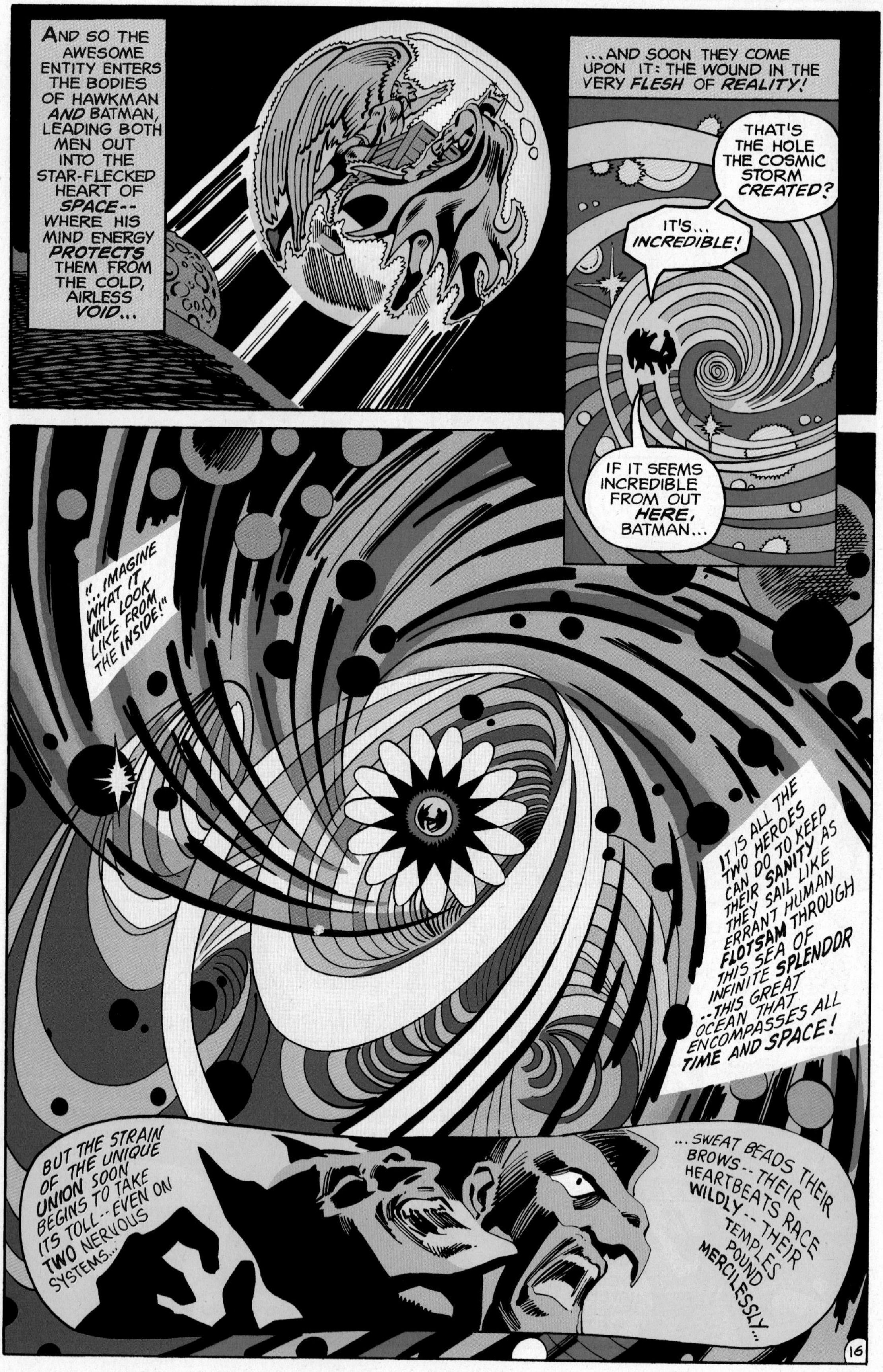

AND SO THE AWESOME ENTITY ENTERS THE BODIES OF HAWKMAN AND BATMAN, LEADING BOTH MEN OUT INTO THE STAR-FLECKED HEART OF SPACE-- WHERE HIS MIND ENERGY PROTECTS THEM FROM THE COLD, AIRLESS VOID...
...AND SOON THEY COME UPON IT: THE WOUND IN THE VERY FLESH OF REALITY!
THAT'S THE HOLE THE COSMIC STORM CREATED?
IT'S... INCREDIBLE!
IF IT SEEMS INCREDIBLE FROM OUT HERE, BATMAN...
"...IMAGINE WHAT IT WILL LOOK LIKE FROM THE INSIDE!"
IT IS ALL THE TWO HEROES CAN DO TO KEEP THEIR SANITY AS THEY SAIL LIKE ERRANT HUMAN FLOTSAM THROUGH THIS SEA OF INFINITE SPLENDOR ..THIS GREAT OCEAN THAT ENCOMPASSES ALL TIME AND SPACE!
BUT THE STRAIN OF THE UNIQUE UNION SOON BEGINS TO TAKE ITS TOLL-- EVEN ON TWO NERVOUS SYSTEMS...
...SWEAT BEADS THEIR BROWS-- THEIR HEARTBEATS RACE WILDLY-- THEIR TEMPLES POUND MERCILESSLY...
16

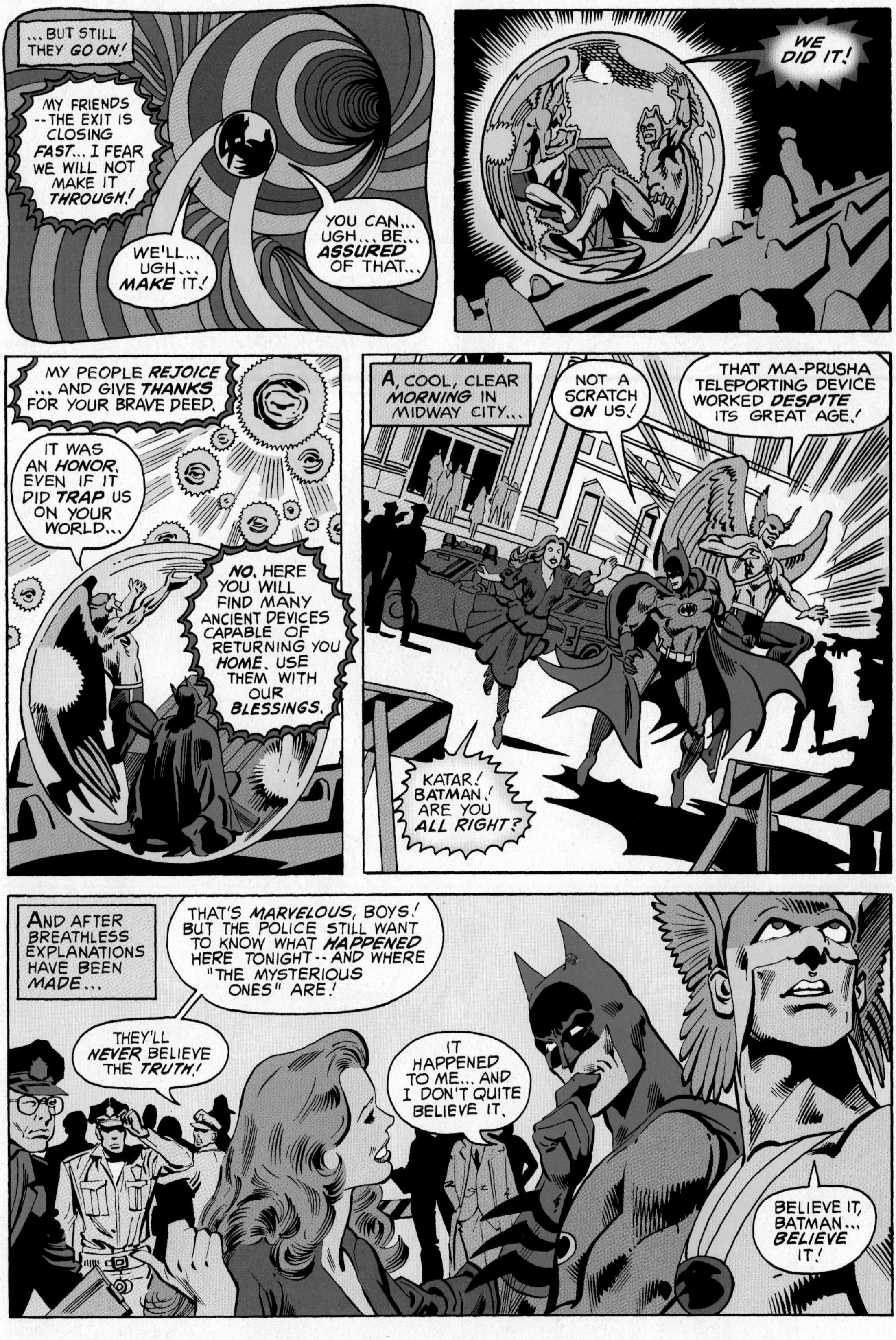
...BUT STILL THEY GO ON!
MY FRIENDS --THE EXIT IS CLOSING FAST... I FEAR WE WILL NOT MAKE IT THROUGH!
WE'LL... UGH... MAKE IT!
YOU CAN... UGH... BE... ASSURED OF THAT...
WE DID IT!
MY PEOPLE REJOICE ... AND GIVE THANKS FOR YOUR BRAVE DEED.
IT WAS AN HONOR, EVEN IF IT DID TRAP US ON YOUR WORLD...
NO. HERE YOU WILL FIND MANY ANCIENT DEVICES CAPABLE OF RETURNING YOU HOME. USE THEM WITH OUR BLESSINGS.
A, COOL, CLEAR MORNING IN MIDWAY CITY...
NOT A SCRATCH ON US!
THAT MA-PRUSHA TELEPORTING DEVICE WORKED DESPITE ITS GREAT AGE!
KATAR! BATMAN! ARE YOU ALL RIGHT?
AND AFTER BREATHLESS EXPLANATIONS HAVE BEEN MADE...
THAT'S MARVELOUS, BOYS! BUT THE POLICE STILL WANT TO KNOW WHAT HAPPENED HERE TONIGHT--AND WHERE "THE MYSTERIOUS ONES" ARE!
THEY'LL NEVER BELIEVE THE TRUTH!
IT HAPPENED TO ME... AND I DON'T QUITE BELIEVE IT.
BELIEVE IT, BATMAN... BELIEVE IT!

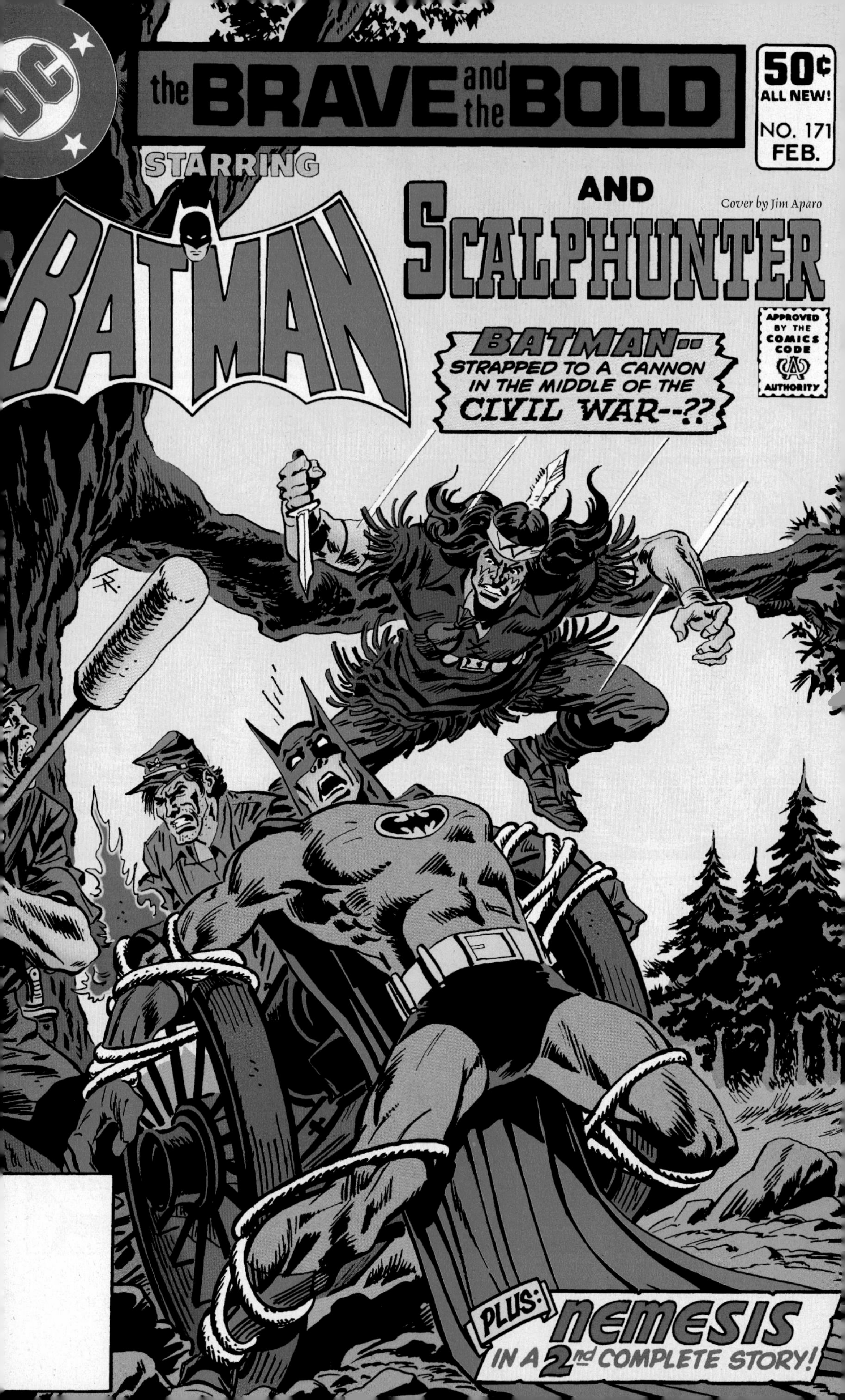
DC
the BRAVE and the BOLD
50¢
ALL NEW!
NO. 171
FEB.
STARRING
BATMAN
AND
SCALPHUNTER
Cover by Jim Aparo
APPROVED BY THE COMICS CODE AUTHORITY
BATMAN--
STRAPPED TO A CANNON
IN THE MIDDLE OF THE
CIVIL WAR--??
PLUS:
nemesis
IN A 2nd COMPLETE STORY!

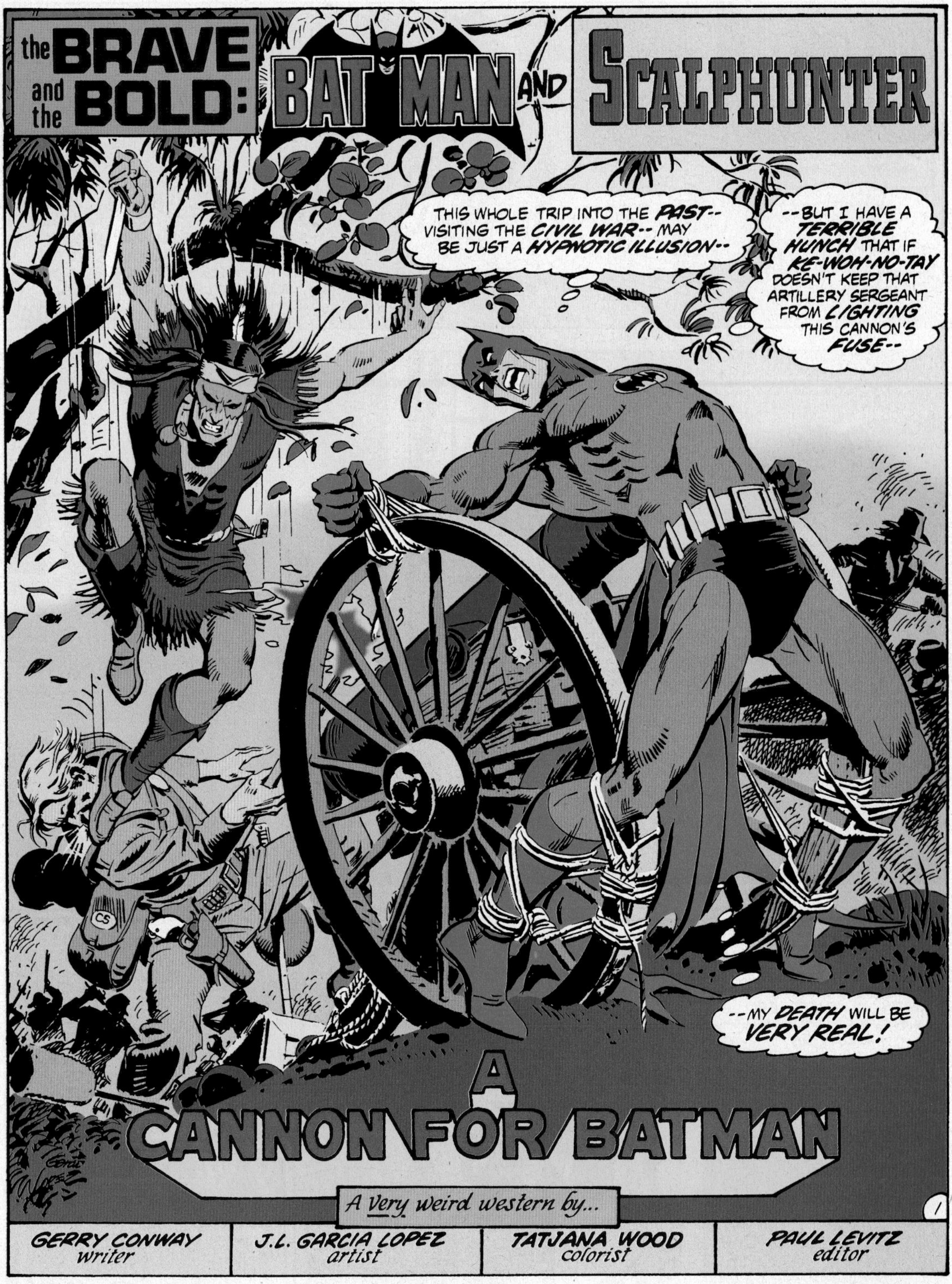
the BRAVE and the BOLD:
BATMAN AND SCALPHUNTER
THIS WHOLE TRIP INTO THE PAST-- VISITING THE CIVIL WAR-- MAY BE JUST A HYPNOTIC ILLUSION--
--BUT I HAVE A TERRIBLE HUNCH THAT IF KE-WOH-NO-TAY DOESN'T KEEP THAT ARTILLERY SERGEANT FROM LIGHTING THIS CANNON'S FUSE--
--MY DEATH WILL BE VERY REAL!
A CANNON FOR BATMAN
A Very weird western by...
1
GERRY CONWAY writer
J.L. GARCIA LOPEZ artist
TATJANA WOOD colorist
PAUL LEVITZ editor

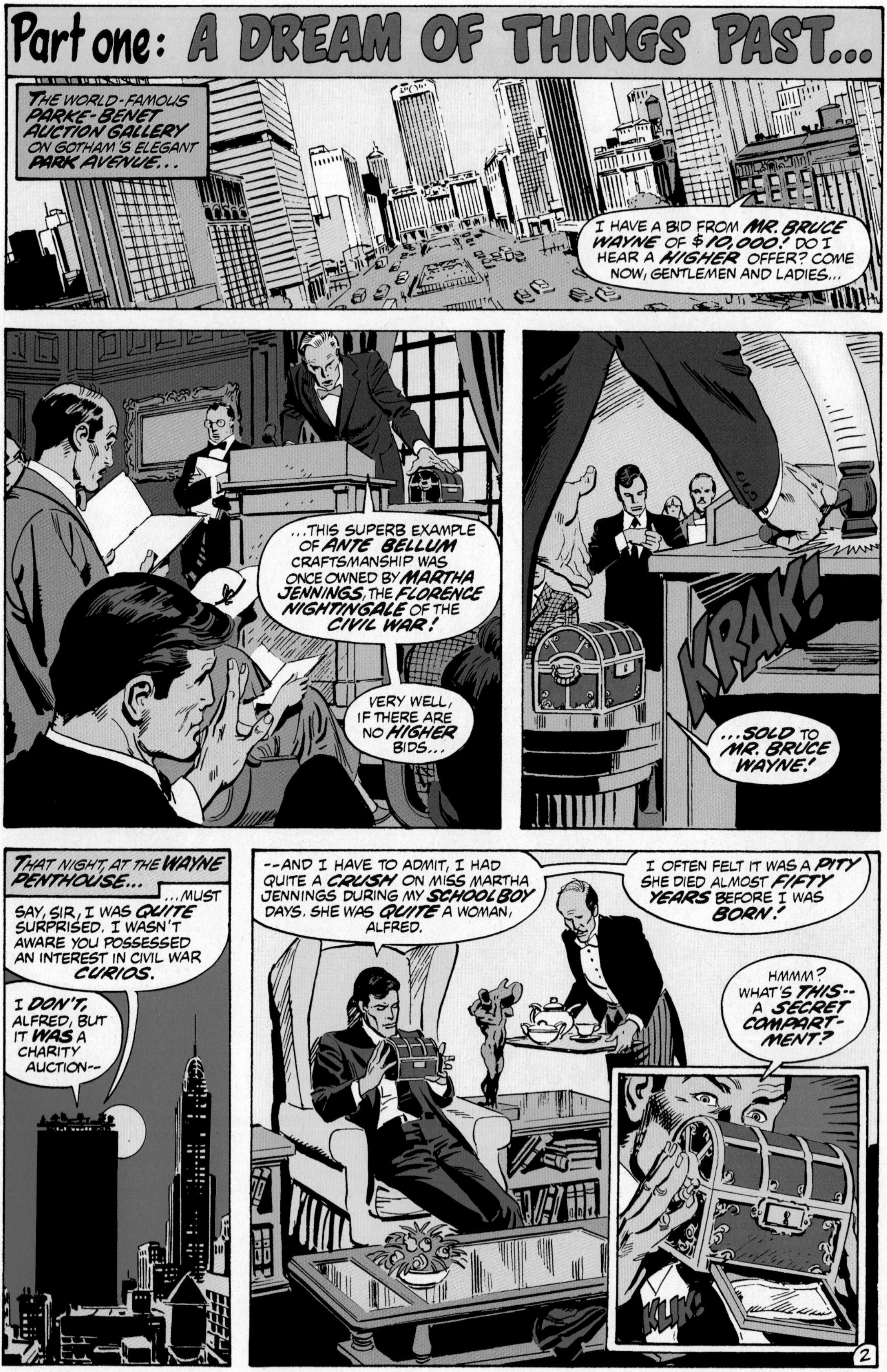
Part one: A DREAM OF THINGS PAST...
THE WORLD-FAMOUS PARKE-BENET AUCTION GALLERY ON GOTHAM'S ELEGANT PARK AVENUE...
I HAVE A BID FROM MR. BRUCE WAYNE OF $10,000! DO I HEAR A HIGHER OFFER? COME NOW, GENTLEMEN AND LADIES...
...THIS SUPERB EXAMPLE OF ANTE BELLUM CRAFTSMANSHIP WAS ONCE OWNED BY MARTHA JENNINGS, THE FLORENCE NIGHTINGALE OF THE CIVIL WAR!
VERY WELL, IF THERE ARE NO HIGHER BIDS...
KRAK!
...SOLD TO MR. BRUCE WAYNE!
THAT NIGHT, AT THE WAYNE PENTHOUSE...
...MUST SAY, SIR, I WAS QUITE SURPRISED. I WASN'T AWARE YOU POSSESSED AN INTEREST IN CIVIL WAR CURIOS.
I DON'T, ALFRED, BUT IT WAS A CHARITY AUCTION--
--AND I HAVE TO ADMIT, I HAD QUITE A CRUSH ON MISS MARTHA JENNINGS DURING MY SCHOOLBOY DAYS. SHE WAS QUITE A WOMAN, ALFRED.
I OFTEN FELT IT WAS A PITY SHE DIED ALMOST FIFTY YEARS BEFORE I WAS BORN!
HMMM? WHAT'S THIS-- A SECRET COMPART-MENT?
KLIK!
2

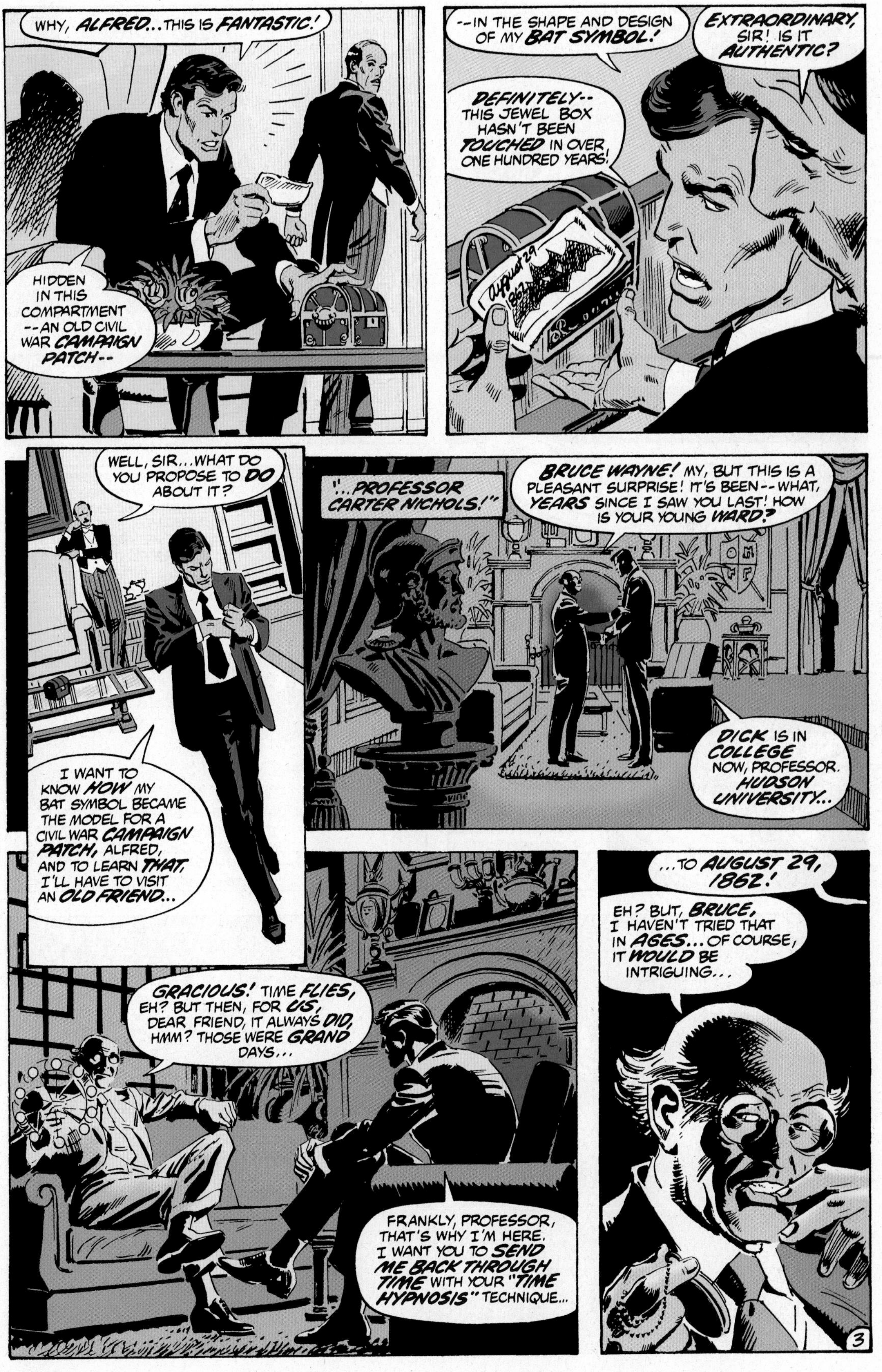

WHY, ALFRED... THIS IS FANTASTIC!
HIDDEN IN THIS COMPARTMENT --AN OLD CIVIL WAR CAMPAIGN PATCH--
--IN THE SHAPE AND DESIGN OF MY BAT SYMBOL!
EXTRAORDINARY, SIR! IS IT AUTHENTIC?
DEFINITELY-- THIS JEWEL BOX HASN'T BEEN TOUCHED IN OVER ONE HUNDRED YEARS!
August 29 1862
WELL, SIR... WHAT DO YOU PROPOSE TO DO ABOUT IT?
I WANT TO KNOW HOW MY BAT SYMBOL BECAME THE MODEL FOR A CIVIL WAR CAMPAIGN PATCH, ALFRED, AND TO LEARN THAT, I'LL HAVE TO VISIT AN OLD FRIEND...
"...PROFESSOR CARTER NICHOLS!"
BRUCE WAYNE! MY, BUT THIS IS A PLEASANT SURPRISE! IT'S BEEN--WHAT, YEARS SINCE I SAW YOU LAST! HOW IS YOUR YOUNG WARD?
DICK IS IN COLLEGE NOW, PROFESSOR. HUDSON UNIVERSITY...
GRACIOUS! TIME FLIES, EH? BUT THEN, FOR US, DEAR FRIEND, IT ALWAYS DID, HMM? THOSE WERE GRAND DAYS...
FRANKLY, PROFESSOR, THAT'S WHY I'M HERE. I WANT YOU TO SEND ME BACK THROUGH TIME WITH YOUR "TIME HYPNOSIS" TECHNIQUE...
...TO AUGUST 29, 1862!
EH? BUT, BRUCE, I HAVEN'T TRIED THAT IN AGES... OF COURSE, IT WOULD BE INTRIGUING...
3

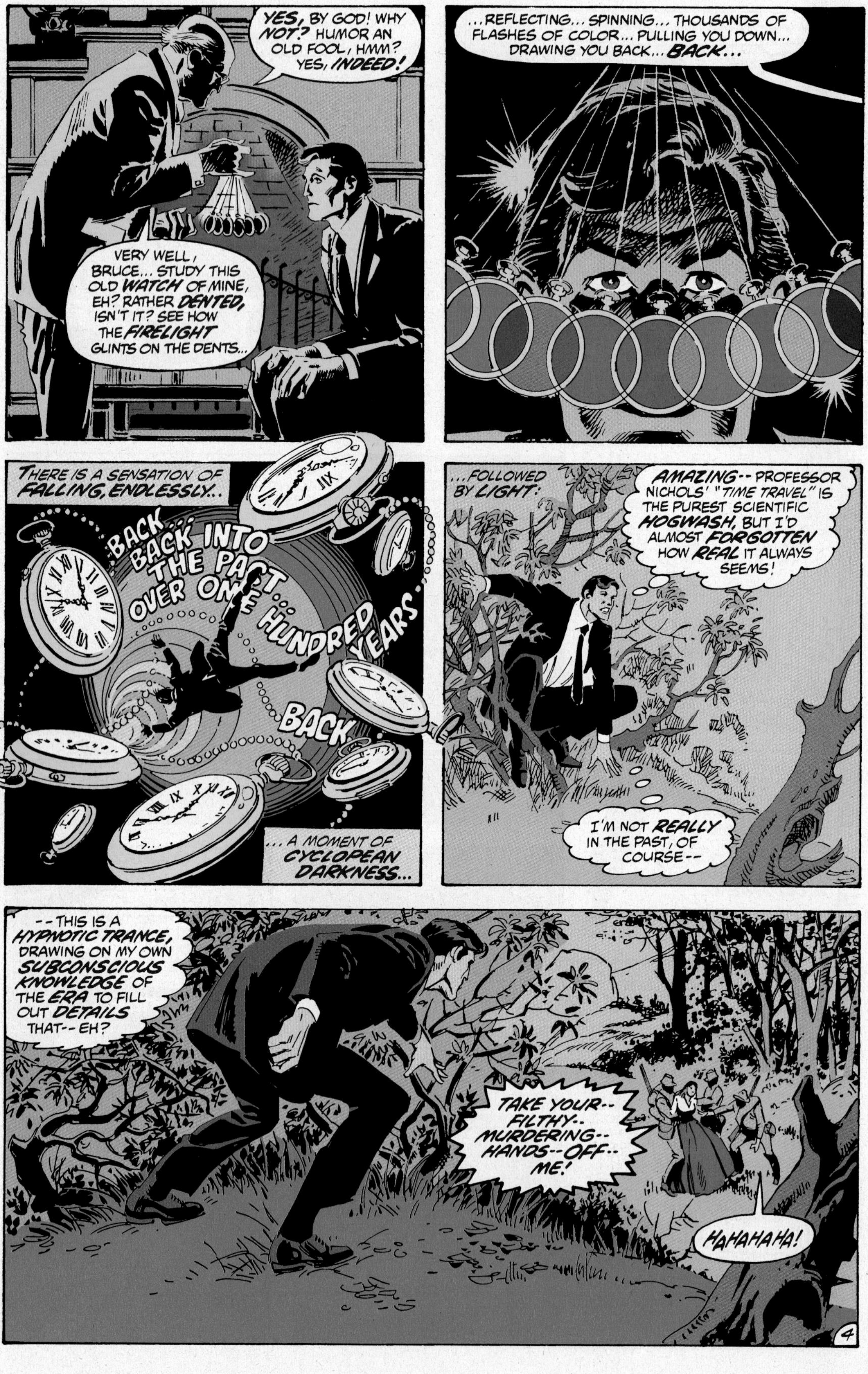
YES, BY GOD! WHY NOT? HUMOR AN OLD FOOL, HMM? YES, INDEED!
VERY WELL, BRUCE... STUDY THIS OLD WATCH OF MINE, EH? RATHER DENTED, ISN'T IT? SEE HOW THE FIRELIGHT GLINTS ON THE DENTS...
...REFLECTING... SPINNING... THOUSANDS OF FLASHES OF COLOR... PULLING YOU DOWN... DRAWING YOU BACK... BACK...
THERE IS A SENSATION OF FALLING, ENDLESSLY...
BACK... BACK INTO THE PAST... OVER ONE HUNDRED YEARS
BACK
...A MOMENT OF CYCLOPEAN DARKNESS...
...FOLLOWED BY LIGHT:
AMAZING-- PROFESSOR NICHOLS' "TIME TRAVEL" IS THE PUREST SCIENTIFIC HOGWASH, BUT I'D ALMOST FORGOTTEN HOW REAL IT ALWAYS SEEMS!
I'M NOT REALLY IN THE PAST, OF COURSE--
--THIS IS A HYPNOTIC TRANCE, DRAWING ON MY OWN SUBCONSCIOUS KNOWLEDGE OF THE ERA TO FILL OUT DETAILS THAT--EH?
TAKE YOUR-- FILTHY-- MURDERING-- HANDS--OFF-- ME!
HAHAHAHA!
4

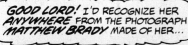

GOOD LORD! I'D RECOGNIZE HER ANYWHERE FROM THE PHOTOGRAPH MATTHEW BRADY MADE OF HER...

...THAT'S MARTHA JENNINGS!

HYPNOTIC TRANCE OR NOT, I CAN'T LET THAT WOMAN BE HURT!

AND I'VE A FEELING THOSE SOLDIERS WOULD BE FAR LESS IMPRESSED BY THE SUDDEN APPEARANCE OF BRUCE WAYNE THAN THEY MIGHT BE BY--

WHO ON EARTH IS THAT?

HE COMES RIDING FROM THE FOREST LIKE SOME PRIMEVAL FORCE CAPTURED IN FLESH, HEELS PLUNGING INTO HIS STALLION'S HEAVING SIDES, BODY LIFTING IN UNISON WITH EACH LONG STRIDE...

AND HIS WAR-CRY IS A WOLF'S MOON-HOWL...

AIIYIY

SWEET LORD IN--

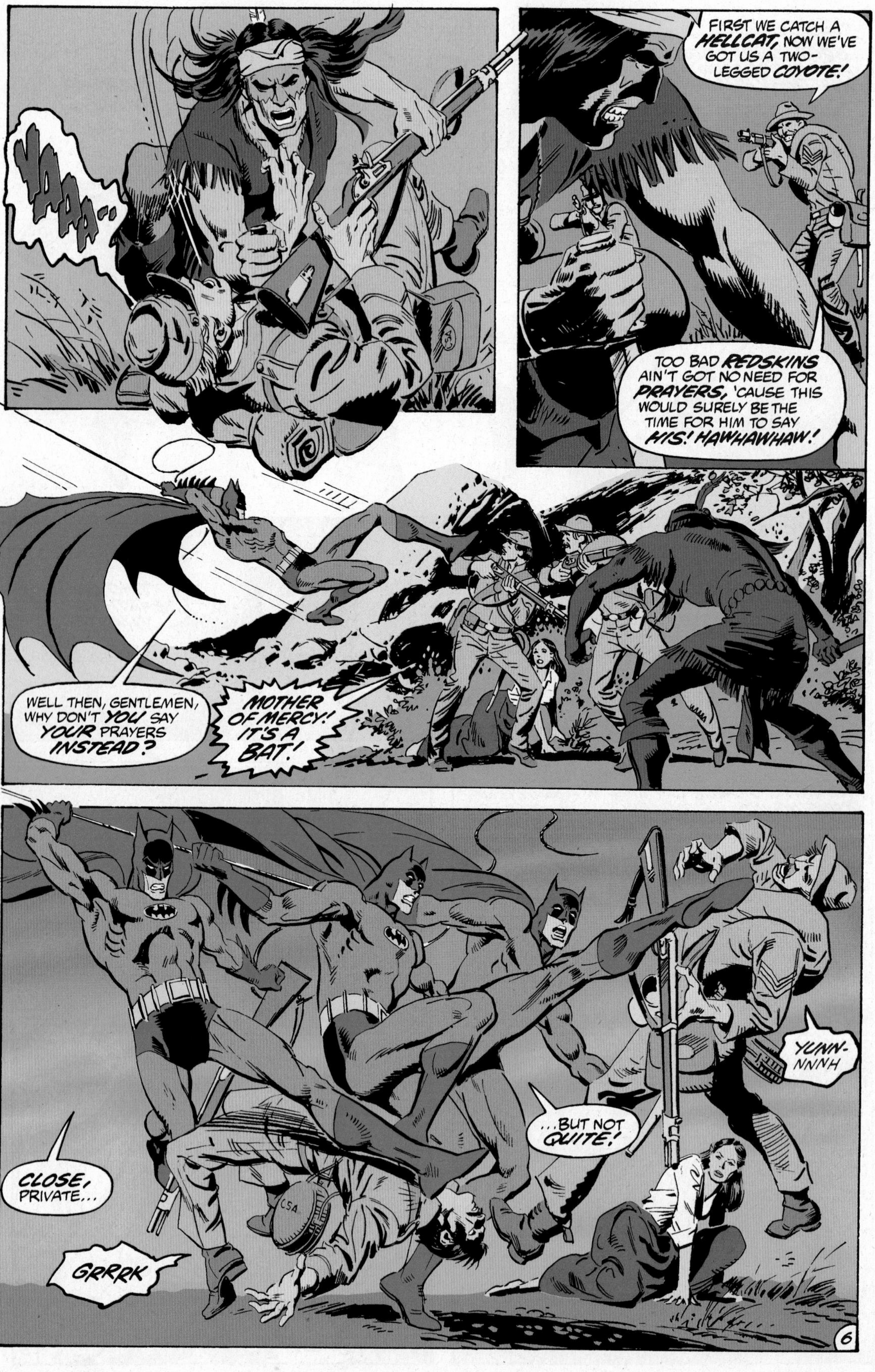

YAAAA..
FIRST WE CATCH A HELLCAT, NOW WE'VE GOT US A TWO-LEGGED COYOTE!
TOO BAD REDSKINS AIN'T GOT NO NEED FOR PRAYERS, 'CAUSE THIS WOULD SURELY BE THE TIME FOR HIM TO SAY HIS! HAWHAWHAW!
WELL THEN, GENTLEMEN, WHY DON'T YOU SAY YOUR PRAYERS INSTEAD?
MOTHER OF MERCY! IT'S A BAT!
YUNN-NNNH
CLOSE, PRIVATE...
...BUT NOT QUITE!
GRRRK
CSA
6

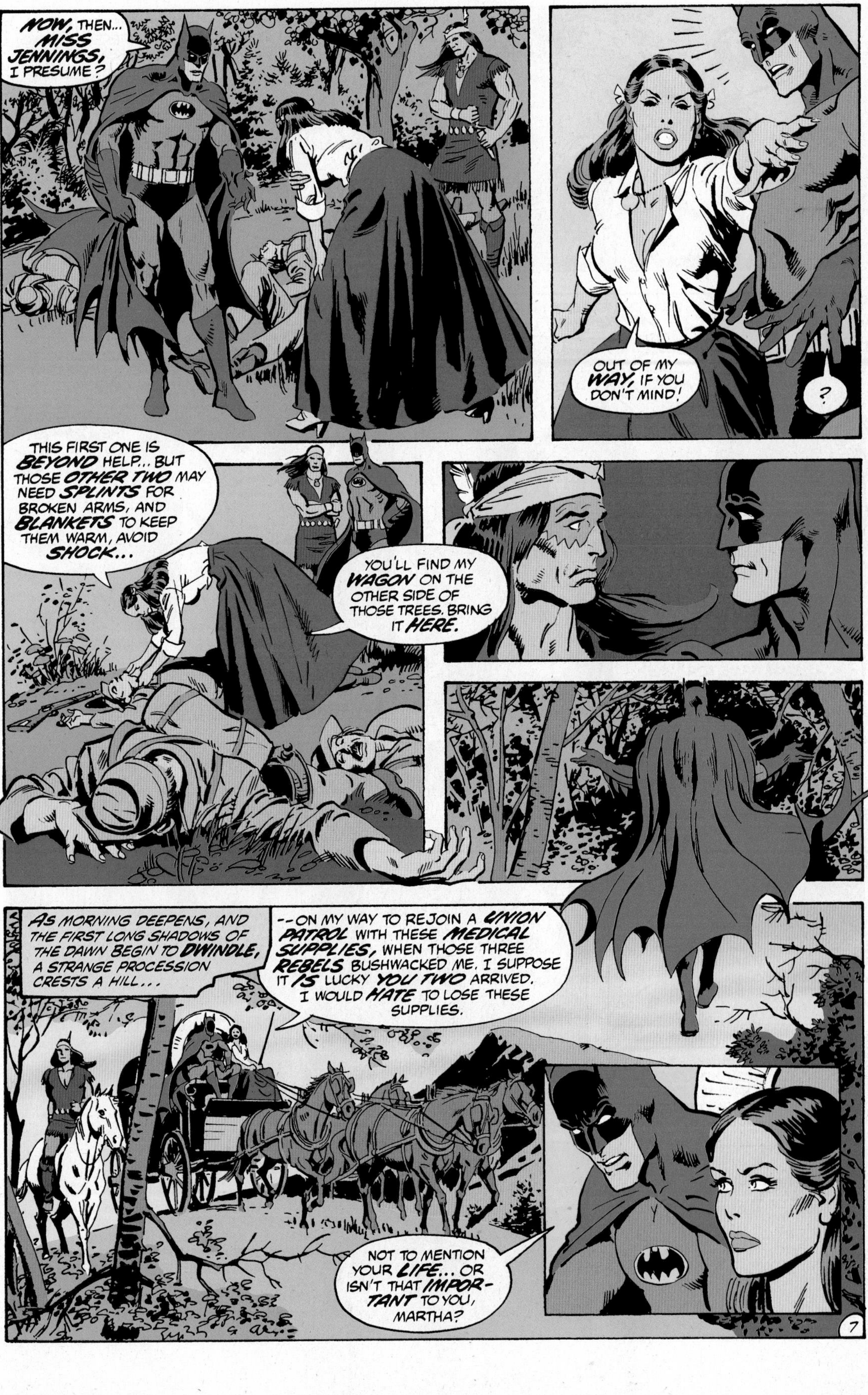
NOW, THEN... MISS JENNINGS, I PRESUME?
OUT OF MY WAY, IF YOU DON'T MIND!
?
THIS FIRST ONE IS BEYOND HELP... BUT THOSE OTHER TWO MAY NEED SPLINTS FOR BROKEN ARMS, AND BLANKETS TO KEEP THEM WARM, AVOID SHOCK...
YOU'LL FIND MY WAGON ON THE OTHER SIDE OF THOSE TREES. BRING IT HERE.
AS MORNING DEEPENS, AND THE FIRST LONG SHADOWS OF THE DAWN BEGIN TO DWINDLE, A STRANGE PROCESSION CRESTS A HILL...
--ON MY WAY TO REJOIN A UNION PATROL WITH THESE MEDICAL SUPPLIES, WHEN THOSE THREE REBELS BUSHWACKED ME. I SUPPOSE IT IS LUCKY YOU TWO ARRIVED. I WOULD HATE TO LOSE THESE SUPPLIES.
NOT TO MENTION YOUR LIFE... OR ISN'T THAT IMPORTANT TO YOU, MARTHA?
7

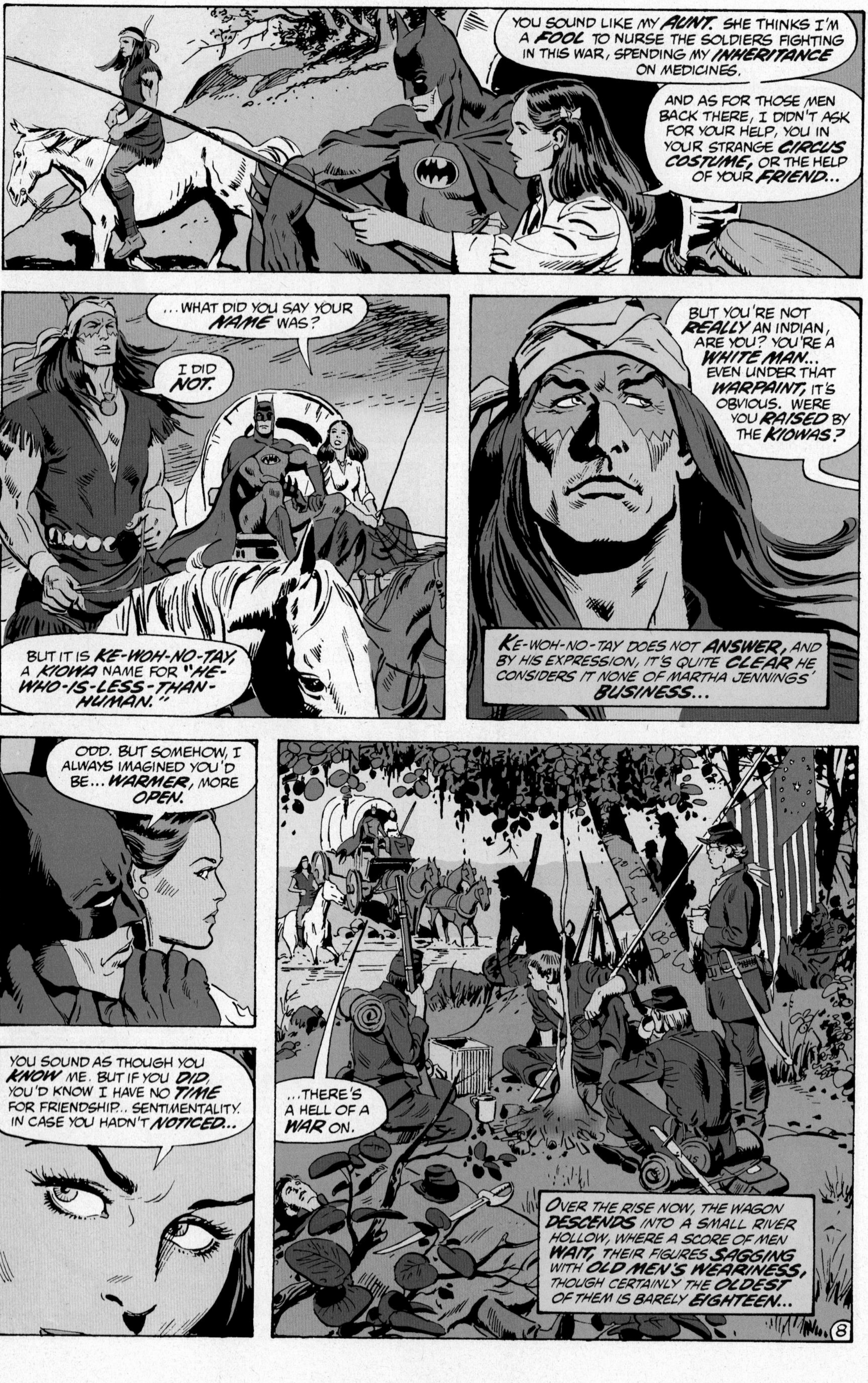
YOU SOUND LIKE MY AUNT. SHE THINKS I'M A FOOL TO NURSE THE SOLDIERS FIGHTING IN THIS WAR, SPENDING MY INHERITANCE ON MEDICINES.
AND AS FOR THOSE MEN BACK THERE, I DIDN'T ASK FOR YOUR HELP, YOU IN YOUR STRANGE CIRCUS COSTUME, OR THE HELP OF YOUR FRIEND...
...WHAT DID YOU SAY YOUR NAME WAS?
I DID NOT.
BUT IT IS KE-WOH-NO-TAY, A KIOWA NAME FOR "HE-WHO-IS-LESS-THAN-HUMAN."
BUT YOU'RE NOT REALLY AN INDIAN, ARE YOU? YOU'RE A WHITE MAN... EVEN UNDER THAT WARPAINT, IT'S OBVIOUS. WERE YOU RAISED BY THE KIOWAS?
KE-WOH-NO-TAY DOES NOT ANSWER, AND BY HIS EXPRESSION, IT'S QUITE CLEAR HE CONSIDERS IT NONE OF MARTHA JENNINGS' BUSINESS...
ODD. BUT SOMEHOW, I ALWAYS IMAGINED YOU'D BE... WARMER, MORE OPEN.
YOU SOUND AS THOUGH YOU KNOW ME. BUT IF YOU DID, YOU'D KNOW I HAVE NO TIME FOR FRIENDSHIP... SENTIMENTALITY. IN CASE YOU HADN'T NOTICED...
...THERE'S A HELL OF A WAR ON.
OVER THE RISE NOW, THE WAGON DESCENDS INTO A SMALL RIVER HOLLOW, WHERE A SCORE OF MEN WAIT, THEIR FIGURES SAGGING WITH OLD MEN'S WEARINESS, THOUGH CERTAINLY THE OLDEST OF THEM IS BARELY EIGHTEEN...
8

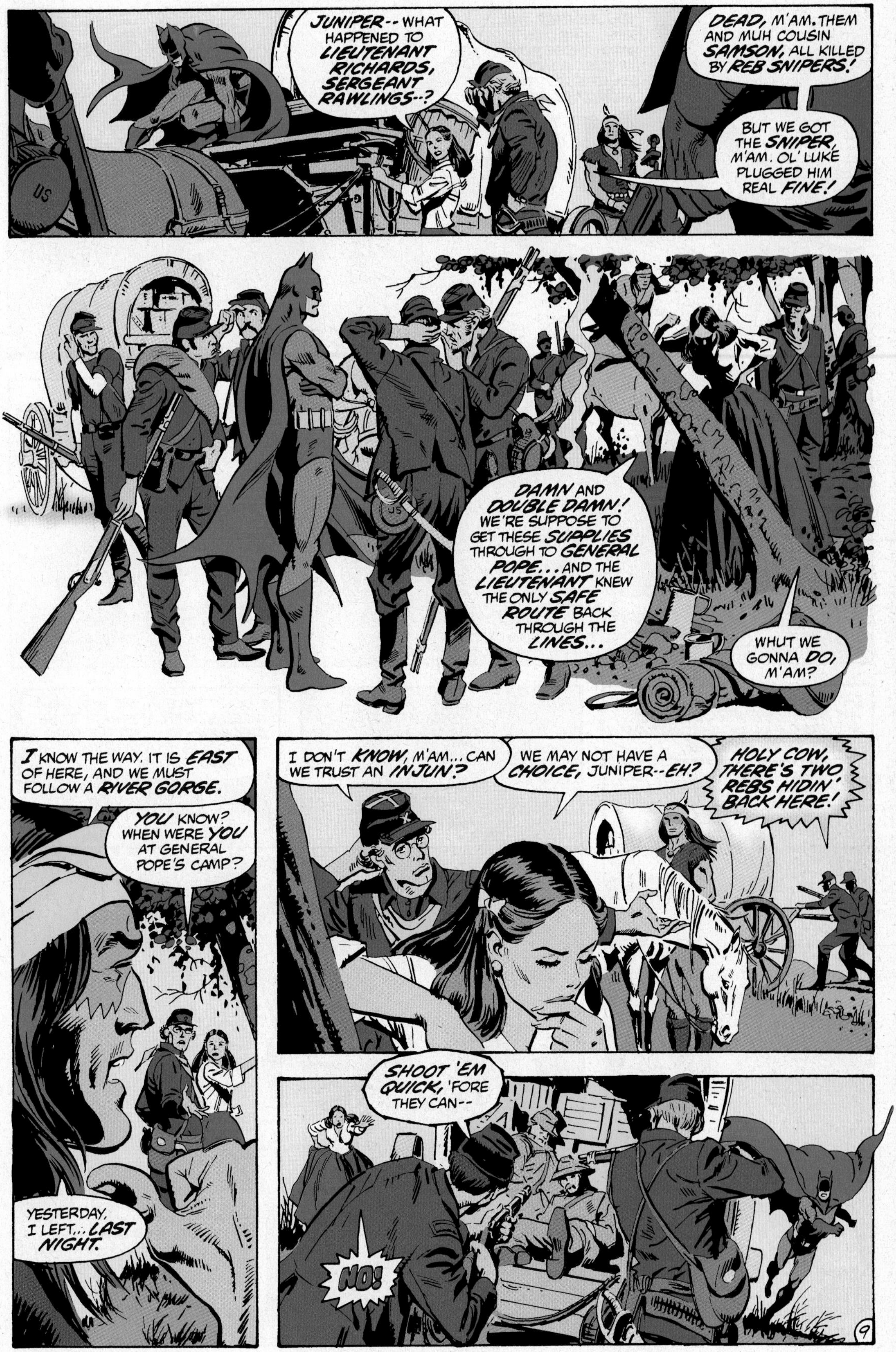
JUNIPER-- WHAT HAPPENED TO LIEUTENANT RICHARDS, SERGEANT RAWLINGS--?
DEAD, M'AM. THEM AND MUH COUSIN SAMSON, ALL KILLED BY REB SNIPERS!
BUT WE GOT THE SNIPER, M'AM. OL' LUKE PLUGGED HIM REAL FINE!
DAMN AND DOUBLE DAMN! WE'RE SUPPOSE TO GET THESE SUPPLIES THROUGH TO GENERAL POPE... AND THE LIEUTENANT KNEW THE ONLY SAFE ROUTE BACK THROUGH THE LINES...
WHUT WE GONNA DO, M'AM?
I KNOW THE WAY. IT IS EAST OF HERE, AND WE MUST FOLLOW A RIVER GORGE.
YOU KNOW? WHEN WERE YOU AT GENERAL POPE'S CAMP?
YESTERDAY, I LEFT... LAST NIGHT.
I DON'T KNOW, M'AM... CAN WE TRUST AN INJUN?
WE MAY NOT HAVE A CHOICE, JUNIPER--EH?
HOLY COW, THERE'S TWO REBS HIDIN' BACK HERE!
SHOOT 'EM QUICK, 'FORE THEY CAN--
NO!
9

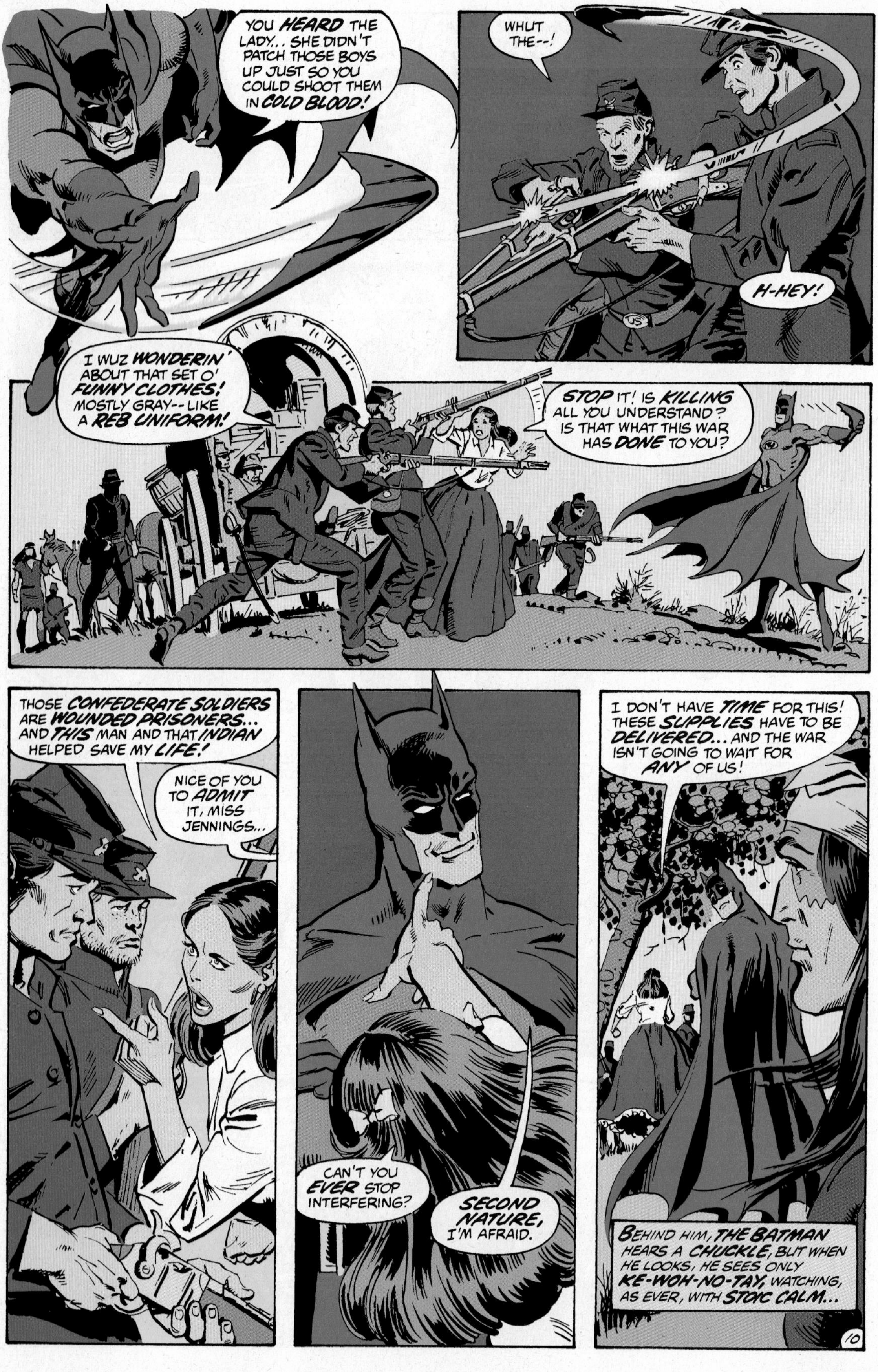

YOU HEARD THE LADY... SHE DIDN'T PATCH THOSE BOYS UP JUST SO YOU COULD SHOOT THEM IN COLD BLOOD!
WHUT THE--!
H-HEY!
I WUZ WONDERIN' ABOUT THAT SET O' FUNNY CLOTHES! MOSTLY GRAY-- LIKE A REB UNIFORM!
STOP IT! IS KILLING ALL YOU UNDERSTAND? IS THAT WHAT THIS WAR HAS DONE TO YOU?
THOSE CONFEDERATE SOLDIERS ARE WOUNDED PRISONERS... AND THIS MAN AND THAT INDIAN HELPED SAVE MY LIFE!
NICE OF YOU TO ADMIT IT, MISS JENNINGS...
CAN'T YOU EVER STOP INTERFERING?
SECOND NATURE, I'M AFRAID.
I DON'T HAVE TIME FOR THIS! THESE SUPPLIES HAVE TO BE DELIVERED... AND THE WAR ISN'T GOING TO WAIT FOR ANY OF US!
BEHIND HIM, THE BATMAN HEARS A CHUCKLE, BUT WHEN HE LOOKS, HE SEES ONLY KE-WOH-NO-TAY, WATCHING, AS EVER, WITH STOIC CALM...
10

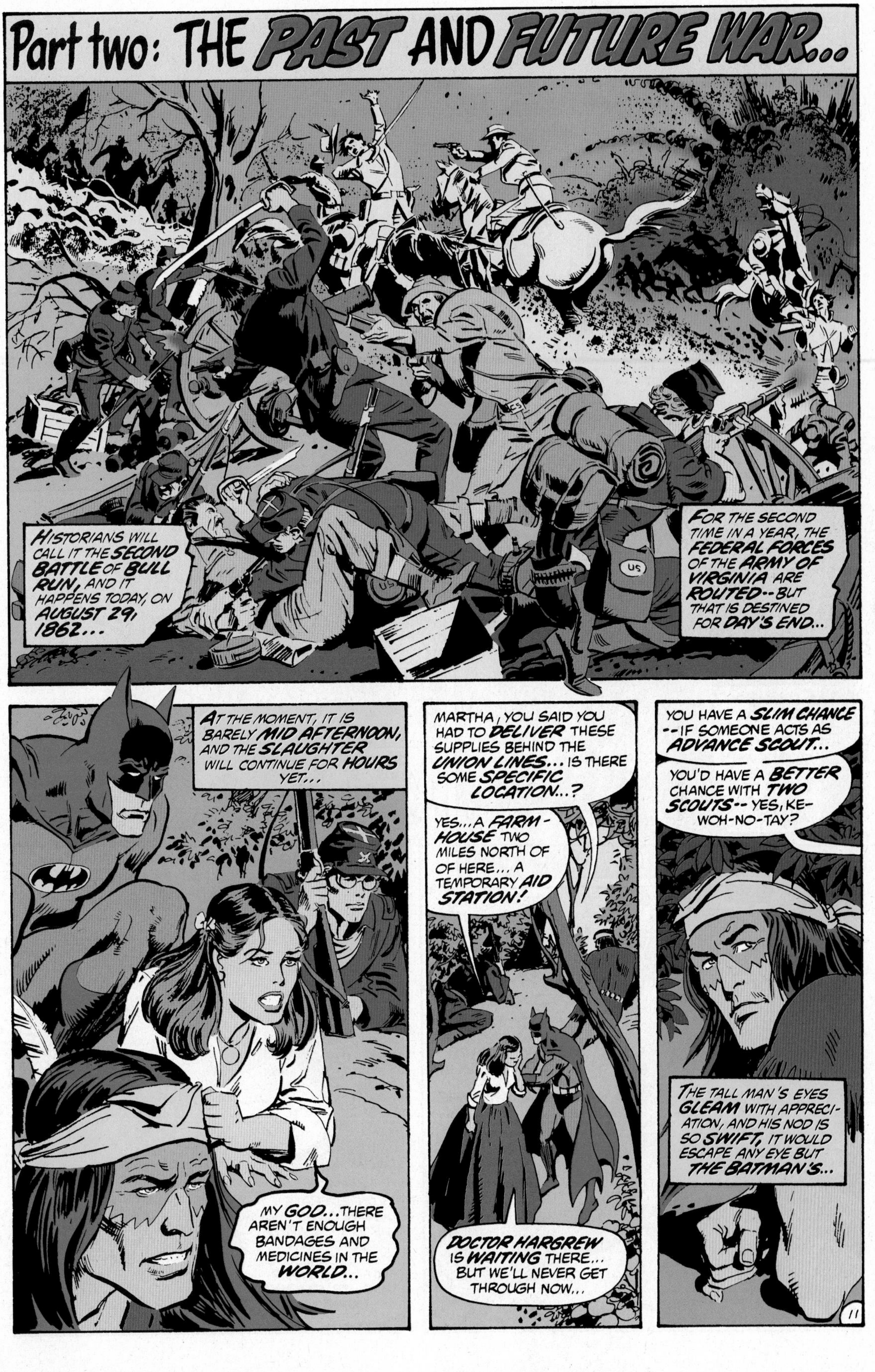
Part two: THE PAST AND FUTURE WAR...
HISTORIANS WILL CALL IT THE SECOND BATTLE OF BULL RUN, AND IT HAPPENS TODAY, ON AUGUST 29, 1862...
FOR THE SECOND TIME IN A YEAR, THE FEDERAL FORCES OF THE ARMY OF VIRGINIA ARE ROUTED--BUT THAT IS DESTINED FOR DAY'S END...
AT THE MOMENT, IT IS BARELY MID AFTERNOON, AND THE SLAUGHTER WILL CONTINUE FOR HOURS YET...
MY GOD...THERE AREN'T ENOUGH BANDAGES AND MEDICINES IN THE WORLD...
MARTHA, YOU SAID YOU HAD TO DELIVER THESE SUPPLIES BEHIND THE UNION LINES... IS THERE SOME SPECIFIC LOCATION...?
YES... A FARM-HOUSE TWO MILES NORTH OF OF HERE... A TEMPORARY AID STATION!
DOCTOR HARGREW IS WAITING THERE... BUT WE'LL NEVER GET THROUGH NOW...
YOU HAVE A SLIM CHANCE --IF SOMEONE ACTS AS ADVANCE SCOUT...
YOU'D HAVE A BETTER CHANCE WITH TWO SCOUTS-- YES, KE-WOH-NO-TAY?
THE TALL MAN'S EYES GLEAM WITH APPRECIATION, AND HIS NOD IS SO SWIFT, IT WOULD ESCAPE ANY EYE BUT THE BATMAN'S...
11

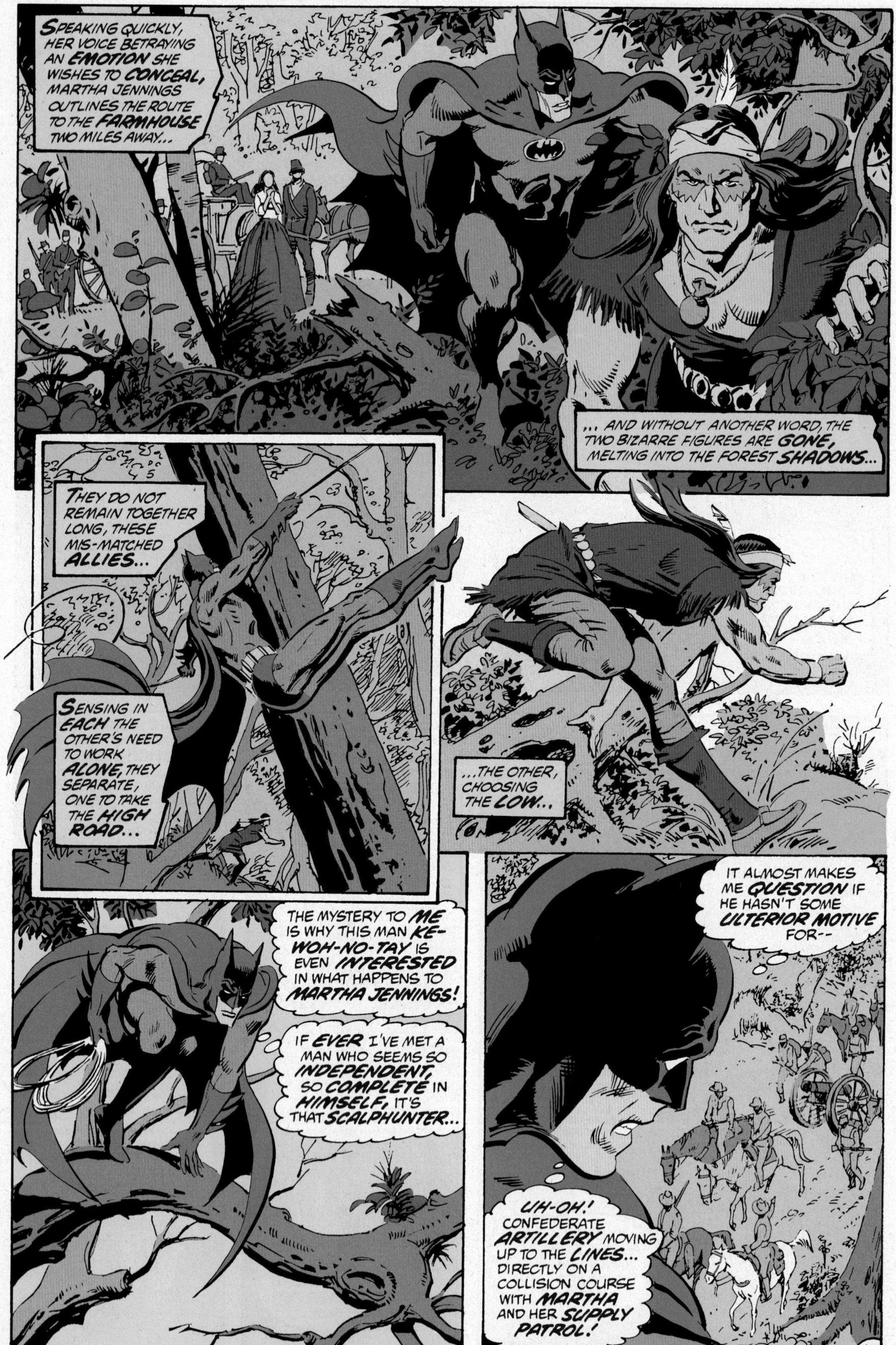
SPEAKING QUICKLY, HER VOICE BETRAYING AN EMOTION SHE WISHES TO CONCEAL, MARTHA JENNINGS OUTLINES THE ROUTE TO THE FARMHOUSE TWO MILES AWAY...
... AND WITHOUT ANOTHER WORD, THE TWO BIZARRE FIGURES ARE GONE, MELTING INTO THE FOREST SHADOWS...
THEY DO NOT REMAIN TOGETHER LONG, THESE MIS-MATCHED ALLIES...
SENSING IN EACH THE OTHER'S NEED TO WORK ALONE, THEY SEPARATE, ONE TO TAKE THE HIGH ROAD...
...THE OTHER, CHOOSING THE LOW...
THE MYSTERY TO ME IS WHY THIS MAN KE-WOH-NO-TAY IS EVEN INTERESTED IN WHAT HAPPENS TO MARTHA JENNINGS!
IF EVER I'VE MET A MAN WHO SEEMS SO INDEPENDENT, SO COMPLETE IN HIMSELF, IT'S THAT SCALPHUNTER...
IT ALMOST MAKES ME QUESTION IF HE HASN'T SOME ULTERIOR MOTIVE FOR--
UH-OH! CONFEDERATE ARTILLERY MOVING UP TO THE LINES... DIRECTLY ON A COLLISION COURSE WITH MARTHA AND HER SUPPLY PATROL!
12

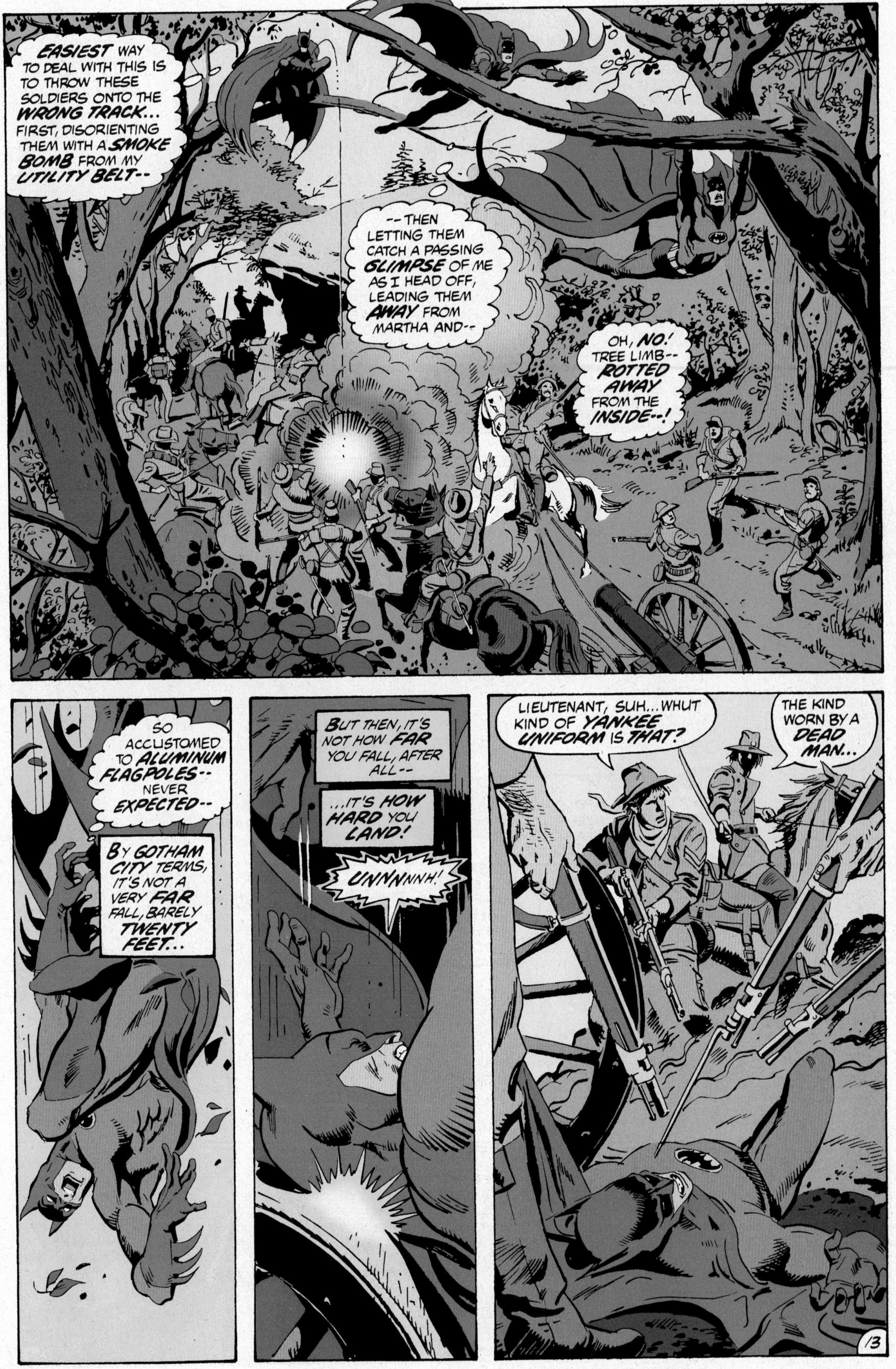
EASIEST WAY TO DEAL WITH THIS IS TO THROW THESE SOLDIERS ONTO THE WRONG TRACK... FIRST, DISORIENTING THEM WITH A SMOKE BOMB FROM MY UTILITY BELT--
--THEN LETTING THEM CATCH A PASSING GLIMPSE OF ME AS I HEAD OFF, LEADING THEM AWAY FROM MARTHA AND--
OH, NO! TREE LIMB--ROTTED AWAY FROM THE INSIDE--!
SO ACCUSTOMED TO ALUMINUM FLAGPOLES--NEVER EXPECTED--
BY GOTHAM CITY TERMS, IT'S NOT A VERY FAR FALL, BARELY TWENTY FEET...
BUT THEN, IT'S NOT HOW FAR YOU FALL, AFTER ALL--
...IT'S HOW HARD YOU LAND!
UNNNNNH!
LIEUTENANT, SUH...WHUT KIND OF YANKEE UNIFORM IS THAT?
THE KIND WORN BY A DEAD MAN...
13

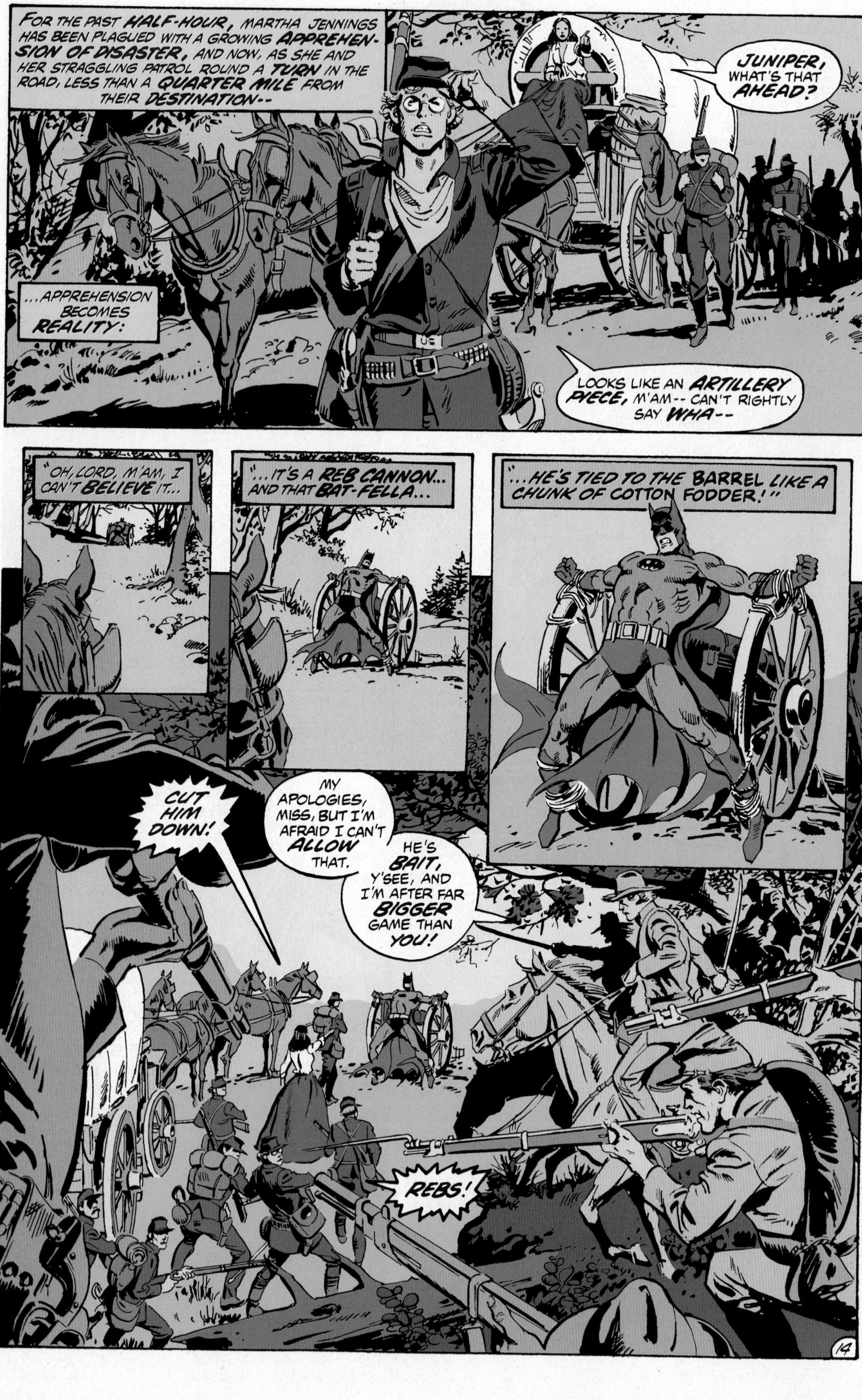

FOR THE PAST HALF-HOUR, MARTHA JENNINGS HAS BEEN PLAGUED WITH A GROWING APPREHENSION OF DISASTER, AND NOW, AS SHE AND HER STRAGGLING PATROL ROUND A TURN IN THE ROAD, LESS THAN A QUARTER MILE FROM THEIR DESTINATION--
JUNIPER, WHAT'S THAT AHEAD?
...APPREHENSION BECOMES REALITY:
LOOKS LIKE AN ARTILLERY PIECE, M'AM-- CAN'T RIGHTLY SAY WHA--
"OH, LORD, M'AM, I CAN'T BELIEVE IT...
"...IT'S A REB CANNON... AND THAT BAT-FELLA...
"...HE'S TIED TO THE BARREL LIKE A CHUNK OF COTTON FODDER!"
CUT HIM DOWN!
MY APOLOGIES, MISS, BUT I'M AFRAID I CAN'T ALLOW THAT.
HE'S BAIT, Y'SEE, AND I'M AFTER FAR BIGGER GAME THAN YOU!
REBS!
14

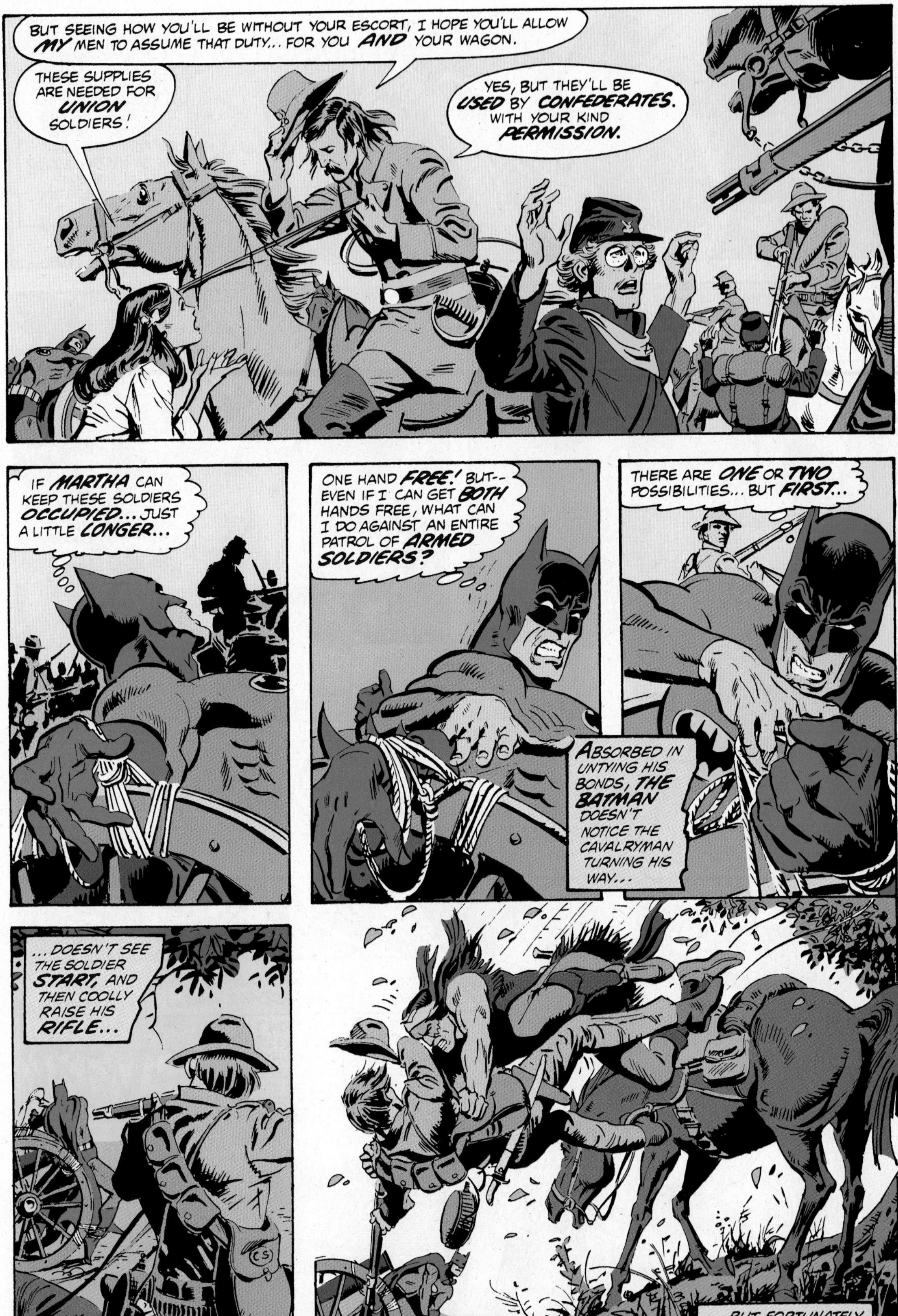
BUT SEEING HOW YOU'LL BE WITHOUT YOUR ESCORT, I HOPE YOU'LL ALLOW MY MEN TO ASSUME THAT DUTY... FOR YOU AND YOUR WAGON.
THESE SUPPLIES ARE NEEDED FOR UNION SOLDIERS!
YES, BUT THEY'LL BE USED BY CONFEDERATES. WITH YOUR KIND PERMISSION.
IF MARTHA CAN KEEP THESE SOLDIERS OCCUPIED... JUST A LITTLE LONGER...
ONE HAND FREE! BUT-- EVEN IF I CAN GET BOTH HANDS FREE, WHAT CAN I DO AGAINST AN ENTIRE PATROL OF ARMED SOLDIERS?
THERE ARE ONE OR TWO POSSIBILITIES... BUT FIRST...
ABSORBED IN UNTYING HIS BONDS, THE BATMAN DOESN'T NOTICE THE CAVALRYMAN TURNING HIS WAY...
...DOESN'T SEE THE SOLDIER START, AND THEN COOLLY RAISE HIS RIFLE...
...BUT FORTUNATELY, OTHER EYES DO...
15

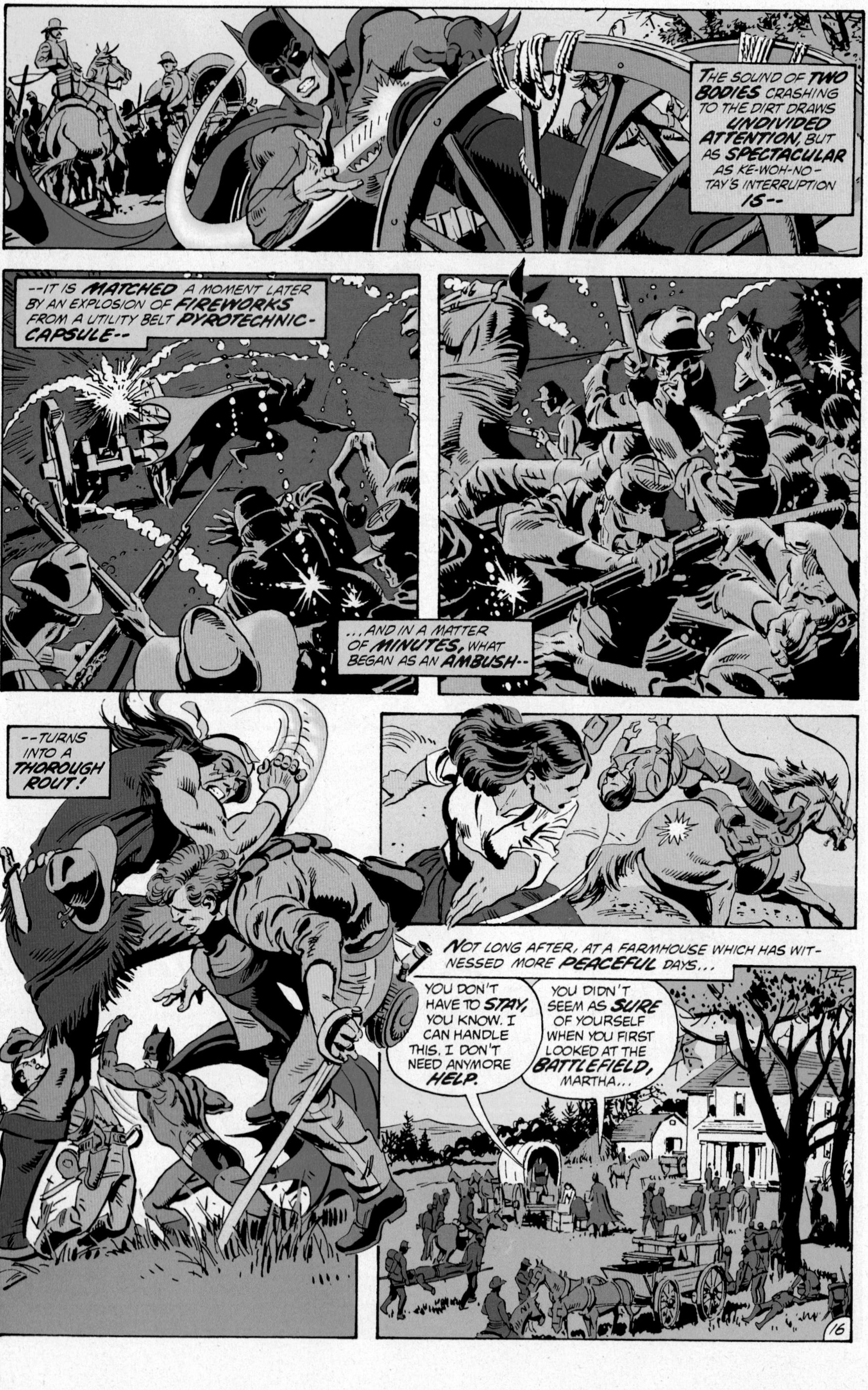

THE SOUND OF TWO BODIES CRASHING TO THE DIRT DRAWS UNDIVIDED ATTENTION, BUT AS SPECTACULAR AS KE-WOH-NO-TAY'S INTERRUPTION IS--
--IT IS MATCHED A MOMENT LATER BY AN EXPLOSION OF FIREWORKS FROM A UTILITY BELT PYROTECHNIC-CAPSULE--
...AND IN A MATTER OF MINUTES, WHAT BEGAN AS AN AMBUSH--
--TURNS INTO A THOROUGH ROUT!
NOT LONG AFTER, AT A FARMHOUSE WHICH HAS WITNESSED MORE PEACEFUL DAYS...
YOU DON'T HAVE TO STAY, YOU KNOW. I CAN HANDLE THIS. I DON'T NEED ANYMORE HELP.
YOU DIDN'T SEEM AS SURE OF YOURSELF WHEN YOU FIRST LOOKED AT THE BATTLEFIELD, MARTHA...
16

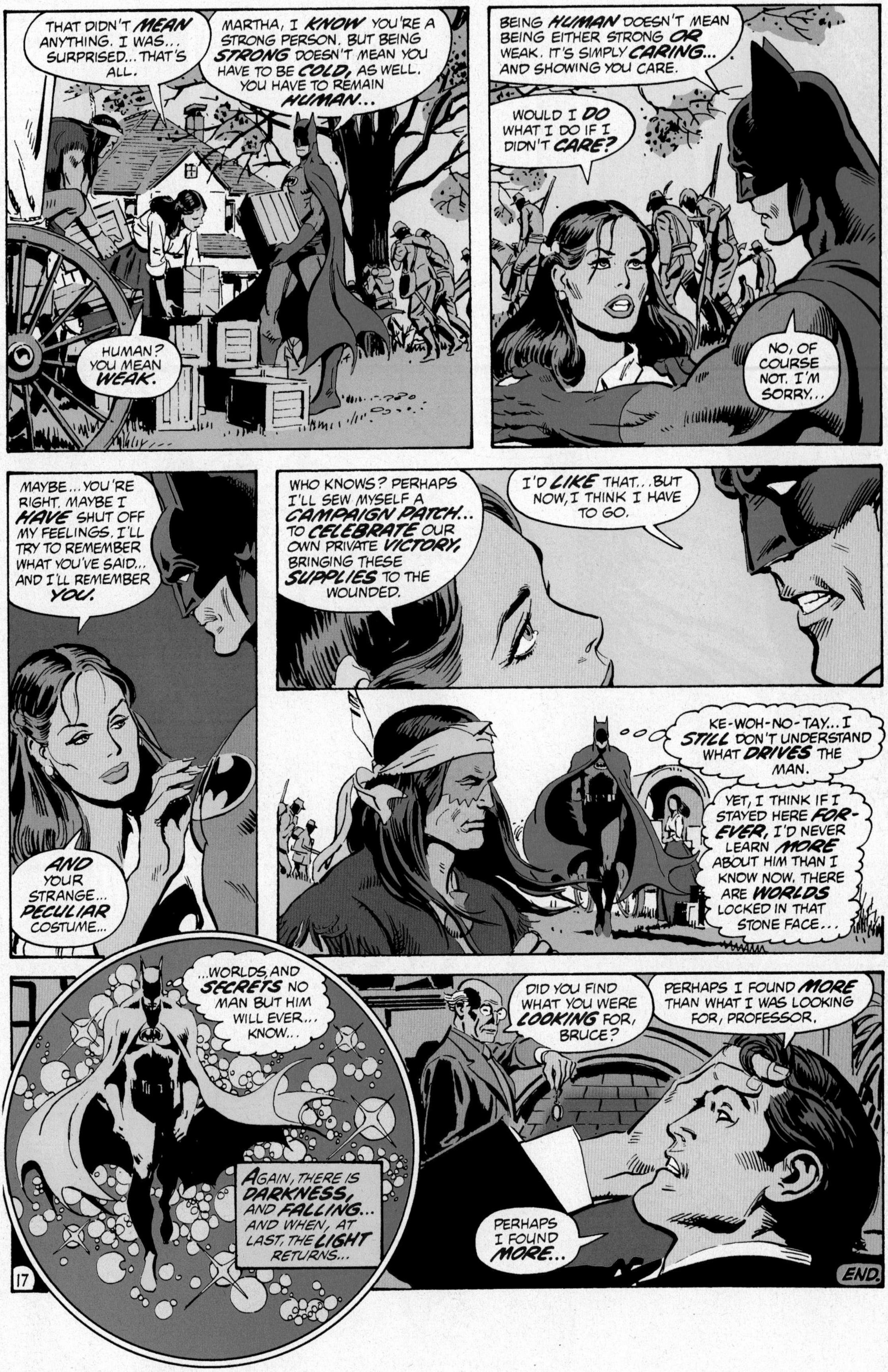
THAT DIDN'T MEAN ANYTHING. I WAS... SURPRISED... THAT'S ALL.
MARTHA, I KNOW YOU'RE A STRONG PERSON. BUT BEING STRONG DOESN'T MEAN YOU HAVE TO BE COLD, AS WELL. YOU HAVE TO REMAIN HUMAN...
HUMAN? YOU MEAN WEAK.
BEING HUMAN DOESN'T MEAN BEING EITHER STRONG OR WEAK. IT'S SIMPLY CARING... AND SHOWING YOU CARE.
WOULD I DO WHAT I DO IF I DIDN'T CARE?
NO, OF COURSE NOT. I'M SORRY...
MAYBE... YOU'RE RIGHT. MAYBE I HAVE SHUT OFF MY FEELINGS. I'LL TRY TO REMEMBER WHAT YOU'VE SAID... AND I'LL REMEMBER YOU.
AND YOUR STRANGE... PECULIAR COSTUME...
WHO KNOWS? PERHAPS I'LL SEW MYSELF A CAMPAIGN PATCH... TO CELEBRATE OUR OWN PRIVATE VICTORY, BRINGING THESE SUPPLIES TO THE WOUNDED.
I'D LIKE THAT... BUT NOW, I THINK I HAVE TO GO.
KE-WOH-NO-TAY... I STILL DON'T UNDERSTAND WHAT DRIVES THE MAN.
YET, I THINK IF I STAYED HERE FOR-EVER, I'D NEVER LEARN MORE ABOUT HIM THAN I KNOW NOW. THERE ARE WORLDS LOCKED IN THAT STONE FACE...
...WORLDS, AND SECRETS NO MAN BUT HIM WILL EVER... KNOW...
AGAIN, THERE IS DARKNESS, AND FALLING... AND WHEN, AT LAST, THE LIGHT RETURNS...
17
DID YOU FIND WHAT YOU WERE LOOKING FOR, BRUCE?
PERHAPS I FOUND MORE THAN WHAT I WAS LOOKING FOR, PROFESSOR.
PERHAPS I FOUND MORE...
END.

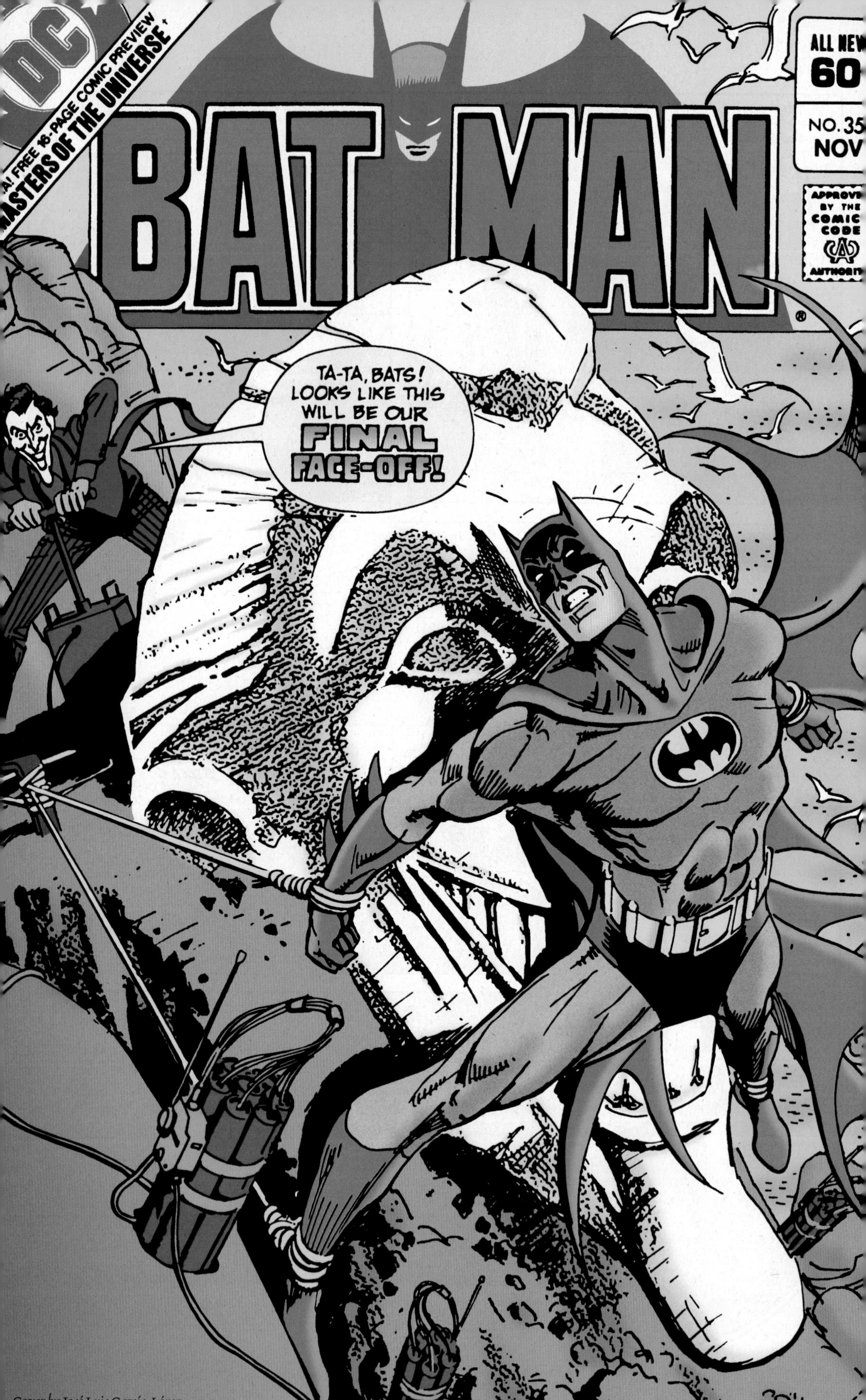
DC
FREE 16-PAGE COMIC PREVIEW
MASTERS OF THE UNIVERSE
BATMAN
ALL NEW
60
NO.35
NOV
APPROVED BY THE COMICS CODE AUTHORITY
TA-TA, BATS! LOOKS LIKE THIS WILL BE OUR FINAL FACE-OFF!

Cover by José Luis García-López

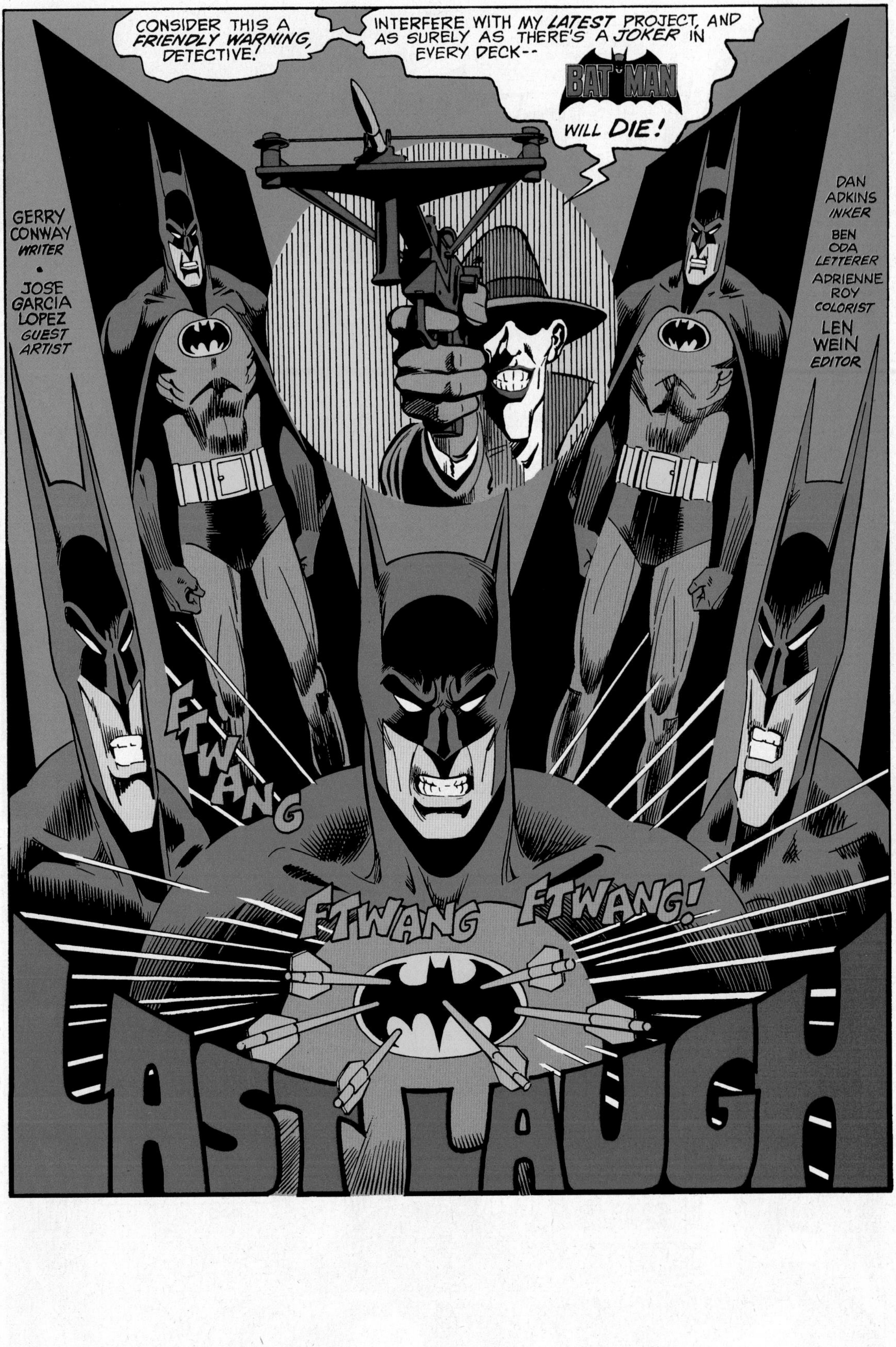
CONSIDER THIS A FRIENDLY WARNING, DETECTIVE!
INTERFERE WITH MY LATEST PROJECT, AND AS SURELY AS THERE'S A JOKER IN EVERY DECK--
BATMAN
WILL DIE!
GERRY CONWAY WRITER
JOSE GARCIA LOPEZ GUEST ARTIST
DAN ADKINS INKER
BEN ODA LETTERER
ADRIENNE ROY COLORIST
LEN WEIN EDITOR
FTWANG
FTWANG
FTWANG!
LAST LAUGH

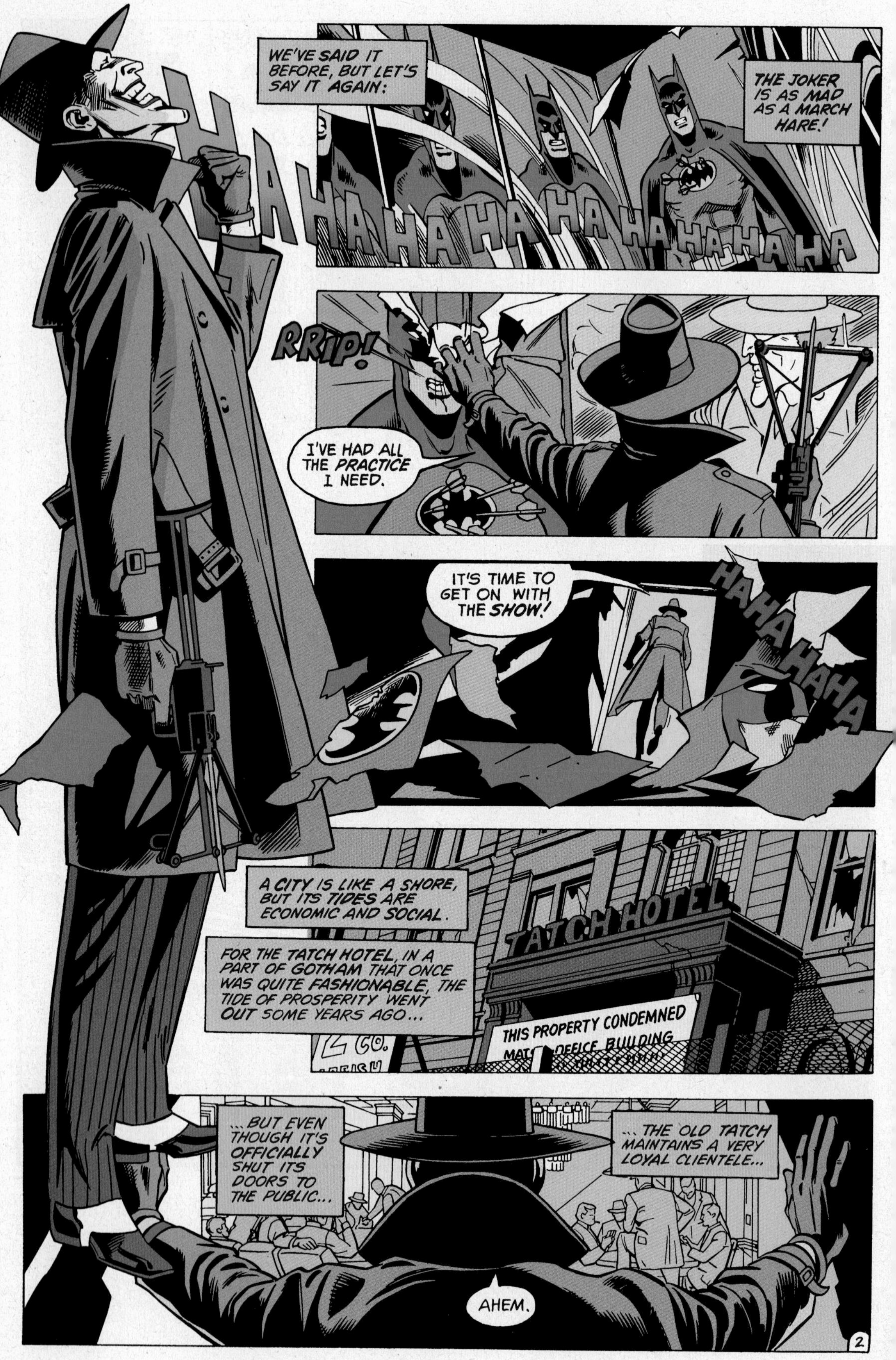

WE'VE SAID IT BEFORE, BUT LET'S SAY IT AGAIN:
THE JOKER IS AS MAD AS A MARCH HARE!
HA HA HA HA HA HA HA HA HA HA HA HA HA
RRIP!
I'VE HAD ALL THE PRACTICE I NEED.
IT'S TIME TO GET ON WITH THE SHOW!
HAHAHAHA
A CITY IS LIKE A SHORE, BUT ITS TIDES ARE ECONOMIC AND SOCIAL.
TATCH HOTEL
FOR THE TATCH HOTEL, IN A PART OF GOTHAM THAT ONCE WAS QUITE FASHIONABLE, THE TIDE OF PROSPERITY WENT OUT SOME YEARS AGO...
THIS PROPERTY CONDEMNED
...BUT EVEN THOUGH IT'S OFFICIALLY SHUT ITS DOORS TO THE PUBLIC...
...THE OLD TATCH MAINTAINS A VERY LOYAL CLIENTELE...
AHEM.
2

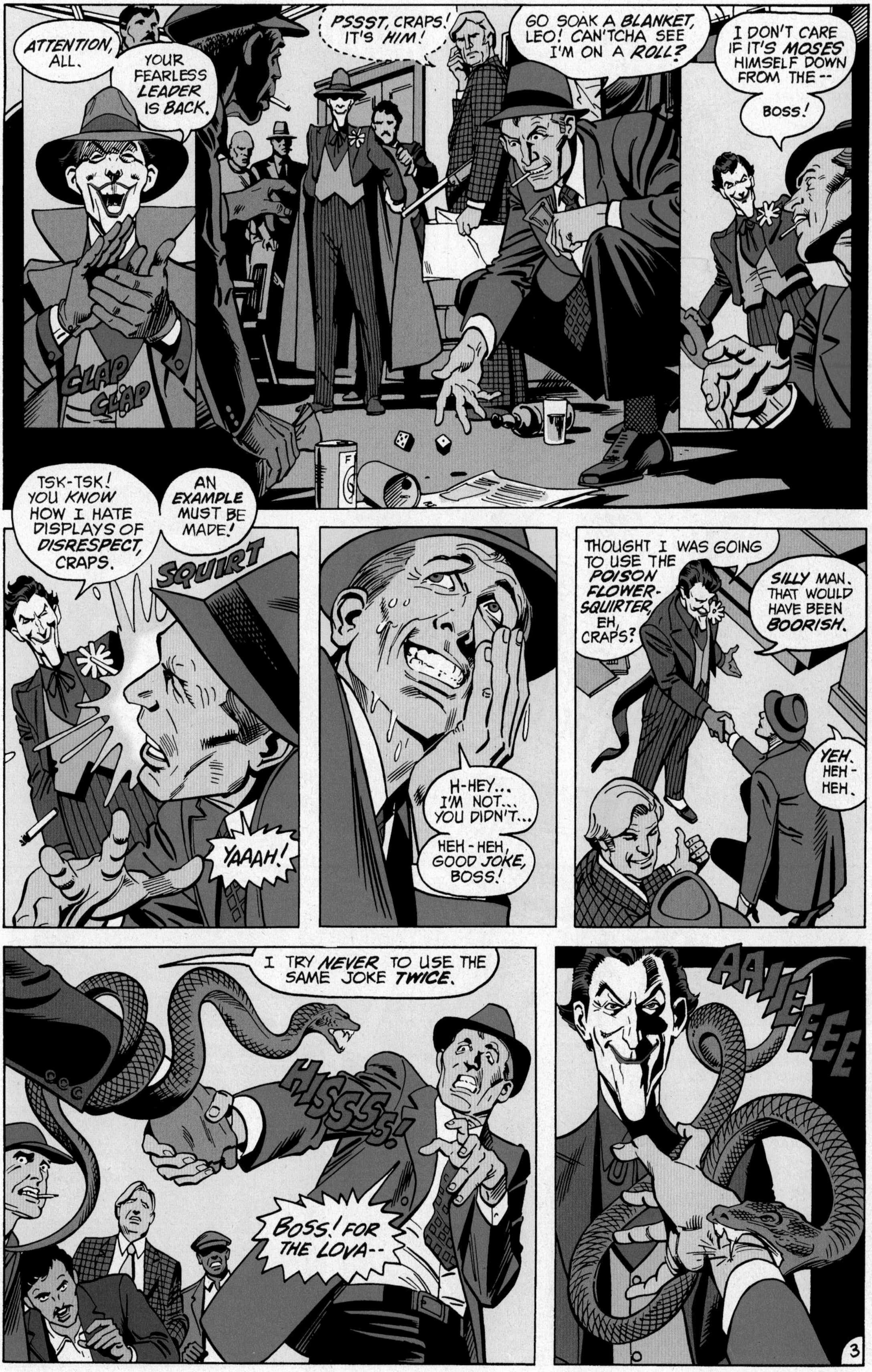
ATTENTION, ALL.
YOUR FEARLESS LEADER IS BACK.
CLAP CLAP
PSSST, CRAPS! IT'S HIM!
GO SOAK A BLANKET, LEO! CAN'TCHA SEE I'M ON A ROLL?
I DON'T CARE IF IT'S MOSES HIMSELF DOWN FROM THE --
BOSS!
TSK-TSK! YOU KNOW HOW I HATE DISPLAYS OF DISRESPECT, CRAPS.
AN EXAMPLE MUST BE MADE!
SQUIRT
YAAAH!
H-HEY... I'M NOT... YOU DIDN'T...
HEH-HEH, GOOD JOKE, BOSS!
THOUGHT I WAS GOING TO USE THE POISON FLOWER-SQUIRTER, EH, CRAPS?
SILLY MAN. THAT WOULD HAVE BEEN BOORISH.
YEH. HEH-HEH.
I TRY NEVER TO USE THE SAME JOKE TWICE.
HISSSS!
BOSS! FOR THE LOVA--
AAIIEEEEE
3

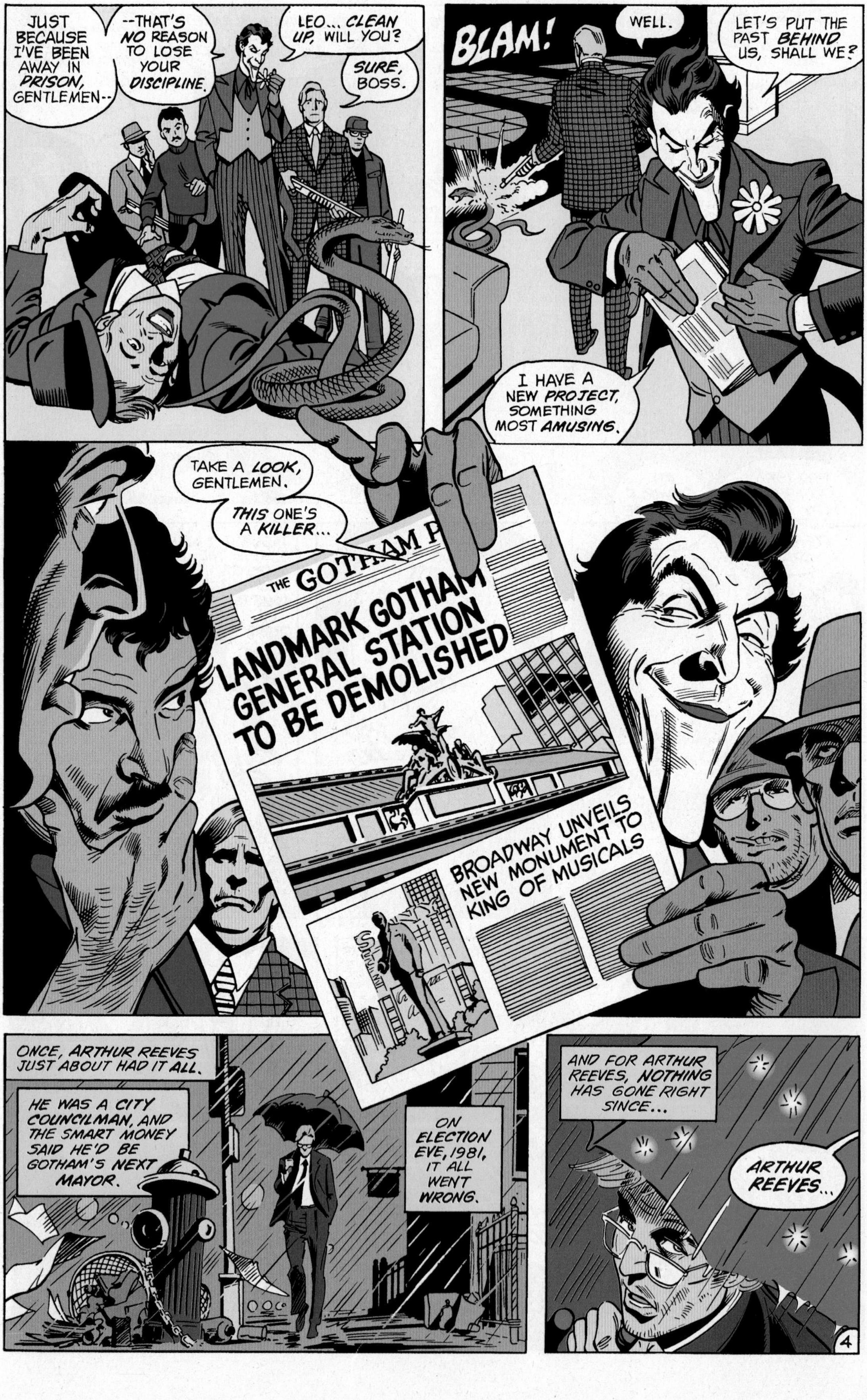
JUST BECAUSE I'VE BEEN AWAY IN PRISON, GENTLEMEN--
--THAT'S NO REASON TO LOSE YOUR DISCIPLINE.
LEO... CLEAN UP, WILL YOU?
SURE, BOSS.
BLAM!
WELL.
LET'S PUT THE PAST BEHIND US, SHALL WE?
I HAVE A NEW PROJECT, SOMETHING MOST AMUSING.
TAKE A LOOK, GENTLEMEN.
THIS ONE'S A KILLER...
THE GOTHAM P
LANDMARK GOTHAM GENERAL STATION TO BE DEMOLISHED
BROADWAY UNVEILS NEW MONUMENT TO KING OF MUSICALS
ONCE, ARTHUR REEVES JUST ABOUT HAD IT ALL.
HE WAS A CITY COUNCILMAN, AND THE SMART MONEY SAID HE'D BE GOTHAM'S NEXT MAYOR.
ON ELECTION EVE, 1981, IT ALL WENT WRONG.
AND FOR ARTHUR REEVES, NOTHING HAS GONE RIGHT SINCE...
ARTHUR REEVES...
4

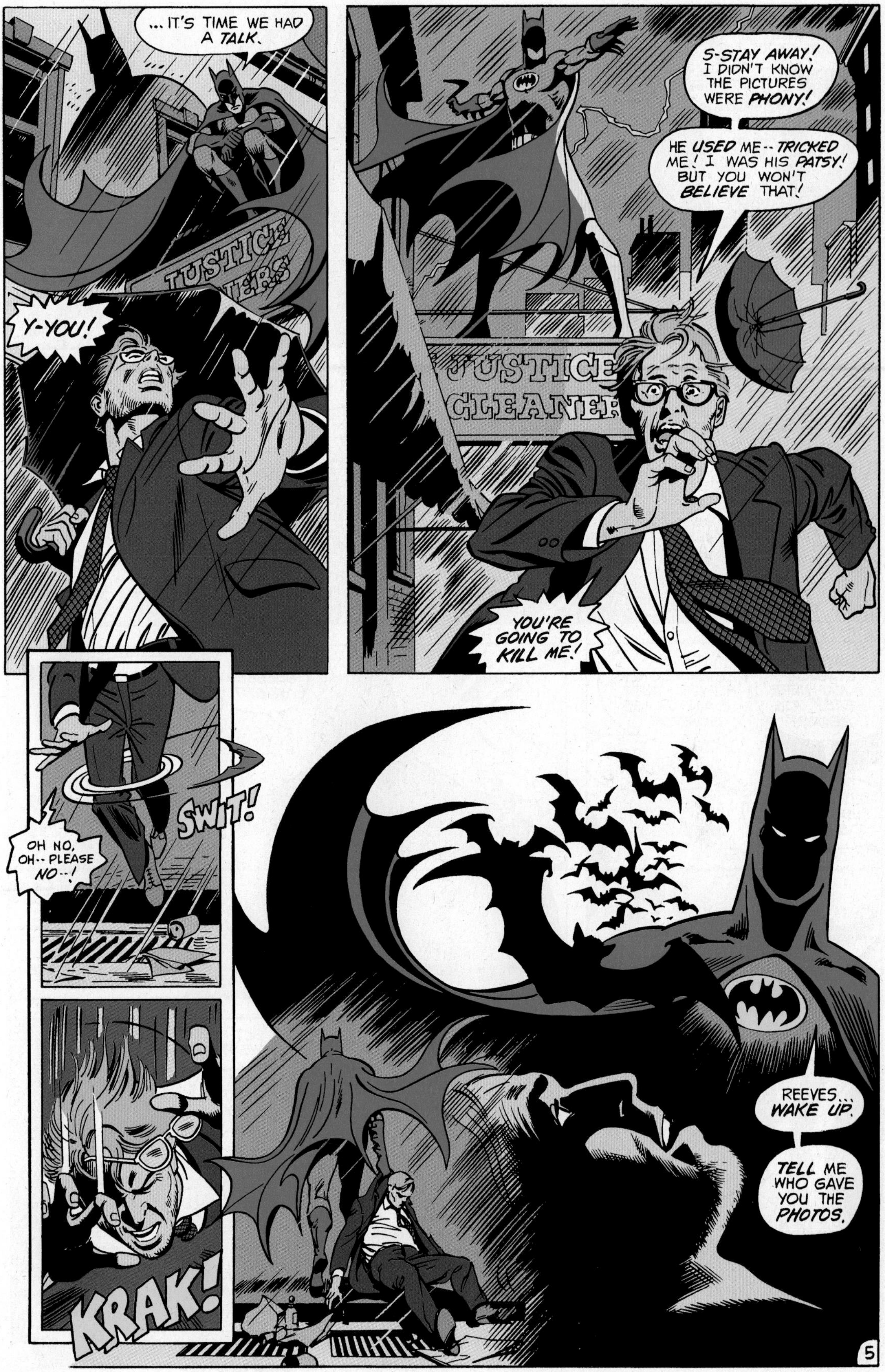

...IT'S TIME WE HAD A TALK.
JUSTICE CLEANERS
Y-YOU!
S-STAY AWAY! I DIDN'T KNOW THE PICTURES WERE PHONY!
HE USED ME--TRICKED ME! I WAS HIS PATSY! BUT YOU WON'T BELIEVE THAT!
JUSTICE CLEANER
YOU'RE GOING TO KILL ME!
SWIT!
OH NO, OH--PLEASE NO--!
KRAK!
REEVES... WAKE UP.
TELL ME WHO GAVE YOU THE PHOTOS.
5

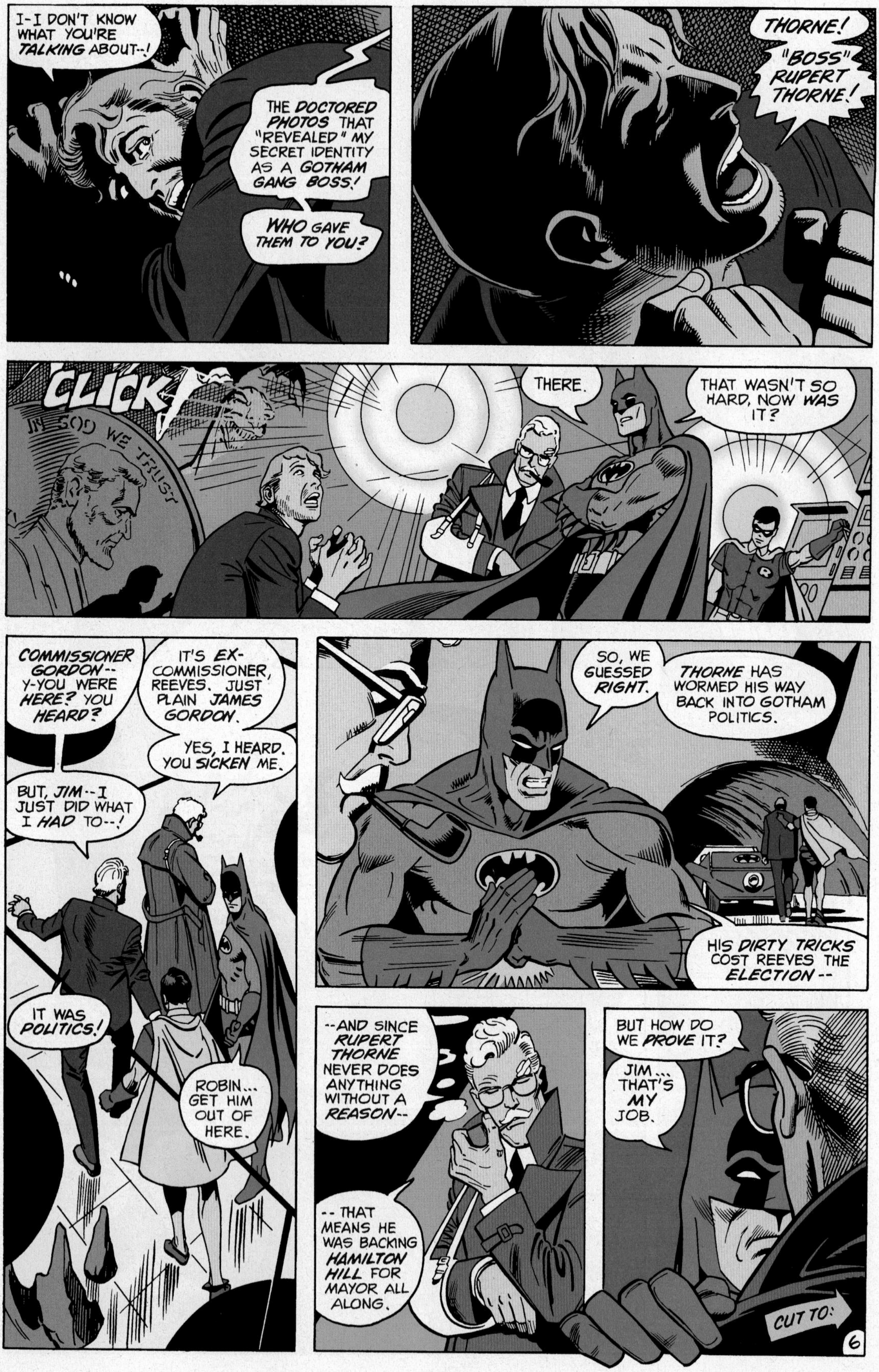
I-I DON'T KNOW WHAT YOU'RE TALKING ABOUT--!
THE DOCTORED PHOTOS THAT "REVEALED" MY SECRET IDENTITY AS A GOTHAM GANG BOSS!
WHO GAVE THEM TO YOU?
THORNE! "BOSS" RUPERT THORNE!
CLICK
IN GOD WE TRUST
THERE.
THAT WASN'T SO HARD, NOW WAS IT?
COMMISSIONER GORDON-- Y-YOU WERE HERE? YOU HEARD?
IT'S EX-COMMISSIONER, REEVES. JUST PLAIN JAMES GORDON.
YES, I HEARD. YOU SICKEN ME.
BUT, JIM--I JUST DID WHAT I HAD TO--!
IT WAS POLITICS!
ROBIN... GET HIM OUT OF HERE.
SO, WE GUESSED RIGHT.
THORNE HAS WORMED HIS WAY BACK INTO GOTHAM POLITICS.
HIS DIRTY TRICKS COST REEVES THE ELECTION--
--AND SINCE RUPERT THORNE NEVER DOES ANYTHING WITHOUT A REASON--
--THAT MEANS HE WAS BACKING HAMILTON HILL FOR MAYOR ALL ALONG.
BUT HOW DO WE PROVE IT?
JIM... THAT'S MY JOB.
CUT TO:
6

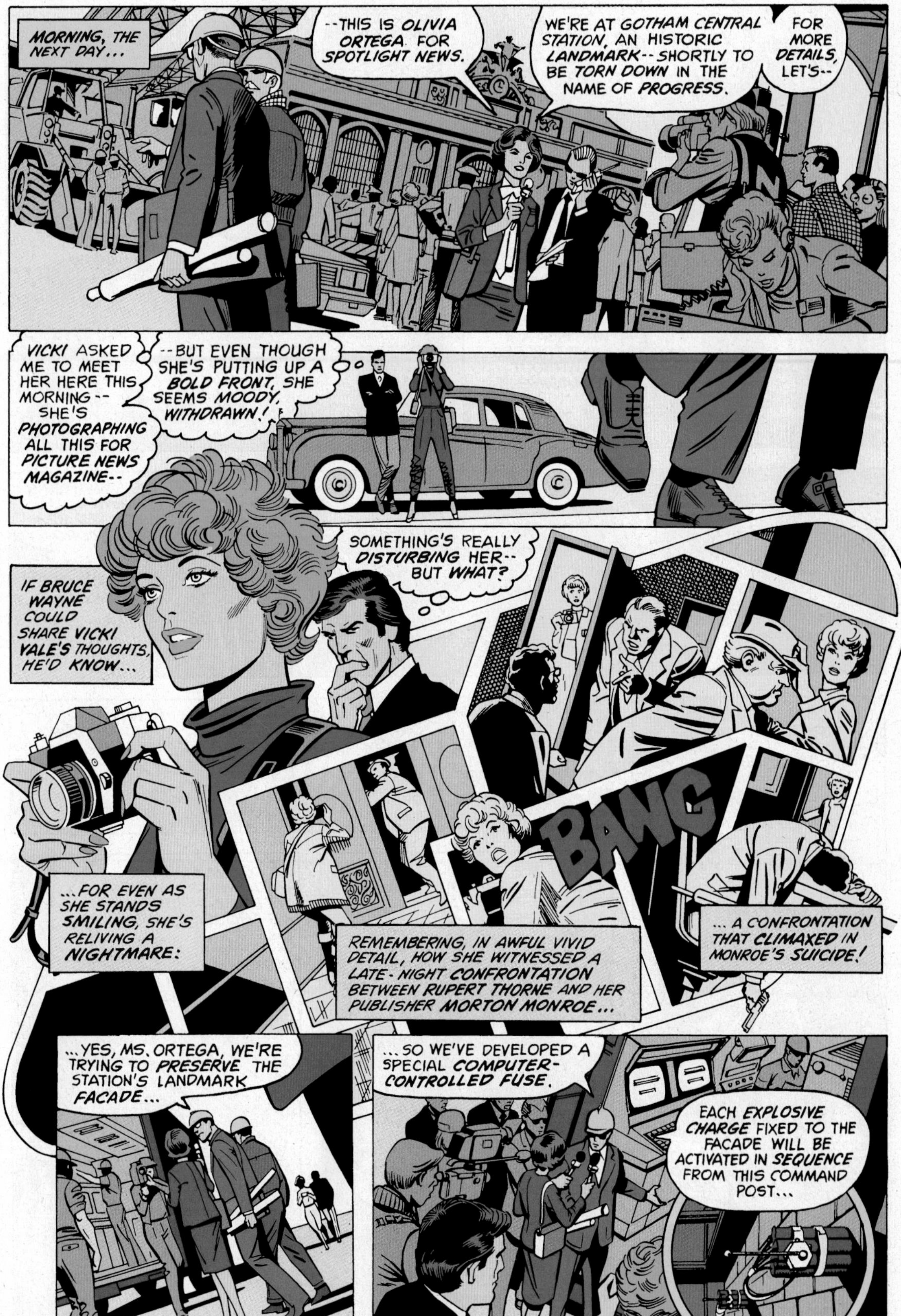
MORNING, THE NEXT DAY...
--THIS IS OLIVIA ORTEGA FOR SPOTLIGHT NEWS.
WE'RE AT GOTHAM CENTRAL STATION, AN HISTORIC LANDMARK-- SHORTLY TO BE TORN DOWN IN THE NAME OF PROGRESS.
FOR MORE DETAILS, LET'S--
VICKI ASKED ME TO MEET HER HERE THIS MORNING-- SHE'S PHOTOGRAPHING ALL THIS FOR PICTURE NEWS MAGAZINE--
--BUT EVEN THOUGH SHE'S PUTTING UP A BOLD FRONT, SHE SEEMS MOODY, WITHDRAWN!
IF BRUCE WAYNE COULD SHARE VICKI YALE'S THOUGHTS, HE'D KNOW...
SOMETHING'S REALLY DISTURBING HER-- BUT WHAT?
...FOR EVEN AS SHE STANDS SMILING, SHE'S RELIVING A NIGHTMARE:
REMEMBERING, IN AWFUL VIVID DETAIL, HOW SHE WITNESSED A LATE-NIGHT CONFRONTATION BETWEEN RUPERT THORNE AND HER PUBLISHER MORTON MONROE...
BANG
...A CONFRONTATION THAT CLIMAXED IN MONROE'S SUICIDE!
...YES, MS. ORTEGA, WE'RE TRYING TO PRESERVE THE STATION'S LANDMARK FACADE...
...SO WE'VE DEVELOPED A SPECIAL COMPUTER-CONTROLLED FUSE.
EACH EXPLOSIVE CHARGE FIXED TO THE FACADE WILL BE ACTIVATED IN SEQUENCE FROM THIS COMMAND POST...
7

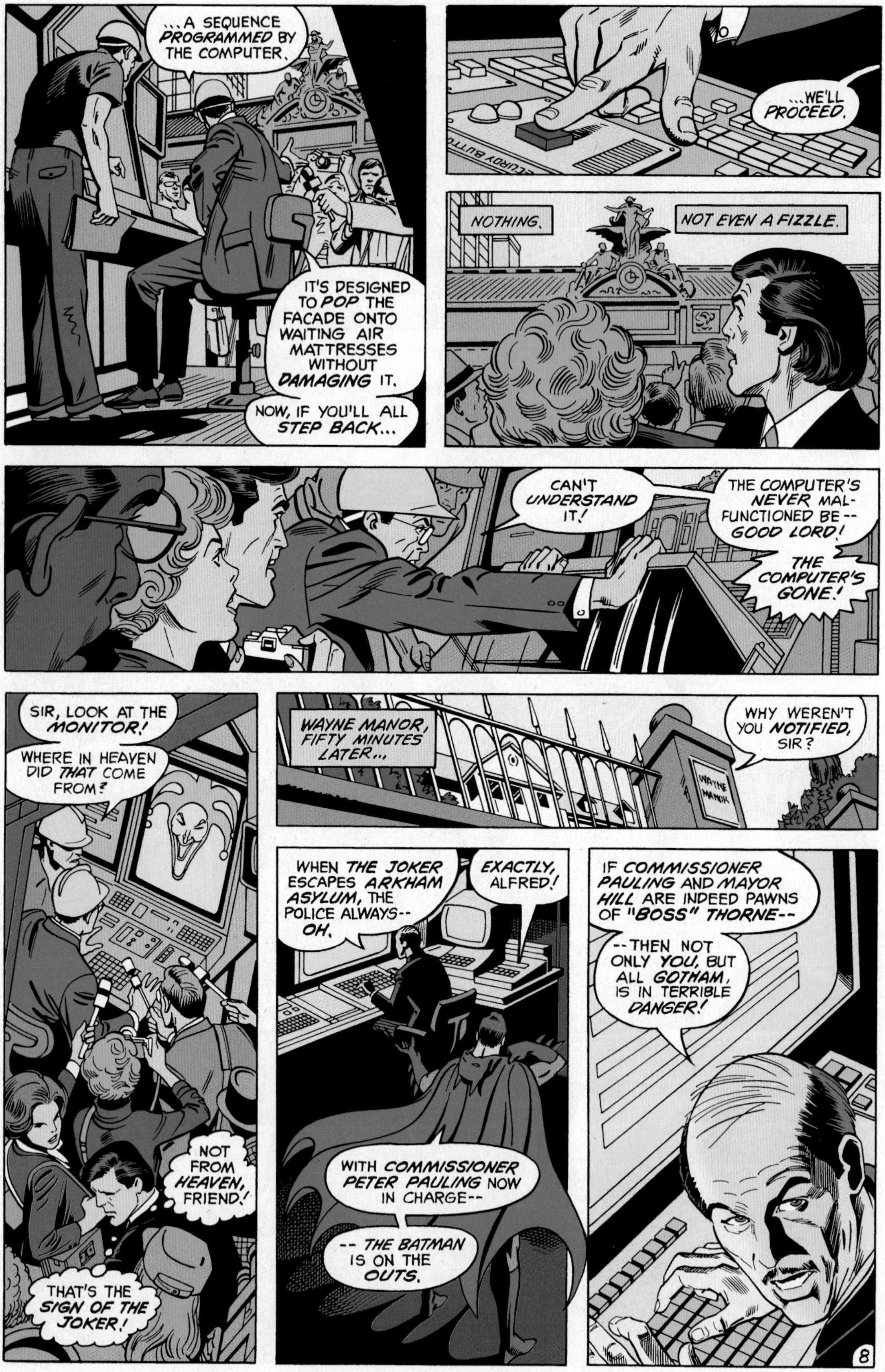
...A SEQUENCE PROGRAMMED BY THE COMPUTER.
IT'S DESIGNED TO POP THE FACADE ONTO WAITING AIR MATTRESSES WITHOUT DAMAGING IT.
NOW, IF YOU'LL ALL STEP BACK...
...WE'LL PROCEED.
NOTHING.
NOT EVEN A FIZZLE.
CAN'T UNDERSTAND IT!
THE COMPUTER'S NEVER MAL-FUNCTIONED BE--GOOD LORD!
THE COMPUTER'S GONE!
SIR, LOOK AT THE MONITOR!
WHERE IN HEAVEN DID THAT COME FROM?
NOT FROM HEAVEN, FRIEND!
THAT'S THE SIGN OF THE JOKER!
WAYNE MANOR, FIFTY MINUTES LATER...
WHY WEREN'T YOU NOTIFIED, SIR?
WHEN THE JOKER ESCAPES ARKHAM ASYLUM, THE POLICE ALWAYS--OH.
EXACTLY, ALFRED!
WITH COMMISSIONER PETER PAULING NOW IN CHARGE--
--THE BATMAN IS ON THE OUTS.
IF COMMISSIONER PAULING AND MAYOR HILL ARE INDEED PAWNS OF "BOSS" THORNE--
--THEN NOT ONLY YOU, BUT ALL GOTHAM, IS IN TERRIBLE DANGER!
8

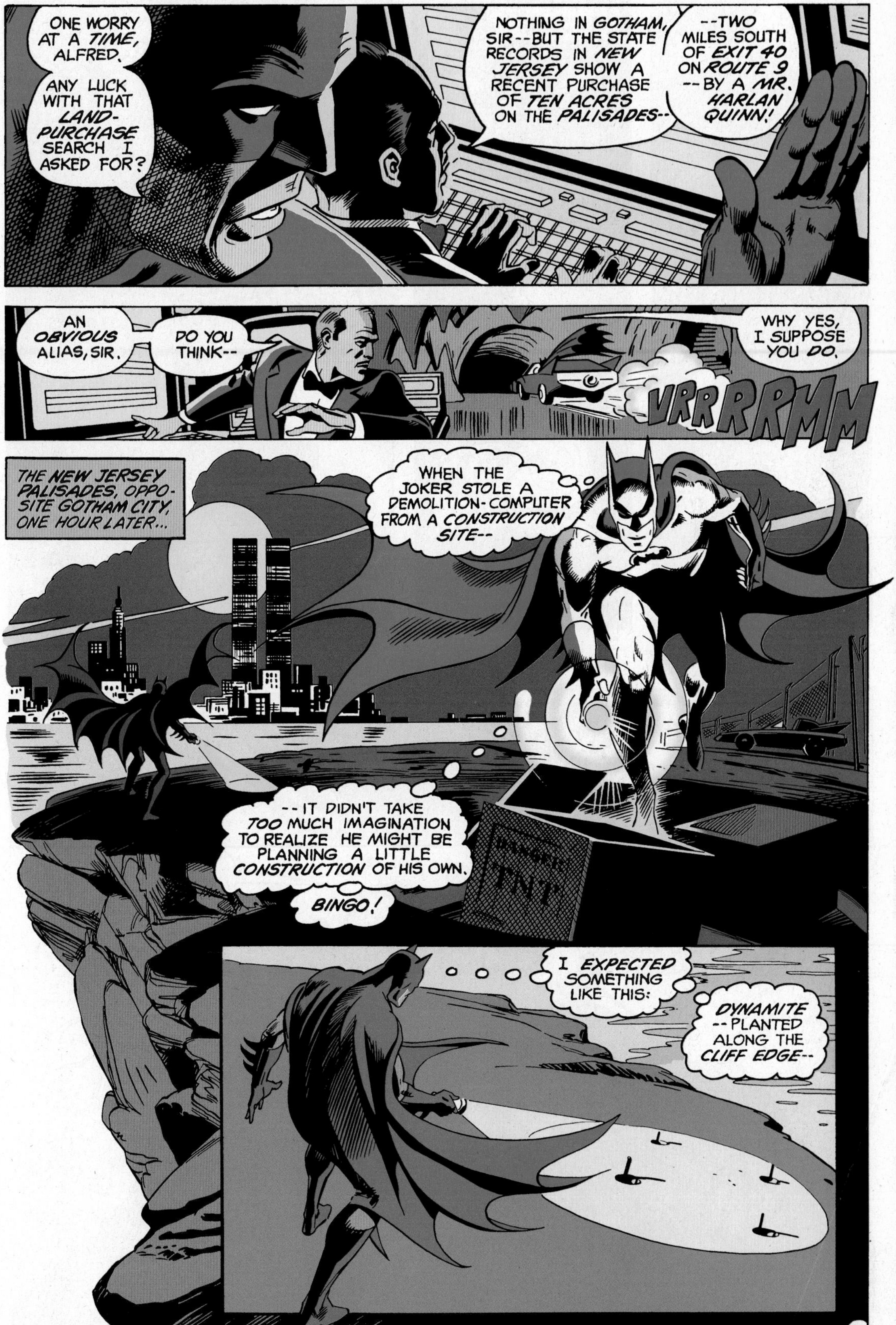
ONE WORRY AT A TIME, ALFRED.
ANY LUCK WITH THAT LAND-PURCHASE SEARCH I ASKED FOR?
NOTHING IN GOTHAM, SIR--BUT THE STATE RECORDS IN NEW JERSEY SHOW A RECENT PURCHASE OF TEN ACRES ON THE PALISADES--
--TWO MILES SOUTH OF EXIT 40 ON ROUTE 9 --BY A MR. HARLAN QUINN!
AN OBVIOUS ALIAS, SIR.
DO YOU THINK--
WHY YES, I SUPPOSE YOU DO.
VRRRRMM
THE NEW JERSEY PALISADES, OPPOSITE GOTHAM CITY, ONE HOUR LATER...
WHEN THE JOKER STOLE A DEMOLITION-COMPUTER FROM A CONSTRUCTION SITE--
--IT DIDN'T TAKE TOO MUCH IMAGINATION TO REALIZE HE MIGHT BE PLANNING A LITTLE CONSTRUCTION OF HIS OWN.
BINGO!
TNT
I EXPECTED SOMETHING LIKE THIS:
DYNAMITE --PLANTED ALONG THE CLIFF EDGE--
9

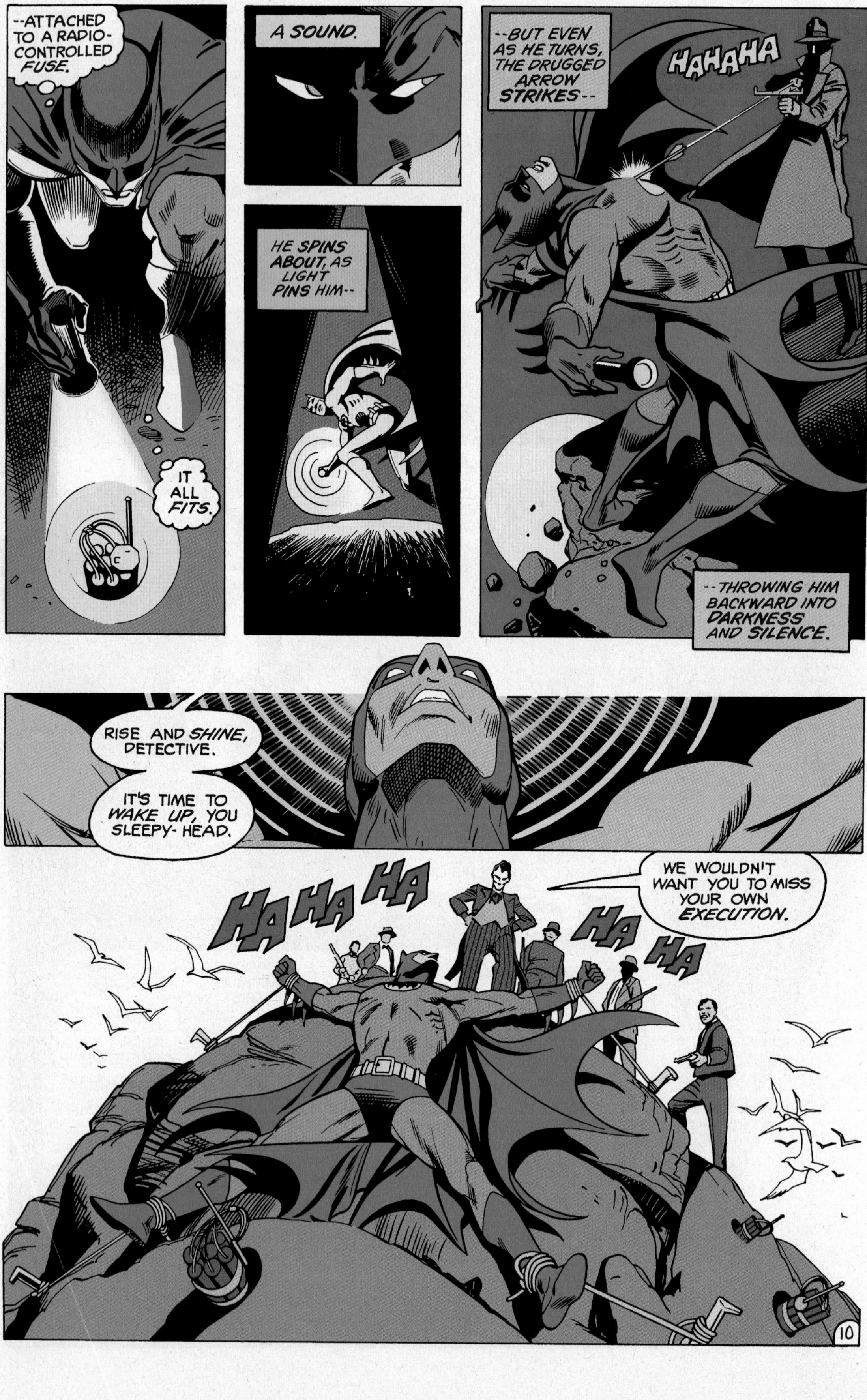
--ATTACHED TO A RADIO-CONTROLLED FUSE.
IT ALL FITS.
A SOUND.
HE SPINS ABOUT, AS LIGHT PINS HIM--
--BUT EVEN AS HE TURNS, THE DRUGGED ARROW STRIKES--
HAHAHA
--THROWING HIM BACKWARD INTO DARKNESS AND SILENCE.
RISE AND SHINE, DETECTIVE.
IT'S TIME TO WAKE UP, YOU SLEEPY- HEAD.
HAHAHA
WE WOULDN'T WANT YOU TO MISS YOUR OWN EXECUTION.
HA HA
10

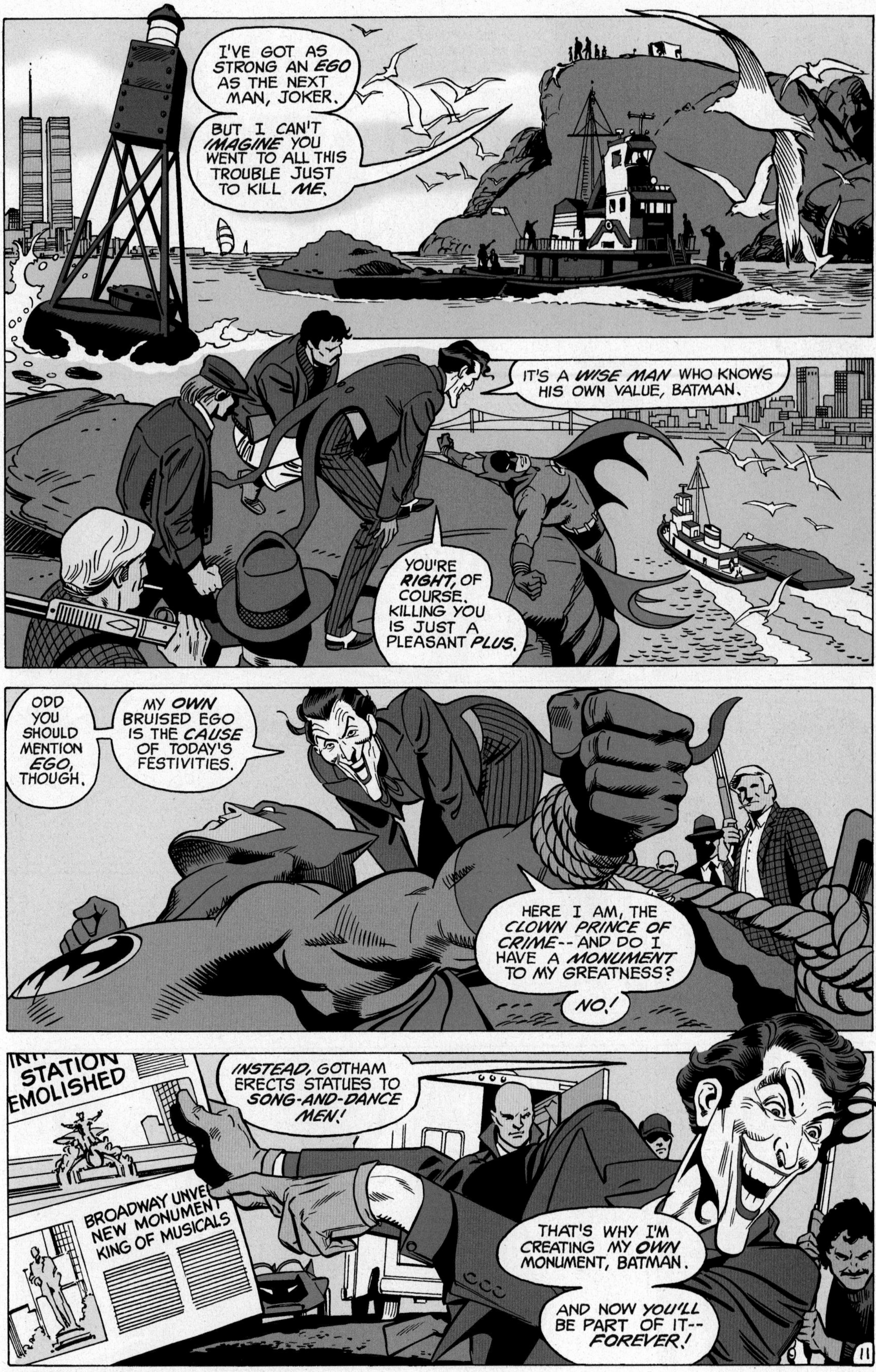
I'VE GOT AS STRONG AN EGO AS THE NEXT MAN, JOKER.
BUT I CAN'T IMAGINE YOU WENT TO ALL THIS TROUBLE JUST TO KILL ME.
IT'S A WISE MAN WHO KNOWS HIS OWN VALUE, BATMAN.
YOU'RE RIGHT, OF COURSE. KILLING YOU IS JUST A PLEASANT PLUS.
ODD YOU SHOULD MENTION EGO, THOUGH.
MY OWN BRUISED EGO IS THE CAUSE OF TODAY'S FESTIVITIES.
HERE I AM, THE CLOWN PRINCE OF CRIME-- AND DO I HAVE A MONUMENT TO MY GREATNESS?
NO!
STATION
EMOLISHED
INSTEAD, GOTHAM ERECTS STATUES TO SONG-AND-DANCE MEN!
BROADWAY UNVE
NEW MONUMENT
KING OF MUSICALS
THAT'S WHY I'M CREATING MY OWN MONUMENT, BATMAN.
AND NOW YOU'LL BE PART OF IT-- FOREVER!
11

CRACKLING WITH GLEE, THE JOKER TURNS AWAY--

THIS COMPUTER IS A *MARVELOUS* DEVICE, BATMAN.

BY FIRING THE *EXPLOSIVES* ALONG THIS CLIFF-EDGE AT JUST THE *RIGHT* INTERVALS--

--AND THE BATMAN ACTS.

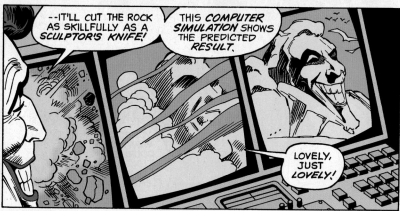

--IT'LL CUT THE ROCK AS SKILLFULLY AS A *SCULPTOR'S KNIFE!*

THIS *COMPUTER SIMULATION* SHOWS THE PREDICTED *RESULT.*

LOVELY, JUST *LOVELY!*

ROPE FRAYS-- AND BREAKS.

IMAGINE HOW GOTHAM WILL *REACT*--

--WHEN ITS CITIZENS RISE TO SEE *MY* IMAGE WATCHING OVER THEM.

IT'LL BE *GLORIOUS!*

ONLY ONE HAND IS FREE--

--BUT ONE HAND IS ALL HE NEEDS.

CLK

HMMM

12

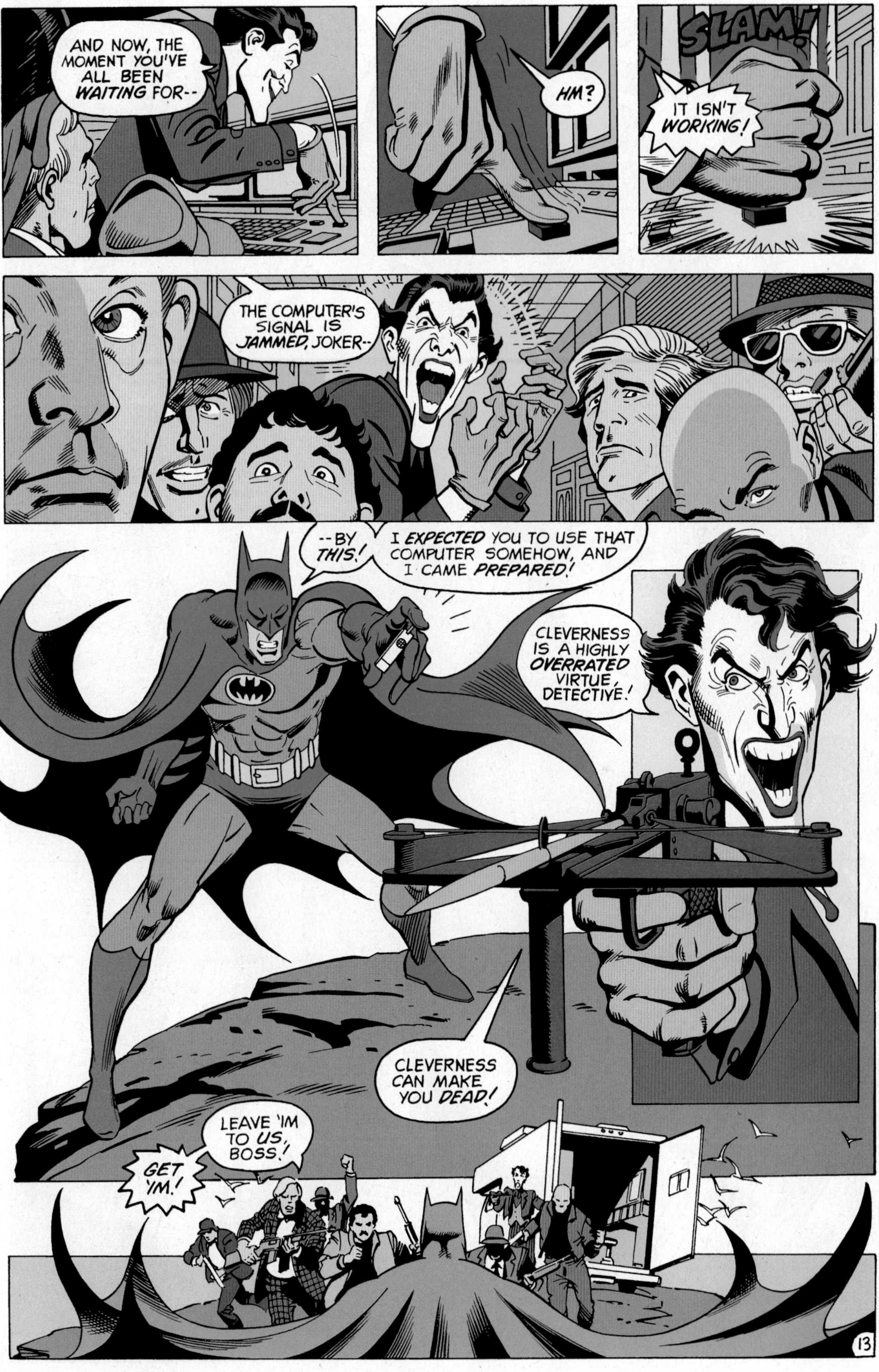
AND NOW, THE MOMENT YOU'VE ALL BEEN WAITING FOR--
HM?
SLAM!
IT ISN'T WORKING!
THE COMPUTER'S SIGNAL IS JAMMED, JOKER--
--BY THIS!
I EXPECTED YOU TO USE THAT COMPUTER SOMEHOW, AND I CAME PREPARED!
CLEVERNESS IS A HIGHLY OVERRATED VIRTUE, DETECTIVE!
CLEVERNESS CAN MAKE YOU DEAD!
LEAVE 'IM TO US, BOSS!
GET 'IM!
13

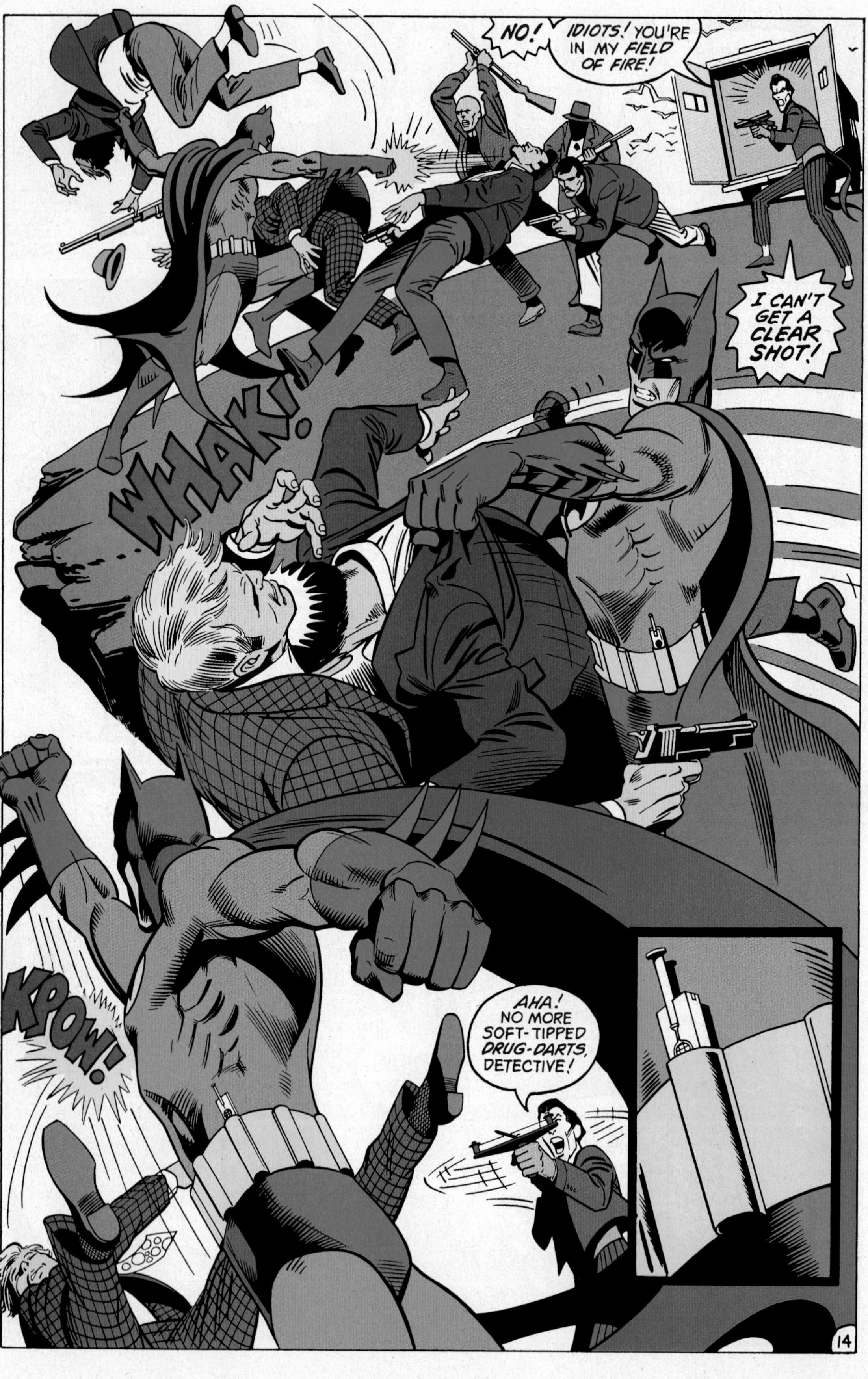
NO!
IDIOTS! YOU'RE IN MY FIELD OF FIRE!
I CAN'T GET A CLEAR SHOT!
WHAK!
KPOW!
AHA! NO MORE SOFT-TIPPED DRUG-DARTS, DETECTIVE!
14

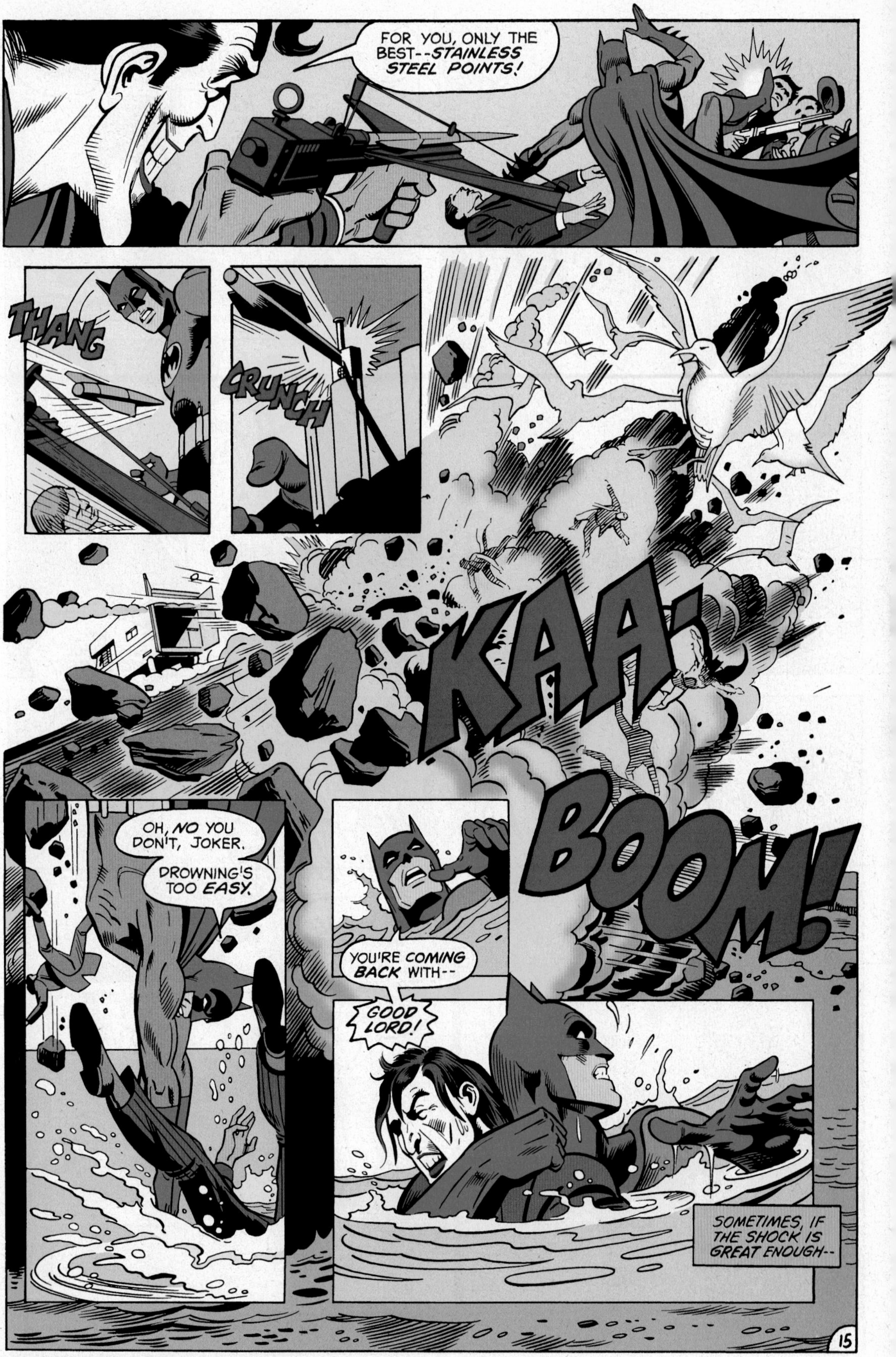
FOR YOU, ONLY THE BEST--STAINLESS STEEL POINTS!
THANG
CRUNCH
KAA-BOOM!
OH, NO YOU DON'T, JOKER.
DROWNING'S TOO EASY.
YOU'RE COMING BACK WITH--
GOOD LORD!
SOMETIMES, IF THE SHOCK IS GREAT ENOUGH--
15

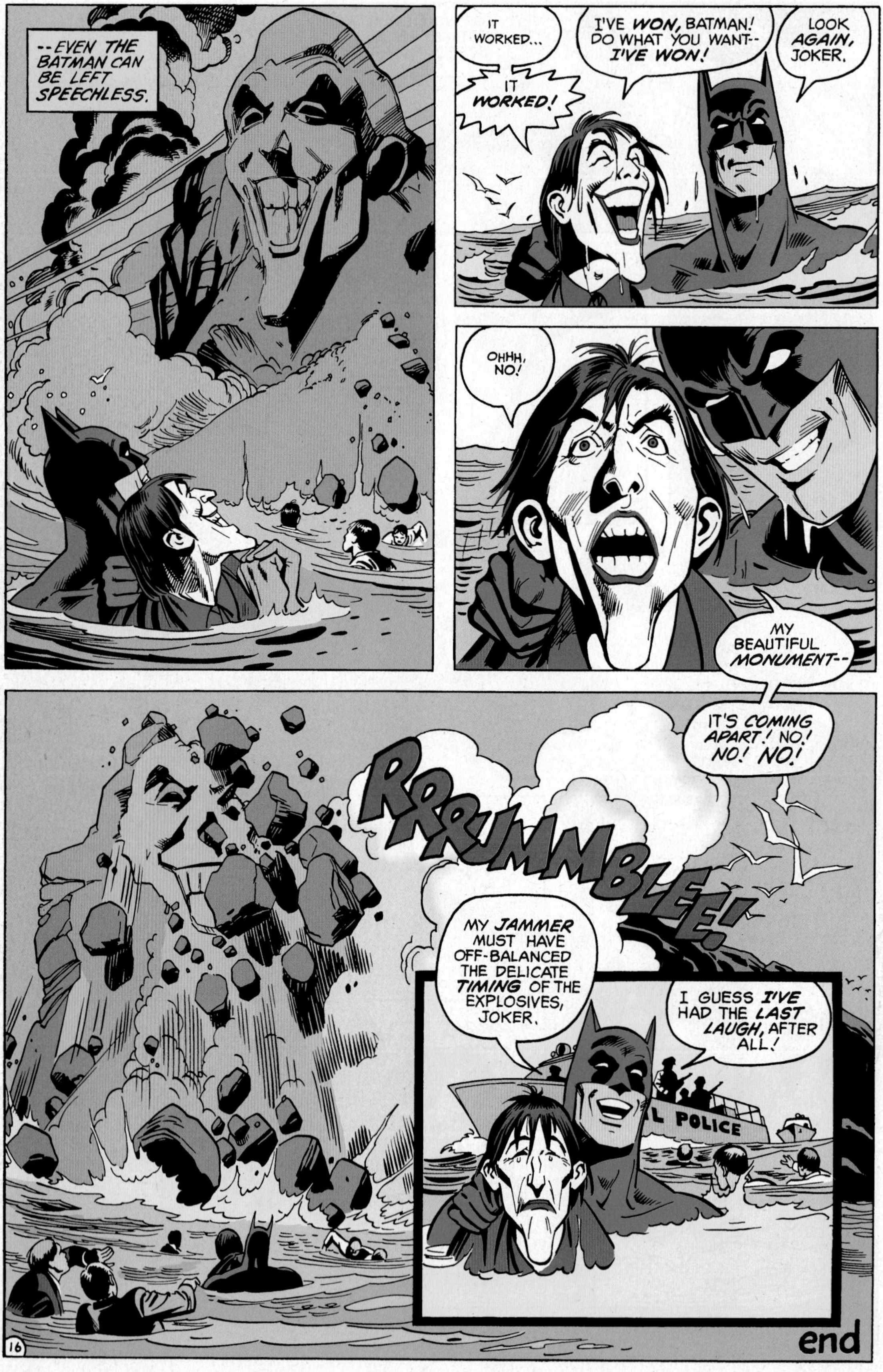
--EVEN THE BATMAN CAN BE LEFT SPEECHLESS.
IT WORKED...
IT WORKED!
I'VE WON, BATMAN! DO WHAT YOU WANT-- I'VE WON!
LOOK AGAIN, JOKER.
OHHH, NO!
MY BEAUTIFUL MONUMENT--
IT'S COMING APART! NO! NO! NO!
RRRRUMMMBLEE!
MY JAMMER MUST HAVE OFF-BALANCED THE DELICATE TIMING OF THE EXPLOSIVES, JOKER.
I GUESS I'VE HAD THE LAST LAUGH, AFTER ALL!
L POLICE
16
end

**FROM THE WRITER OF
300 & SIN CITY**

FRANK MILLER

Frank Miller's classic graphic novel features a Gotham City that has sunk into decadence and lawlessness ten years after an aging Batman retired. The Dark Knight returns in a blaze of glory when his city needs him most to end the threat of a brutal new generation of criminals while encountering the Joker, Two-Face and the Man of Steel for the final time.

"Groundbreaking."
– USA TODAY

"It's film noir in cartoon panels."
–VANITY FAIR

BATMAN: THE DARK KNIGHT RETURNS

FRANK MILLER
WITH KLAUS JANSON and LYNN VARLEY

BATMAN:
THE DARK KNIGHT
STRIKES AGAIN

BATMAN: YEAR ONE

ALL STAR BATMAN & ROBIN,
THE BOY WONDER VOL. I

with
DAVID MAZZUCCHELLI

with
JIM LEE

SEARCH THE GRAPHIC NOVELS SECTION OF
DCCOMICS.COM
FOR ART AND INFORMATION ON ALL OF OUR BOOKS!

"What's not to love? Dynamic art, riveting storytelling and two heroes who exist at polar opposites of the spectrum!"
— WIZARD

"A real treat for any lover of the superhero genre of comics."
— THE WASHINGTON TIMES

JEPH LOEB
with ED McGUINNESS

SUPERMAN / BATMAN:
SUPERGIRL

SUPERMAN / BATMAN:
ABSOLUTE POWER

SUPERMAN / BATMAN:
VENGEANCE

with
MICHAEL TURNER

with
CARLOS PACHECO

with
ED McGUINNESS

SEARCH THE GRAPHIC NOVELS SECTION OF
DCCOMICS.COM
FOR ART AND INFORMATION ON ALL OF OUR BOOKS!